新 セルフスタディ
IELTS
アイエルツ
ライティング
完全攻略

Anthony Allan 著

the japan times 出版

はじめに

　IELTSのライティングセクションは、テストの中で最も難しいパートだとよく言われます。1時間という限られた時間内に2つのエッセイを作成する中で、受験者は様々な壁にぶつかり、このセクションのスコアが一番低くなってしまうことが多いのです。そのため私は、ライティングセクションに特化したIELTSの対策書が必要だと感じました。本書は、受験者が直面する問題を解決し、より良い結果を得る助けになることを目指しています。

　『新セルフスタディ IELTSライティング完全攻略』は、IELTSのペーパー版、またはコンピューター版に向けて学習者が学べるように、タスク1とタスク2のサンプルエッセイを50本以上掲載しました。本書の手法は、多くのエッセイに触れること、解説、分析、そして再現を基本としています。まず各タスクの全問題タイプについて、サンプルエッセイを、導入、本体、結論のパーツごとに解説しています。そして「Self-Study!」ユニットでは、各問題タイプに3〜4本のサンプルエッセイを用意しました。学習者はエッセイの構造を理解し、内容のアイデアを抽出するためにサンプルエッセイを分析して、その結果を使ってエッセイを再現・再構築します。

　各ユニットには、重要語彙や表現に関するエクササイズを掲載し、学習者がエッセイを書く時に行いがちな間違いも取り上げています。さらに、巻末と別冊にはタスク2のエッセイ問題例50問や、タスク2のトピック20に関する語彙などを収録しました。受験者の皆さんは、普段の学習はもちろん、IELTSテストの直前にこの特別付録を参照することで、長文のライティングタスクに必要なアイデアを頭の中で思い起こすことができます。さらに、全エッセイの読み上げ音声もご利用いただけます。繰り返し聴いて、語句や表現、そしてエッセイのアイデアを記憶から引き出す助けにしてください。

以下は、IELTS受験者を助けることを目標とした本書の要約です：

- 28本のIELTSタスク1エッセイ（全問題タイプ）を学習する
- 25本のIELTSタスク2エッセイ（全問題タイプ）を学習する
- エッセイの構造を分析し、理解する
- IELTSのエッセイを再現し、書く練習をする
- エッセイの種類別（タスク1）およびトピック別（タスク2）の語彙を増強する
- IELTSのエッセイを書く際の典型的なミスを回避する
- タスク2のエッセイのためにアイデアを収集する
- 50本以上のタスク1とタスク2のエッセイを読んで、聞く

　本書は、IELTSの特定のレベルを対象としたものではありません。様々なレベルの学習者が、それぞれの望む結果に到達するために必要な知識やスキルを身につけることができます。さらに本書は、学習者が留学を目指すのがどの国であれ、大学でライティングの課題をやり遂げるのに役立つと信じています。

　最後に、本書を書く動機を与えてくれたアフィニティ・ランゲージのIELTS受験生に感謝します。また、ジャパンタイムズ出版、特に本書の編集者である大庭葉子さんの、このプロジェクトを実現するためのプロ意識と献身に、心から感謝の意を表します。最後になりましたが、英文の翻訳を担当された春日聡子さんの素晴らしい仕事ぶりにも、深く感謝いたします。

Anthony Allan

Contents

Task 1

Task 2

本書の構成と使い方

　Task 1 と Task 2 それぞれに、本番のエッセイの書き方、タイプ別攻略、タイプ別セルフスタディがあります。特典音声（p. 8参照）や巻末の Task 2 問題例50、別冊「IELTS ミニ辞典」も活用してください。

Task 1／Task 2　本番のエッセイの書き方

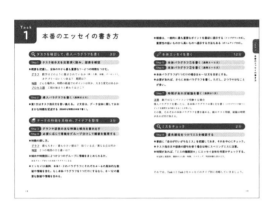

　試験本番でのライティングで**最も効率的な流れと時間配分、注意事項**を紹介しています。普段の学習の前はもちろん、試験当日にも見直して活用してください。

Task 1／Task 2　タイプ別攻略

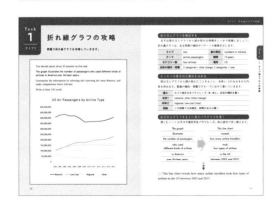

　各タスクの全タイプについて、例題で攻略していきます。

　Task 1でグラフや図のどこに注目するか、Task 2で**アイデアをどう構成していけばよいか**がわかります。

Task 1 / Task 2　タイプ別セルフスタディ

　各タスクの全タイプについて、**計41個のモデルエッセイ**を使って学習します。

　質問に答えてエッセイを分析し、再構成することで、**グラフ・図の説明力、アイデアを展開する力**を鍛えます。

　「タイプ別攻略」と「タイプ別セルフスタディ」には、**エッセイの重要語句・表現**を復習できるエクササイズがついています。

　各テーマの重要語句はもちろん、**エッセイを構成するのに不可欠な表現**もしっかり身につけます。

Extra　**Task 2問題例50**

　巻末には、Task 2の問題例を50個用意しました。本書で鍛えたライティング力に、さらに磨きをかけてください。
　※問題のみです。モデルエッセイはついていません。

別冊　**【保存版】IELTSミニ辞典**

　別冊付録として、Task 1に役立つ「トレンドを表す表現」や、Task 2頻出トピック別の重要語句・表現（計563）を1冊にまとめました。

特典音声について

　Task 1、Task 2のモデルエッセイ53本の音声をご利用いただけます。音声の速度はやや遅めにしています。繰り返し聴いて語句や表現を確認する、ディクテーションを行うなど、様々な形で活用してください。

📱 スマートフォン

1 ジャパンタイムズ出版の音声アプリ「OTO Navi」をインストール

2 アプリ内で本書を検索

3 音声をダウンロードし、再生

3秒早送り・早戻し、繰り返し再生などの便利機能つきです。学習にお役立てください。

💻 パソコン

1 ブラウザからジャパンタイムズ出版のサイト「BOOK CLUB」にアクセス

https://bookclub.japantimes.co.jp/book/b607619.html

2 音声をダウンロードし、iTunesなどに取り込んで再生

※音声はzipファイルを展開（解凍）してご利用ください。

IELTSとライティングタスクの概要

　IELTSは、英語圏に留学・移住を目指す人々の英語力を測定する4技能（ライティング、リーディング、リスニング、スピーキング）の試験です。主に大学・大学院留学のための「アカデミック・モジュール」と研修・移住のための「ジェネラル・トレーニング・モジュール」があり、本書はアカデミック・モジュールを受ける人に向けて書かれています。

　試験の日程や申込方法の詳細は、日本英語検定協会のウェブサイトでご確認ください。https://www.eiken.or.jp/ielts/

　本書は4技能のうち、「ライティング」の対策書です。問題形式や採点基準について見ていきましょう。

■ 問題形式

　60分でTask 1とTask 2のエッセイを1つずつ完成させなければなりません。それぞれの問題・解答用紙が配られ、どちらから書き始めても構いません。

	Task 1（目安：20分）	Task 2（目安：40分）
内容	グラフや表、プロセス図、地図について説明する	1つのトピックについて、自分の意見を述べる
設問タイプ	①折れ線グラフ ②棒グラフ ③表 ④円グラフ ⑤プロセス図 ⑥地図・図解 ⑦異なるタイプの組み合わせ	①賛成・反対を述べる ②物事の両面と意見を述べる ③問題と解決策を提示する ④議論を評価する ⑤原因とその影響を述べる
ワード数	150語以上 ＊語数＋10％（＝165語）が目安	250語以上 ＊語数＋10％（＝275語）が目安

■ 出題されるテーマ

Task 1	Task 2	
・人口、旅行者、観客の動向 ・生産量や失業率の変遷 ・器具や装置の仕組み ・作業手順の説明 ・地図の解説 <div align="right">など</div>	・人間関係、文化 ・観光、旅行 ・メディア ・教育、学習 ・動物保護 ・芸術 ・犯罪	・消費動向 ・人口の増減 ・テクノロジー ・環境問題、汚染 ・健康、運動 ・雇用、退職 <div align="right">など</div>

■ ライティングの採点基準

ライティングは、以下の4つの基準で評価されます。

① タスク達成力 (Task 1) ／タスク対応力 (Task 2)

Task 1：タスクを理解し、グラフや図表に含まれる情報を過不足なく解説しているか。

Task 2：タスクに適切に対応しているか。トピックに即したアイデアを裏づけや具体例とともに発展・補強し、それが明快かつ効果的な文章になっているか。

② 首尾一貫性とつながり (Task 1/Task 2)

内容が論理的で、情報やアイデアを適切につないで論旨を展開しているか。

③ 豊富な語彙 (Task 1/Task 2)

豊富な語彙を、適切・正確に使うことができているか。同じ単語を何度も使わずに表現できているか。

④ 文法知識と正確な運用 (Task 1/Task 2)

文法知識を用いて、長い文を適切・正確に書いているか。多様な構文を正

確に使っているか。

■ ライティングのスコア

　IELTSでは、ライティング、リーディング、リスニング、スピーキングそれぞれに、1〜9までの「バンドスコア」(0.5刻み)が与えられます。ライティングは、Task 1、Task 2それぞれで、前項の①〜④について、このバンドスコアで評価されます。Task 1とTask 2のスコアを1：2の比率で平均したものがライティングのバンドスコアとなります。

■ エッセイの基本構成

　典型的なパラグラフの構成は以下の通りです。

Task 1	Task 2
Introduction（導入）	Introduction（導入）
Body 1（本体1）	Body 1（本体1）
Body 2（本体2）	Body 2（本体2）
Conclusion（結論）	Body 3（本体3）
	Conclusion（結論）

※Task 1の本体は通例1〜2つ。Task 2は同様に2〜3つ。
　Task 1では結論が必須ではないので、時間がなければ書かなくてOK。

　各パラグラフにどんな内容をどのように書いていくか、本体パラグラフをいくつ書くのがよいかなど、詳細はこの後のタスク・設問タイプごとの例題と分析ステップを通して学習していきます。

■ 総合バンドスコア

　IELTSでは、4技能それぞれの「バンドスコア」（0.5刻み）を加算平均した「総合バンドスコア」が与えられます。総合バンドスコアは、最終的に.0か.5の近い方に切り捨て・切り上げられます（例：6.25→6.5）。

9	Expert user	英語を十分に、自在に操ることができる。表現を完全に理解し、適切、正確、流暢に使うことができる。
8	Very good user	英語を十分に操ることができるが、時に不正確・不適切な表現が見られる。慣れない状況下での誤解も散見されるが、複雑で細かい議論が行える。
7	Good user	英語を操ることができるが、時々、不正確・不適切な表現が見られる。状況によって誤解が生じる可能性もあるが、複雑な表現をよく使いこなし、細かい筋道も理解する。
6	Competent user	おおむね、通用する程度に英語を操ることができるが、不正確さ・不適切さ・誤解がある。慣れた状況下では、複雑な表現を使い、理解することもできる。
5	Modest user	限定的に英語を使うことができるが、ほとんどの場合だいたいの意味を汲みとることができる程度で、ミスも多い。得意な領域で、基本的なコミュニケーションができる。
4	Limited user	慣れた状況にかぎって、基本的な英語を使うことができる。理解と表現に問題がたびたび生じる。複雑な言葉や表現を使うことができない。
3	Extremely limited user	きわめて慣れた状況下で、おおまかな意味を伝え、理解する。頻繁にコミュニケーション不能に陥る。

| 2 | Intermittent user | 慣れた状況下で、単語や短い決まり文句で簡単なことを伝える以外、実質的なコミュニケーションができない。話された英語や書かれた英語の理解が困難。 |
| 1 | Non user | いくつかの単語を知っているだけで、基本的に英語の使用能力を有していない。 |

大学などの入学時に必要な標準スコアの目安は、以下の通りです。

・Postgraduate level（大学院レベル）
　 ＝ 6.5〜7.0

・Undergraduate level（大学学部レベル）
　 ＝ 6.0〜6.5

・Vocational course（専門学校）
　 ＝ 5.5〜6.0

・Foundation course（一般教養課程）
　 ＝ 4.5〜5.5

■ IELTSはイギリス英語のテスト？

　イギリス英語圏のテスト、というイメージが強いIELTSですが、特定の英語での解答を要求されることはありません。解答にイギリス英語やアメリカ英語、その他、英語が第一言語の国々の特徴（つづりなど）が含まれていても、得点には影響しません。

　なお、本書のつづりや音声はイギリス英語を採用しています。

エッセイ・ライティングの基本戦略

戦略 1 最初に1と2両方のタスクに目を通す

書きやすいものがあれば、そちらから始める。時間配分に注意（Task 1：20分、Task 2：40分目安）。

戦略 2 エッセイの基本構成を確認しておく

導入→本体（1～3）→結論（Task 2のみ必須）。Task 2では必ず結論を書く。すべてを記述できず、単語数が十分でなくても、結論があることでエッセイの形式が整う。

戦略 3 読みやすく美しい字で

ブロック体で読みやすく書く。上を閉じないaやgはuやyに、丸みのないfはtに、上が開きすぎているrはvに見えるので注意。kは左右を離さないように書く（1<にならないように）。

小文字のg, j, p, q, yのぶら下がり部分は文字のラインの下に出るように注意。ピリオドはコンマとしっかり区別する。大文字は小文字の2倍の高さで書く。

戦略 4 フォーマルでアカデミックな英語を使う

くだけた表現は使わない。Task 2では身近な出来事や事象を挙げて理由や具体例を示すが、I think/feel/believe ... を連発する個人的な文章にはしないこと。これらは意見表明や結論を書く時にとどめる。

世間によく知られている事実を述べる場合を除き、alwaysやnever、willなど極端な、あるいは断定する表現を避けて、代わりにoftenやrarely、could、mightなどを使う。※別冊「IELTSミニ辞典」参照。

戦略 5 タスク指示文・トピック説明文をうまく利用する

ただし、節や文をそのまま使うのはNG。書き換えて活用する。

戦略 6　導入部分はタスクに応じた書き方を覚える

導入部分の内容はタスクでほぼ決まるので、タイプに応じた書き方を覚えておく。

戦略 7　本体は最初に構成を決める

パラグラフをいくつにして、そこに何を書くか、アイデアをまとめてから書く。

戦略 8　文の長さを変えて変化をつける

主節のみで成り立つ単文は新たなポイントの紹介や、ポイントの強調に使う。

エッセイの大半は2節から成る文。and や but、because、although などを使って情報を2つ紹介したり、関連する情報をつなげたりする。

3節の文は、情報をさらに広げたい場合に使う。

戦略 9　できるだけ多様な語彙を使う

名詞と動詞は、なるべく同義語を使って反復を避ける。各エッセイのエクササイズや別冊「IELTS ミニ辞典」で、語彙を増やしておこう。

戦略 10　動詞の時制に注意

Task 1 のグラフや図が過去の情報なら過去形に。プロセスの説明なら現在形が適切。Task 2 は様々な時制の動詞を使えるとよいが、中心になるのは現在形。

戦略 11　単語の総数は「行数」を目安にする

A4用紙に英文を書き、その1行が何語になるかを確認しておく。通例は9〜12語。1行10語なら Task 1 は約19行、Task 2 は約30行（いずれもパラグラフ間のあきを含む）。

本番で書き始める際に、目標の行数に☆などの印をつけておくのも効果的。エッセイを書き終えたら印を消し忘れないように。

戦略 12　パラグラフの区切りは1行あける

①パラグラフ冒頭を数文字下げるインデントで示す伝統的な方法と、②パラグラフ間に1行あける方法がある。エッセイがいくつのパラグラフから成るかがひと目でわかる②がおすすめ。

戦略 13　ミスのチェックはタイプ別に優先順位をつける

自分が犯しがちなミスを把握しておき、まずはそれを中心にチェック。「冠詞と複数形」「動詞の3人称」「スペリング」「判別困難な書き文字」「時制」など、タイプ別にエッセイ全体をスキャニングすると時短になる。

戦略 14　Task 1のグラフや表の大文字と数字の扱い

グラフや図に登場する項目は大文字になっていることが多いが、エッセイでは、固有名詞や文頭でなければ小文字にする。

棒グラフや折れ線グラフでは、書きたい部分の数字がわかりづらい場合、自分なりに読み取って書く（例：80と90の真ん中より90寄りに見える場合は「86」または「87」と決めてOK）。

Task 1

本番のエッセイの書き方

🔍 タスクを確認して、導入パラグラフを書く　　3分

Step 1　タスク指示文を注意深く読み、図表を確認

● 概要を把握し、全体の中から最も重要な1〜2つの特徴をつかむ。

　<u>グラフ</u>　数字はどのように提示されているか（例：人数、金額、パーセント）、
　　　　　　カテゴリーはいくつある？　期間は？

　<u>地図</u>　どんな場所か、時間の経過でのポイントは何か、大きな変化はあるか

　<u>プロセス図</u>　工程の始まりと終わりはどこ？

Step 2　導入パラグラフを書く（通例は2文）

● 第1文はタスク指示文を言い換える。2文目は、データ全体に関しておおまかな特徴を記述する（具体的な特徴は本体で書く）。

📚 データの特徴を見極め、アイデアを整理　　3分

Step 3　グラフや図表の主な特徴と傾向を書き出す

Step 4　必要に応じて情報をグループ分けして順番を整理する

● 特徴の探し方。

　<u>グラフ</u>　最も大きい／最も小さい値は？　似ている点／異なる点は何か

　<u>地図</u>　2つの地図の主な違いは？

● 傾向や特徴別に2つか3つのグループに情報をまとめられるか。

　※各グループが1つの本体パラグラフになる

● エッセイは通例、本体1・2のパラグラフにそれぞれ4〜6の具体的な数値や情報を含む。もし本体パラグラフを1つだけにするなら、8〜12の重要な数値や情報を含める。

- 順番は、一般的に最も重要なポイントを最初に提示する（トップダウン方式）。重要性の低いものから高いものへ提示する方法もある（ボトムアップ方式）。

✎ 本体エッセイを書く　　　　　　　　　　12分

Step 5　本体パラグラフ①を書く（通例3〜5文）

Step 6　本体パラグラフ②を書く（通例3〜5文）

- 本体パラグラフが1つだけの場合は6〜12文を目安とする。
- 必要があれば、さらに本体パラグラフを書く。ただし、2つで十分なことが多い。

Step 7　時間があれば結論を書く（通例は1文）

<u>注意</u>　紙ではなくパソコンで受験する場合

導入パラグラフを書いたら、各本体パラグラフの第1文を書く（パラグラフで扱うトピックを説明する内容となることが多い）。

その後、それぞれの本体パラグラフを書き進める。紙のテスト同様、結論は時間があれば付け加える。

🔍 ミスをチェック　　　　　　　　　　　　2分

Step 8　優先順位をつけてミスを確認する

- 事前に「自分が行いがちなミス」を把握しておき、それを中心にチェック。
- タスク指示文や図表の語句を使う場合は特にスペリングミスに注意。
- 時間があれば、「ミスの種類別※」にエッセイ全体を何度かチェックする。

　　※冠詞と複数形、動詞の3人称・時制、スペリング、判別困難な書き文字。

それでは、Task 1をエッセイのタイプ別に攻略していきましょう。

折れ線グラフの攻略

例題で折れ線グラフを攻略していきます。

You should spend about 20 minutes on this task.

The graph illustrates the number of passengers who used different kinds of airlines in America over thirteen years.

Summarise the information by selecting and reporting the main features, and make comparisons where relevant.

Write at least 150 words.

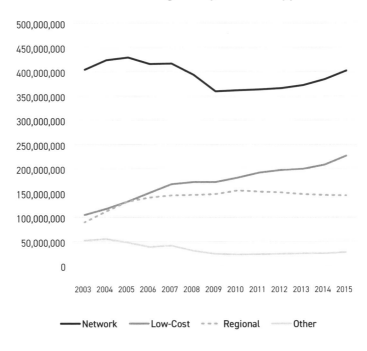

US Air Passengers by Airline Type

指示文とグラフを確認する

まずは指示文とグラフから読み取れる情報をしっかり把握しましょう。折れ線グラフは、ある時期の傾向やパターンの推移を示します。

タイプ	line	数の単位	numbers in millions
テーマ	airline passengers	期間	13 years
カテゴリー数	four airlines	場所	US
全体の傾向・特徴	2 categories = little change, 2 categories = rose		

エッセイの基本的な構成を決める

指示文とグラフから読み取れたことをもとに、本体1・2のおおまかな内容を決めます。数値の傾向・特徴でグループに分けて書いていきます。

導入	タスク指示文をパラフレーズ（言い換え）。全体の傾向を書く
本体1	network, other (little change)
本体2	regional, low-cost (rose)
結論	この段階では未確定。時間があれば書く

指示文とグラフをもとに導入パラグラフを書く

第1文（＝[1]）はタスク指示文をパラフレーズ。別の語句で言い換えます。

The graph	This line chart
illustrates	reveals
the number of passengers	how many airline travellers
who used different kinds of airlines	took four types of airlines
in America	in the US
over thirteen years.	between 2003 and 2015.

[1] This line chart reveals how many airline travellers took four types of airlines in the US between 2003 and 2015.

2文目（= [2]）は"According to the XXXX※"（～によれば）を使って、グラフからわかる全体の傾向や特徴を記述します。

※XXXXには、graph/chart/information/details/data/statistics などを使う。

今回の折れ線グラフなら、最も人気がある・最も人気がない航空会社は最初と最後の年で乗客数があまり変わらないこと、ほかの2社は乗客数が増えていることがわかります。

[2] According to the data, during the thirteen years the most popular and the least popular airlines saw little change in passenger numbers while the remaining two experienced rises.

本体1は最も人気がある・ない航空会社の傾向と数字について、本体2は、ほかの2社について書いていきます。

本体パラグラフ用に情報を書き出し、整理する

2つの本体パラグラフ用に、**具体的な情報やデータ**を書き出します。グラフ上ではっきりしない数字は自分なりに読み取って（決めて）書いて構いません。

本体1 英文 [3]～[7]

[3] every year: most popular = network airlines

[4] 400 mil. passengers in initial year

[5] figure increased, dipped by 50 mil. in 2009

[6] climbed, 2015 = 2003 level

[7] other airlines = lowest, started at 50 mil., fell to half

本体2 英文 [8]～[10]

[8] regional & low-cost airlines = begin with 100 million each, rose over thirteen years

[9] regional airlines = up by 50 million

[10] low-cost carriers = consistent growth, 225 million in last year

メモを使って実際の段落を書いていきます。

※下線はメモで書き出した語句です。

[3] Every year, the most popular way to travel was by using network airlines. [4] Specifically, 400 million passengers used them in the initial year. [5] Then the figure temporarily increased before dipping by 50 million in 2009. [6] Thereafter, it steadily climbed and in 2015 returned to the 2003 level. [7] At the opposite end of the scale, other airlines consistently experienced the lowest figure, which started at approximately 50 million and gradually fell to finish with half of that number.

[8] In contrast, beginning with roughly 100 million each, the number of passengers using regional and low-cost airlines rose over the thirteen years. [9] In the case of regional airlines, the figure went up by 50 million. [10] As to low-cost carriers, passenger numbers experienced consistent growth, reaching 225 million in the last year.

結論も本体同様に情報をメモし、書く（任意）

[11] network airlines = highest number of passengers

　　　popularity of regional and low-cost airline companies grew

[11] Overall, while network airlines retained the highest number of passengers, the popularity of regional, and especially low-cost airline companies, grew.

This line chart reveals how many airline travellers took four types of airlines in the US between 2003 and 2015. According to the data, during the thirteen years the most popular and the least popular airlines saw little change in passenger numbers while the remaining two experienced rises.

Every year, the most popular way to travel was by using network airlines. Specifically, 400 million passengers used them in the initial year. Then the figure temporarily increased before dipping by 50 million in 2009. Thereafter, it steadily climbed and in 2015 returned to the 2003 level. At the opposite end of the scale, other airlines consistently experienced the lowest figure, which started at approximately 50 million and gradually fell to finish with half of that number.

In contrast, beginning with roughly 100 million each, the number of passengers using regional and low-cost airlines rose over the thirteen years. In the case of regional airlines, the figure went up by 50 million. As to low-cost carriers, passenger numbers experienced consistent growth, reaching 225 million in the last year.

(176 words – 10 sentences)

Overall, while network airlines retained the highest number of passengers, the popularity of regional, and especially low-cost airline companies, grew.

(196 words – 11 sentences)

　この折れ線グラフは、2003年から2015年の間に、アメリカで4種類の航空会社を利用した旅行者の数を明らかにしたものだ。データによると、13年間で最も人気がある航空会社と最も人気がない航空会社にはほとんど変化がなく、残り2つの航空会社は乗客数が増加した。

　どの年も最も人気がある旅行手段は、ネットワーク航空会社を利用することだった。具体的に言うと、初年度は4億人の乗客がネットワーク航空を利用した。そして2009年に5000万人減少する前には、一時的に増加している。それ以降は着実に上昇し、2015年には2003年の数値に戻った。目盛りの反対側では、その他航空会社が一貫して最低の数値で推移しており、およそ5000万人で始まり、徐々に減少して、その半分の数で終了した。

　対照的に、地域航空会社と格安航空会社を利用する乗客の数は、それぞれおよそ1億人で始まり、13年の間にどちらの数値も上昇した。地域航空の場合は、5000万人増加した。格安航空会社については、乗客数は安定して伸び続け、最終年は2億2500万人に達した。

　全体的には、ネットワーク航空が最も多くの乗客者数を維持している一方で、地域航空会社、そして特に格安航空会社の人気が高まった。

エクササイズ

エッセイ中の重要語句と表現をエクササイズで確認します。

語句に当てはまる訳の番号を選んでください。

_____ the most popular   _____ temporarily

_____ the least popular   _____ Thereafter,

_____ little change   _____ At the opposite end of the scale,

_____ the remaining two   _____ the lowest figure

_____ Specifically,   _____ In the case of

_____ the initial year   _____ As to

1. 目盛りの反対側では	4. …については	7. 初年度	10. 最も人気がある
2. …の場合は	5. 具体的に言うと	8. それ以降	11. 一時的に
3. 最も人気がない	6. 最小の数値	9. ほとんど変化がない	12. 残りの2つ

同じ意味の単語を記入してください。

- graph   =   c _ _ _ _
- travellers   =   p _ _ _ _ _ _ _ _ _
- number   =   f _ _ _ _ _

正しい単語を選んでください。

- This line chart reveals [what / how / why] many airline travellers …
- Every year, the most popular way [to / for / in] travel was …
- … the figure went up by 50 [millions / million].

棒グラフの攻略

例題で棒グラフを攻略していきます。

You should spend about 20 minutes on this task.

This chart shows the amounts of some types of cheese produced in Canada during 2019.

Summarise the information by selecting and reporting the main features, and make comparisons where relevant.

Write at least 150 words.

Cheese Types（tons）

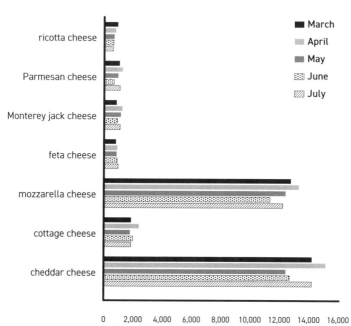

指示文とグラフを確認する

　棒グラフは、折れ線グラフ同様、ある時期の傾向やパターンの推移を示すことが多いです。数値が一番高いものから低いもの、低いものから高いものなど、どの順番で説明するかを決めます。傾向が同じか似ているものをまとめて説明してもいいでしょう。

タイプ	bar	**数の単位**	tons in thousands
テーマ	types of cheese	**期間**	five months in 2019
カテゴリー数	seven	**場所**	Canada
全体の傾向・特徴	2 categories = high figures, 5 categories = low figures		

エッセイの基本的な構成を決める

　指示文とグラフから読み取れたことをもとに、本体1・2のおおまかな内容を決めます。ここでは数値が低いものと高いものに分けて書いていきます。

導入	タスク指示文をパラフレーズ。全体の傾向を書く
本体1	ricotta, Parmesan, Monterey jack, feta, cottage (low figures)
本体2	mozzarella, cheddar (high figures)
結論	この段階では未確定。時間があれば書く

指示文とグラフをもとに導入パラグラフを書く

　第1文（= [1]）は**タスク指示文をパラフレーズ**。別の語句で言い換えます。

This chart		The horizontal bar graph
shows		reveals
the amounts of		how many tons of
some types of cheese		seven kinds of cheese
produced in Canada		were made in Canada
during 2019.		from March to July, 2019.

[1] The horizontal bar graph reveals how many tons of seven kinds of

cheese were made in Canada from March to July, 2019.

2文目（＝[2]）は、グラフからわかる全体の傾向や特徴を記述します。今回の棒グラフなら、最初の「全体の傾向・特徴」にあるように、2つのカテゴリーがほかのものより生産量が多いことがわかります。

[2] According to the information, it is clear that two types had much higher rates of production than the others.

前項で決めた通り、本体1は生産量が少ないカテゴリーの傾向と数字について、本体2は生産量が多い2つのカテゴリーについて書いていきます。

本体パラグラフ用に情報を書き出し、整理する

2つの本体パラグラフ用に、**具体的な情報やデータ**を書き出します。グラフ上ではっきりしない数字は自分なりに読み取って（決めて）書いて構いません。

本体1 英文[3]〜[5]

[3] ricotta, Parmesan, Monterey jack, feta: 1,000 tons per month

[4] cottage cheese = double: 2,000 tons per month

[5] April = peak, 2,400 tons

本体2 英文[6]〜[9]

[6] mozzarella, cheddar = higher than other kinds

[7] mozzarella: average = 12,000, lowest = 11,500 in June,
    highest = 13,500 in April

[8] cheddar: 2,000 tons more than mozzarella every month except May

[9] peak = 15,500 in April

メモを使って実際の段落を書いていきます。

※下線はメモで書き出した語句です。

[3] Four types of cheese, <u>ricotta, Parmesan, Monterey jack</u> and <u>feta</u> cheese, had similar figures over the five-month period, at approximately <u>1,000 tons per month</u>. [4] Following these, the figures for <u>cottage cheese</u> were almost <u>double</u>, at just under <u>2,000 tons</u> each <u>month</u>. [5] However, there was an exception in <u>April</u>, when production reached a <u>peak</u> of <u>2,400 tons</u>.

[6] In sharp contrast, the levels of production of <u>mozzarella</u> and <u>cheddar</u> cheese were significantly <u>higher than</u> those of the <u>other</u> five <u>kinds</u>. [7] The <u>average</u> amount for <u>mozzarella</u> cheese was roughly <u>12,000</u> tons, with the <u>lowest</u> figure being <u>11,500 in June</u> while the <u>highest</u> was <u>13,500 in April</u>. [8] Compared with mozzarella, around <u>2,000 tons more cheddar</u> cheese was produced each <u>month except</u> in <u>May</u>. [9] In addition, the <u>peak</u> of production was <u>in April</u>, when the figure registered <u>15,500</u> tons.

結論も本体同様に情報をメモし、書く（任意）

[10] chart demonstrates the overwhelming popularity of mozzarella and
　　　cheddar cheese

[10] In summary, the <u>chart demonstrates the overwhelming popularity of mozzarella and cheddar cheese</u> among consumers during the given period.

The horizontal bar graph reveals how many tons of seven kinds of cheese were made in Canada from March to July, 2019. According to the information, it is clear that two types had much higher rates of production than the others.

Four types of cheese, ricotta, Parmesan, Monterey jack and feta cheese, had similar figures over the five-month period, at approximately 1,000 tons per month. Following these, the figures for cottage cheese were almost double, at just under 2,000 tons each month. However, there was an exception in April, when production reached a peak of 2,400 tons.

In sharp contrast, the levels of production of mozzarella and cheddar cheese were significantly higher than those of the other five kinds. The average amount for mozzarella cheese was roughly 12,000 tons, with the lowest figure being 11,500 in June while the highest was 13,500 in April. Compared with mozzarella, around 2,000 tons more cheddar cheese was produced each month except in May. In addition, the peak of production was in April, when the figure registered 15,500 tons.

(175 words – 9 sentences)

In summary, the chart demonstrates the overwhelming popularity of mozzarella and cheddar cheese among consumers during the given period.

(194 words – 10 sentences)

　この横棒グラフは、2019年3月から7月にかけて、カナダで7種類のチーズが何トン作られたかを表している。情報によると、2種類がほかの種類よりもはるかに高い生産率だったことがわかる。
　4種類のチーズ、リコッタ、パルメザン、モントレー・ジャック、そしてフェタチーズは、5カ月の期間を通して、月約1000トンという似た数字を示している。続くカッテージチーズは、ほぼ2倍の毎月2000トン弱となっている。ただし、4月には例外的に、生産量が2400トンという最高値をつけた。

　対照的に、モッツァレラとチェダーチーズの生産水準は、ほかの5種類のチーズに比べて、大幅に高かった。モッツァレラチーズの平均量はざっと1万2000トンで、最も少なかったのは6月の1万1500トン、最も多かったのは4月の1万3500トンだった。モッツァレラと比較すると、チェダーチーズは5月を除いて、毎月約2000トン多く生産された。また、生産量のピークは4月で、数値は1万5500トンを記録した。
　まとめると、このグラフは、期間中、消費者の間でモッツァレラとチェダーチーズが圧倒的な人気を博したことを示している。

エクササイズ

エッセイ中の重要語句と表現をエクササイズで確認します。

語句に当てはまる訳の番号を選んでください。

_____ it is clear that

_____ similar figures

_____ approximately

_____ an exception

_____ reached a peak of

_____ In sharp contrast,

_____ were significantly higher

_____ The average amount

_____ Compared with

_____ except in May

_____ In addition,

_____ In summary,

_____ overwhelming popularity

1. 似た数字	4. 5月を除いて	8. また	12. 平均量
2. 大幅に高かった	5. 対照的に	9. 圧倒的な人気	13. 例外
3. …がわかる、…が明らかだ	6. まとめると	10. …と比較すると	
	7. 約	11. …の最高値をつけた	

正しいつづりを選んでください。

• According / Accoding

• infomation / information

• demonstrates / demonstraits

正しい単語を選んでください。

• ... were made in Canada [from / by] March [over / to] July, 2019.

• Following these, the figures for cottage cheese [was / were] almost double, at ...

• ... popularity of cheddar cheese [in / among] consumers during ...

表 の 攻 略

例題で表を攻略していきます。

You should spend about 20 minutes on this task.

The graph indicates how much money was used to pay for outsourced research and development in Canada over four years.

Summarise the information by selecting and reporting the main features, and make comparisons where relevant.

Write at least 150 words.

Outsourced R&D expenditure in Canada

(millions of dollars)

	Businesses	Government	Universities	Hospitals	Other Organisations /Individuals
2014	2697	37	170	108	173
2015	3414	58	239	111	209
2016	3589	28	288	67	235
2017	3655	157	643	169	254

指示文と表を確認する

表は数値に特徴があるもの、似た傾向のあるものをまとめて説明するといいでしょう。数値を比較する際は計算に注意します。

タイプ	table	数の単位	dollars in millions
テーマ	outsourced R & D expenditure	期間	four years
カテゴリー数	five	場所	Canada
全体の傾向・特徴	3 categories = increased every year, 2 categories = up & down but increased		

エッセイの基本的な構成を決める

指示文と表から読み取れたことをもとに、本体1・2のおおまかな内容を決めます。ここでは毎年増えているものと増減があるものに分けて書いていきます。

導入	タスク指示文をパラフレーズ。全体の傾向を書く
本体1	businesses, universities, other organisations & individuals (increased every year)
本体2	hospitals, government (up & down but increased)
結論	この段階では未確定。時間があれば書く

指示文と表をもとに導入パラグラフを書く

第1文（= [1]）は**タスク指示文をパラフレーズ**。別の語句で言い換えます。

The graph	*This table*
indicates	*presents*
how much money was used to pay for outsourced research and development	*figures relating to spending on contracted research and development (R & D) for five categories*
in Canada	*in Canada*
over four years.	*from 2014 to 2017.*

[1] This table presents figures relating to spending on contracted research and development (R & D) for five categories in Canada from 2014 to 2017.

2文目（＝[2]）は、表からわかる全体の傾向や特徴を記述します。今回の表は、どのカテゴリーも結局は数値が増えていることがわかります。

[2] According to the details, expenditure rose among all the groups over the designated period.

本体パラグラフ用に情報を書き出し、整理する

2つの本体パラグラフ用に、**具体的な情報やデータ**を書き出します。グラフ上ではっきりしない数字は自分なりに読み取って（決めて）書いて構いません。

本体1 英文 [3]〜[6]

[3] businesses spent most on R & D every year

[4] 2014 = $2,697 million, grew annually, $3,655 = 2017

[5] universities = yearly rises: $170 ↗ $643 million

[6] similar pattern for other organisations & individuals: $173 ↗ $254 million

本体2 英文 [7]〜[10]

[7] although two categories fluctuated, expenditure grew

[8] hospitals: $108 million in 2014, slightly more in 2015,
     less ($67 million) in following year

[9] final year = $169 million

[10] spending by government: exp. fluctuations but up just over fourfold,

$37 ↗ $157 million = most significant proportional rise among all categories

メモを使って実際の段落を書いていきます。

※下線はメモで書き出した語句です。

[3] Clearly, <u>businesses spent</u> the <u>most on R & D every year</u>. [4] In <u>2014</u>, the figure constituted <u>$2,697 million</u>, and the amount <u>grew annually</u>, reaching <u>$3,655</u> million in <u>2017</u>. [5] Spending by <u>universities</u> also saw <u>yearly rises</u>, from <u>$170</u> to <u>$643 million</u>. [6] A <u>similar pattern</u> can be seen in the figures <u>for other organisations and individuals</u>, whose spending surged from <u>$173</u> to <u>$254 million</u> over the four years.

[7] <u>Although</u> the pattern for <u>two categories fluctuated</u>, their <u>expenditure</u> also <u>grew</u> over the whole period. [8] <u>Hospitals</u> spent <u>$108 million in 2014</u>, <u>slightly more in 2015</u>, but far <u>less ($67 million)</u> the <u>following year</u>. [9] However, in the <u>final year</u>, spending shot up to <u>$169 million</u>. [10] <u>Spending by</u> the <u>government</u> also <u>experienced fluctuations but</u> went <u>up just over fourfold</u>, from <u>$37</u> to <u>$157 million</u>, which represented the <u>most significant proportional rise among all categories</u>.

結論も本体同様に情報をメモし、書く（任意）

[11] R & D expenditure by businesses = highest, but government & universities dramatically raised spending

[11] To conclude, while it is evident that <u>R & D expenditure by businesses</u> was the <u>highest</u>, the Canadian <u>government and universities dramatically raised</u> their levels of <u>spending</u> during the given period.

This table presents figures relating to spending on contracted research and development (R & D) for five categories in Canada from 2014 to 2017. According to the details, expenditure rose among all the groups over the designated period.

Clearly, businesses spent the most on R & D every year. In 2014, the figure constituted $2,697 million, and the amount grew annually, reaching $3,655 million in 2017. Spending by universities also saw yearly rises, from $170 to $643 million. A similar pattern can be seen in the figures for other organisations and individuals, whose spending surged from $173 to $254 million over the four years.

Although the pattern for two categories fluctuated, their expenditure also grew over the whole period. Hospitals spent $108 million in 2014, slightly more in 2015, but far less ($67 million) the following year. However, in the final year, spending shot up to $169 million. Spending by the government also experienced fluctuations but went up just over fourfold, from $37 to $157 million, which represented the most significant proportional rise among all categories.

(176 words – 10 sentences)

To conclude, while it is evident that R & D expenditure by businesses was the highest, the Canadian government and universities dramatically raised their levels of spending during the given period.

(206 words – 11 sentences)

この表は、2014年から2017年までの、カナダにおける5つのカテゴリーの委託研究開発（R&D）への支出に関連する数値を示している。その詳細によると、指定期間中にすべてのカテゴリーで支出が増加した。

明らかに、企業が毎年最も多くの費用を研究開発に費やしている。2014年の金額は26億9700万ドルで、総額は毎年増えて2017年には36億5500万ドルに達した。大学の支出も年々増加しており、1億7000万ドルから6億4300万ドルになった。その他の団体や個人の金額についても同じ傾向が見られ、その支出は4年間で1億7300万ドルから2億5400万ドルへと急増した。

2つのカテゴリーについては傾向に変動があったものの、全期間を通しては同じように支出が増加した。病院は、2014年に1億800万ドルを支出し、2015年にはわずかに増えたものの、翌年ははるかに少ない金額（6700万ドル）だった。しかし最終年は、1億6900万ドルと支出が急増した。政府の支出も変動があったが、3700万ドルから1億5700万ドルへと、4倍強増加しており、これはすべてのカテゴリーの中で最も大きな比率の増加となった。

全体として、企業の研究開発費が最も多かったことは確かだが、カナダの政府と大学がこの期間中、劇的に研究開発費への支出水準を上げている。

エクササイズ

エッセイ中の重要語句と表現をエクササイズで確認します。

語句に当てはまる訳の番号を選んでください。

_____ relating to

_____ categories

_____ the details

_____ expenditure

_____ the designated period

_____ Clearly,

_____ yearly rises

_____ A similar pattern can be seen

_____ fluctuated

_____ over the whole period

_____ fourfold

_____ proportional rise

_____ To conclude,

_____ it is evident that

1. 比率の増加	4. 毎年の増加	8. 変動があった	12. 4倍
2. 似た傾向が見られる	5. 明らかに	9. カテゴリー	13. …に関連する
	6. 詳細	10. 支出	14. 指定期間
3. 結論として	7. 全期間を通して	11. …は確かだ	

正しいつづりを選んでください。

• businesses / busineses

• univercities / universities

• organisations / organisatons

間違いをそれぞれ1箇所探してください。 ※表と見比べた内容の間違いも含まれます。

• In 2014, the figure constituted £2,697 million, and ....

• However in the final year, spending ...

• ... the canadian government and universities ...

円グラフの攻略

例題で円グラフを攻略していきます。

You should spend about 20 minutes on this task.

The charts reveal the percentage of tourists who arrived in different parts of the world in two different years.

Summarise the information by selecting and reporting the main features, and make comparisons where relevant.

Write at least 150 words.

International Tourist Arrivals

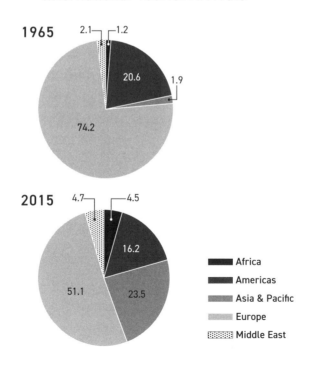

指示文とグラフを確認する

　円グラフは各セグメントの値について見ていきます。セグメントは通常5つほどですが、それ以上の場合は重要ないくつかについて触れればいいでしょう。今回のように2つの円グラフが提示される場合は、2つを比較します。

タイプ	pie × 2	**数の単位**	percentages
テーマ	international tourist arrivals	**期間**	1965, 2015
カテゴリー数	five	**場所**	(five) different parts of the world
全体の傾向・特徴	2 categories = decreased, 3 categories = increased		

エッセイの基本的な構成を決める

　指示文とグラフから読み取れたことをもとに、本体1・2のおおまかな内容を決めます。ここでは割合が減ったものと増えたものに分けて書いていきます。

導入	タスク指示文をパラフレーズ。全体の傾向を書く
本体1	decreases: Europe, the Americas
本体2	increases: the Middle East, Africa, Asia & Pacific
結論	この段階では未確定。時間があれば書く

指示文とグラフをもとに導入パラグラフを書く

　第1文（= [1]）は**タスク指示文をパラフレーズ**。別の語句で言い換えます。

The charts	*These two pie graphs*
reveal	*compare*
the percentage of tourists	*the proportion of holidaymakers*
who arrived in different parts of the world	*that travelled to five major regions of the world*
in two different years.	*in 1965 and 2015.*

[1] These two pie graphs compare the proportion of holidaymakers that travelled to five major regions of the world in 1965 and 2015.

2文目（＝[2]）は、表からわかる全体の傾向や特徴を記述します。2つのグラフを見ると、数値が減っている・増えているセグメントがあるとわかります。

[2] According to the details, the popularity of some areas grew but that of others declined during the half century.

本体パラグラフ用に情報を書き出し、整理する

2つの本体パラグラフ用に、**具体的な情報やデータ**を書き出します。グラフ上ではっきりしない数字は自分なりに読み取って（決めて）書いて構いません。

本体1 英文 [3]〜[6]

[3] highest rates in initial year = two areas, but dropped

[4] three-quarters of all travellers arrived in Europe

[5] however, proportion ↘ to half, fifty years later

[6] Americas = less dramatic change: 20.6% ↘ 16.2%

本体2 英文 [7]〜[12]

[7] three regions = rises

[8] 1965: the Middle East = 2.1%

[9] 2015: the Middle East = 4.7%

[10] more significant rise = Africa, 1.2% ↗ 4.5%

[11] most substantial growth = Asia and the Pacific region

[12] 1965 = 1.9%, then ↗ to nearly quarter of total

メモを使って実際の段落を書いていきます。

※下線はメモで書き出した語句です。

[3] Despite having the highest rates in the initial year, two areas experienced a drop in their percentage of overseas tourists. [4] Namely, almost three-quarters of all travellers in 1965 arrived in Europe. [5] However, the proportion dwindled to around half, fifty years later. [6] Furthermore, visitors to the Americas saw a much less dramatic change, dipping from 20.6 to 16.2%.

[7] In contrast, three regions experienced rises in their figures. [8] In 1965, the Middle East received only 2.1% of all global tourists. [9] Yet, in 2015, the rate stood at 4.7%. [10] There was an even more significant rise for arrivals to Africa, from 1.2 to 4.5%. [11] However, the most substantial growth was in travellers who landed in Asia and the Pacific region. [12] The 1965 proportion constituted a mere 1.9%, which shot up to nearly a quarter of the total, five decades on.

結論も本体同様に情報をメモし、書く（任意）

[13] percentage of tourists who visited Asia grew, proportion arriving in Europe diminished

[13] In summary, the pie charts primarily reveal that during the given period the percentage of tourists who visited Asia grew substantially while the proportion arriving in Europe diminished.

These two pie graphs compare the proportion of holidaymakers that travelled to five major regions of the world in 1965 and 2015. According to the details, the popularity of some areas grew but that of others declined during the half century.

Despite having the highest rates in the initial year, two areas experienced a drop in their percentage of overseas tourists. Namely, almost three-quarters of all travellers in 1965 arrived in Europe. However, the proportion dwindled to around half, fifty years later. Furthermore, visitors to the Americas saw a much less dramatic change, dipping from 20.6 to 16.2%.

In contrast, three regions experienced rises in their figures. In 1965, the Middle East received only 2.1% of all global tourists. Yet, in 2015, the rate stood at 4.7%. There was an even more significant rise for arrivals to Africa, from 1.2 to 4.5%. However, the most substantial growth was in travellers who landed in Asia and the Pacific region. The 1965 proportion constituted a mere 1.9%, which shot up to nearly a quarter of the total, five decades on.

(178 words – 12 sentences)

In summary, the pie charts primarily reveal that during the given period the percentage of tourists who visited Asia grew substantially while the proportion arriving in Europe diminished.

(206 words – 13 sentences)

　この2つの円グラフは、1965年と2015年に、世界の主要5地域に旅行した行楽客の割合を比べたものだ。詳細によると、この半世紀の間に、人気が高まった地域と下がった地域があることがわかる。

　初年度に最も高い割合だったにもかかわらず、2つの地域では海外旅行者の割合が減少した。すなわち、1965年には全旅行者の4分の3近くが、ヨーロッパを訪れていた。しかし、50年後には約半分にまでその割合は減少している。さらに、アメリカ大陸への旅行者は、それほど劇的な変化はなく、20.6％から16.2％へと減少した。

　対照的に、3つの地域の数値が増加した。1965

年、中東は全世界の観光客の2.1％しか受け入れていなかった。しかし2015年には、その割合は4.7％となった。アフリカはそれ以上に大きく増加し、1.2％から4.5％となった。しかし、最も大きな伸びを示したのは、アジア・太平洋地域に上陸した旅行者だった。1965年にはわずか1.9％だったのが、50年後には、全体の約4分の1近くにまで急増した。

　要約すると、これらの円グラフは主に、指定期間中、アジアを訪れた観光客の割合が大幅に増加した一方で、ヨーロッパに到着した人の割合が減少したことを示している。

エクササイズ

エッセイ中の重要語句と表現をエクササイズで確認します。

語句に当てはまる訳の番号を選んでください。

_____ compare

_____ the proportion of

_____ major regions

_____ that of (= the popularity of)

_____ half century

_____ Namely,

_____ almost three-quarters of all

_____ much less

_____ In contrast,

_____ global

_____ Yet,

_____ a mere

_____ a quarter of the total

_____ five decades on

1. 主要地域	5. すなわち	9. …のそれ(…の人気)	13. 世界の
2. 50年後には	6. わずか	10. 半世紀	14. 対照的に
3. しかし	7. 比べる	11. …の割合	
4. ずっと少ない	8. 全体の4分の1	12. 全体の4分の3近く	

同じ意味の単語を記入してください。

* tourists ＝ h_ _ _ _ _ _ _ _ _ _ ＝ v_ _ _ _ _ _ _ ＝
  t_ _ _ _ _ _ _ _

* half century ＝ f_ _ _ _ y_ _ _ _ ＝ f_ _ _ d_ _ _ _ _ _

カッコ内を正しい順序に並べ替えてください。

* According to the details, [some / popularity / of / the / areas] grew but ...

* There [even / was / significant / more / rise / an] for arrivals to Africa, ...

* However, [was / the / growth most / substantial] in ...

* In summary, [reveal / pie / primarily / that / charts / the] during the

  given period ...

プロセス図の攻略

例題でプロセス図を攻略していきます。

You should spend about 20 minutes on this task.

The diagram gives information on the life cycle of plastic bottles.

Summarise the information by selecting and reporting the main features, and make comparisons where relevant.

Write at least 150 words.

Plastic Bottles

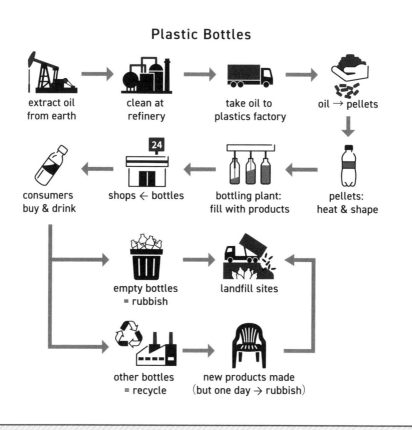

extract oil from earth

clean at refinery

take oil to plastics factory

oil → pellets

pellets: heat & shape

bottling plant: fill with products

shops ← bottles

consumers buy & drink

empty bottles = rubbish

landfill sites

other bottles = recycle

new products made (but one day → rubbish)

指示文と図を確認する

このタイプは、最初から最後まで全プロセスを紹介します。循環している図の場合は、どこから始まり、終わるのかを見極めましょう。

タイプ	process	数の単位	―
テーマ	life cycle of plastic bottle	期間	―
カテゴリー数	12 (images)	場所	―
全体の傾向・特徴	production of plastic bottles, disposal & recycling of plastic bottles		

エッセイの基本的な構成を決める

指示文と図から読み取れたことをもとに、本体1・2のおおまかな内容を決めます。ここでは、本体1で生産工程を、本体2は処分とリサイクルについて書きます。

導入	タスク指示文をパラフレーズ。全体の傾向を書く
本体1	production of plastic bottles
本体2	disposal & recycling of plastic bottles
結論	この段階では未確定。時間があれば書く

指示文と図をもとに導入パラグラフを書く

第1文（= [1]) はタスク指示文をパラフレーズ。別の語句で言い換えます。

The diagram	*This process chart*
gives	*depicts*
information on the life cycle of plastic bottles.	*the various steps in the life of plastic bottles.*

[1] This process chart depicts the various steps in the life of plastic bottles.

プロセス図や地図の場合は、導入パラグラフを1文で終えても構いません。2文目（＝[2]）を書く場合は、全体の傾向や特徴を記述します。"According to"を使い、書き始めましょう。

[2] According to the information, the life cycle begins and ends under the earth's soil.

本体パラグラフ用に情報を書き出し、整理する

2つの本体パラグラフ用に、**具体的な情報やデータ**を書き出します。

本体1 英文 [3]〜[7]

[3] plastic bottles = made from oil, extracted deep underground

[4] oil = cleaned at refinery, transported to plastics factory

[5] factory: oil → pellets → heated & shaped → plastic bottles

[6] bottles filled with water/juice, delivered to shops

[7] consumers purchase & drink

本体2 英文 [8]〜[11]

[8] empty bottles disposed two ways

[9] = thrown into rubbish bins, rubbish → landfill sites
　　→ buried under ground

[10] = recycled at recycling factory & new products made

[11] when products = old, also thrown into landfill sites

メモを使って実際の段落を書いていきます。

※下線はメモで書き出した語句です。

[3] <u>Plastic bottles</u> are <u>made from oil</u>, which is <u>extracted</u> from <u>deep underground</u>. [4] Then the <u>oil</u> is <u>cleaned at</u> a <u>refinery</u> and <u>transported to</u> a <u>plastics factory</u>. [5] At the <u>factory</u>, the <u>oil</u> is used to make <u>pellets</u>, which are <u>heated and shaped</u> into <u>plastic bottles</u>. [6] Following this, the <u>bottles</u> are <u>filled with</u> different liquid products, such as <u>water</u> or <u>juice</u>, and <u>delivered to shops</u>. [7] <u>Consumers</u> then <u>purchase and drink</u> the products.

[8] <u>Empty</u> plastic <u>bottles</u> are <u>disposed</u> of in <u>two ways</u>. [9] On the one hand, some are <u>thrown into rubbish bins</u> and the <u>rubbish</u> is taken to <u>landfill sites</u>, where it is <u>buried under</u> the <u>ground</u>. [10] On the other hand, other plastic bottles are <u>recycled at</u> a <u>recycling factory</u>, <u>and new products</u> (e.g. chairs) are <u>made</u> from the recycled plastic. [11] However, <u>when</u> these <u>products</u> become <u>old</u> and are no longer needed, they are <u>thrown</u> away and <u>also</u> end up in <u>landfill sites</u>.

結論も本体同様に情報をメモし、書く（任意）

[12] plastic bottles and other plastic products end their lives in landfill

[12] In summary, the diagram reveals that <u>plastic bottles and other plastic products</u> ultimately <u>end their lives in landfill</u> sites.

This process chart depicts the various steps in the life of plastic bottles. According to the information, the life cycle begins and ends under the earth's soil.

Plastic bottles are made from oil, which is extracted from deep underground. Then the oil is cleaned at a refinery and transported to a plastics factory. At the factory, the oil is used to make pellets, which are heated and shaped into plastic bottles. Following this, the bottles are filled with different liquid products, such as water or juice, and delivered to shops. Consumers then purchase and drink the products.

Empty plastic bottles are disposed of in two ways. On the one hand, some are thrown into rubbish bins and the rubbish is taken to landfill sites, where it is buried under the ground. On the other hand, other plastic bottles are recycled at a recycling factory, and new products (e.g. chairs) are made from the recycled plastic. However, when these products become old and are no longer needed, they are thrown away and also end up in landfill sites.

(177 words – 11 sentences)

In summary, the diagram reveals that plastic bottles and other plastic products ultimately end their lives in landfill sites.

(196 words – 12 sentences)

　この工程図は、ペットボトルの一生の、様々な段階を描いたものだ。情報によると、そのライフサイクルは、地球の土の下で始まり、終わる。
　ペットボトルは、地下深くから採掘された石油でできている。そして石油は製油所で精製され、プラスチック工場に運ばれる。工場では、石油はペレットの原料となり、それが加熱されてペットボトルが形成される。その後、ペットボトルは水やジュースなどの液体で満たされ、店に配送される。そして消費者がその製品を購入して飲む。

　空のペットボトルは、2つの方法で処分される。一方では、一部のペットボトルがゴミ箱に捨てられ、そのゴミは埋め立て地に運ばれ、地中に埋められる。もう一方では、それ以外のペットボトルがリサイクル工場で再生され、再生されたプラスチックを使って新しい製品（椅子など）が作られる。しかし、これらの製品が古くなって不要になると、捨てられ、同じく埋め立て地に運ばれる。
　要約すると、この図はペットボトルやその他プラスチック製品が、最終的に埋め立て地でその生涯を終えることを示している。

エクササイズ

エッセイ中の重要語句と表現をエクササイズで確認します。

語句に当てはまる訳の番号を選んでください。

＿＿ the various steps		＿＿ liquid products	
＿＿ are made from		＿＿ in two ways	
＿＿ is extracted from		＿＿ On the one hand,	
＿＿ is transported		＿＿ On the other hand,	
＿＿ is used to make		＿＿ e.g. chairs	
＿＿ are shaped into		＿＿ end up	
＿＿ Following this,		＿＿ ultimately	

1. 運ばれる	5. …から採掘される	9. …の原料となる	13. 一方では
2. …に形成される	6. たどり着く	10. もう一方では	14. …でできている
3. 様々な段階	7. 最終的に	11. 液体製品	
4. 2つの方法で	8. その後	12. 椅子など	

which または where を記入してください。

- Plastic bottles are made from oil, (　　　　) is extracted ...

- At the factory, the oil is used to make pellets, (　　　　) are heated ...

- ... the rubbish is taken to landfill sites, (　　　　) it is buried ...

正しい前置詞を記入してください。

- ... the bottles are filled (　　　　) different liquid products, such as ...

- ... new products (e.g. chairs) are made (　　　　) the recycled plastic.

- ... are no longer needed, they are thrown (　　　　) and also ...

地図・図解の攻略

例題で地図・図解を攻略していきます。

You should spend about 20 minutes on this task.

These diagrams reveal how an industrial complex will be redesigned for a local community.

Summarise the information by selecting and reporting the main features, and make comparisons where relevant.

Write at least 150 words.

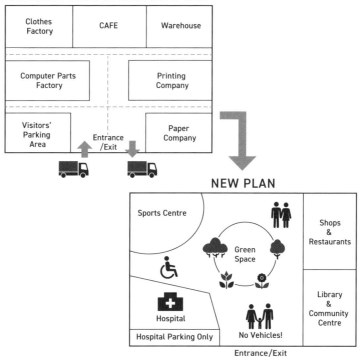

PRESENT INDUSTRIAL COMPLEX

Clothes Factory	CAFE	Warehouse
Computer Parts Factory		Printing Company
Visitors' Parking Area	Entrance /Exit	Paper Company

NEW PLAN

Sports Centre

Green Space

Shops & Restaurants

Hospital

Hospital Parking Only

No Vehicles!

Library & Community Centre

Entrance/Exit

指示文と図を確認する

2つの図の変化を説明していきます。建物や土地の利用でどこ・何が変わったか、位置や方角に注意しながら書きましょう。

タイプ	map	数の単位	—
テーマ	industrial complex redesigned for local community	期間	—
カテゴリー数	seven (clothes factory, etc.)	場所	—
全体の傾向・特徴	complex = change: industrial area → place for local people		

エッセイの基本的な構成を決める

指示文と図から読み取れたことをもとに、本体1・2のおおまかな内容を決めます。ここでは、本体1で現在のレイアウト、本体2で新しいレイアウト案について書きます。

導入	タスク指示文をパラフレーズ。全体の傾向を書く
本体1	present complex layout
本体2	new layout plan
結論	この段階では未確定。時間があれば書く

指示文と図をもとに導入パラグラフを書く

第1文（＝[1]）は**タスク指示文をパラフレーズ**。別の語句で言い換えます。

These diagrams	→	*The two maps*
reveal		*indicate*
how		*the way in which*
an industrial complex		*an industrial site*
will be redesigned		*is going to be redeveloped*
for a local community.		*for local people.*

[1] The two maps indicate the way in which an industrial site is going to

51

be redeveloped for local people.

地図・図解の場合は導入パラグラフを1文で終えても構いません。2文目（＝ [2]）を書く場合は、全体の傾向や特徴を記述します。"According to" で書き始めましょう。

[2] According to the details, the new plan will provide new facilities in the same location.

本体パラグラフ用に情報を書き出し、整理する

2つの本体パラグラフ用に、**具体的な情報やデータ**を書き出します。

本体1 英文 [3]〜[6]

[3] currently, six tenants, parking area by entrance on left

[4] behind parking area = computer parts factory

[5] right side of entrance = paper company & printing company = opposite parts company

[6] back = cafe between clothes factory in left corner & warehouse in right corner

本体2 英文 [7]〜[10]

[7] new site = prohibit vehicles, pedestrians only

[8] circular, green space in middle, surrounded by various facilities

[9] hospital in near-left corner, sports centre in far-left corner

[10] right side: shops, restaurants, library, community centre

メモを使って実際の段落を書いていきます。

※下線はメモで書き出した語句です。

[3] Currently, the industrial complex has six tenants and a parking area for visitors by the entrance, on the left. [4] Behind the parking area, there is a computer parts factory. [5] On the right side of the entrance, there is a paper company, and a printing company stands opposite the parts company. [6] At the back of the site, a cafe is situated between a clothes factory in the left corner and a warehouse in the right one.

[7] Unlike the industrial complex, the new site will prohibit vehicles from entering as it is intended for pedestrians only. [8] There is going to be a circular, green space in the middle that will be surrounded by various facilities. [9] For example, a hospital will be constructed in the near-left corner and a sports centre in the far-left one. [10] The area on the right side will consist of adjacent shops, restaurants, a library and a community centre.

結論も本体同様に情報をメモし、書く（任意）

[11] complex = change from industrial area to place that serves daily needs of local residents

[11] In summary, the complex will change from an industrial area to a place that serves the daily needs of local residents.

The two maps indicate the way in which an industrial site is going to be redeveloped for local people. According to the details, the new plan will provide new facilities in the same location.

Currently, the industrial complex has six tenants and a parking area for visitors by the entrance, on the left. Behind the parking area, there is a computer parts factory. On the right side of the entrance, there is a paper company, and a printing company stands opposite the parts company. At the back of the site, a cafe is situated between a clothes factory in the left corner and a warehouse in the right one.

Unlike the industrial complex, the new site will prohibit vehicles from entering as it is intended for pedestrians only. There is going to be a circular, green space in the middle that will be surrounded by various facilities. For example, a hospital will be constructed in the near-left corner and a sports centre in the far-left one. The area on the right side will consist of adjacent shops, restaurants, a library and a community centre.

(184 words – 10 sentences)

In summary, the complex will change from an industrial area to a place that serves the daily needs of local residents.

(205 words – 11 sentences)

　この2枚の案内図は、ある工業用地が、地元の人々のために再開発される様子を表している。詳細によると、この新計画では同じ場所で新しい施設を提供することになっている。

　現在、この工業団地には6つのテナントが入っており、入り口の左手には来客用の駐車場がある。駐車場の後ろ側には、コンピューターの部品工場がある。入り口の右側には、製紙会社があり、部品会社の反対側には印刷会社が建っている。敷地の奥には、左隅の服飾工場と右隅の倉庫の間に、カフェがある。

　工業団地とは異なり、新しい敷地は歩行者専用となるため、車両の進入は禁止される。中央には円形の緑地があり、それを囲むように様々な施設が配置されることになる。例えば、手前側の左隅には病院、奥の角にはスポーツセンターが建設される。右側の場所は、隣接する店舗やレストラン、図書館、そして公民館で構成される。

　要約すると、この施設は工業地帯から、地域住民の日常的なニーズに応える場所へと変わることになる。

エクササイズ

エッセイ中の重要語句と表現をエクササイズで確認します。

語句に当てはまる訳の番号を選んでください。

____ site	____ Unlike	
____ plan	____ is intended for	
____ facilities	____ will be surrounded by	
____ the same location	____ will be constructed	
____ Currently,	____ far corner	
____ stands opposite	____ will consist of	
____ is situated	____ adjacent	

1. …用である	5. 計画	9. 建設される	13. 同じ場所
2. ある、位置している	6. 隣接する	10. 奥の角	14. 施設
3. …で構成される	7. 反対側に立っている	11. 土地、場所	
4. …に囲まれる予定だ	8. 現在	12. …とは異なり	

正しい単語を選んでください。

- [Behind / On] the parking area ...
- [On / At] the back of the site ...
- ... [in / at] the left corner ...
- ... [at / in] the middle ...
- The area [on / at] the right side ...

There is a ... の未来形になるよう記入してください（例：There will be a ...）。

- There (　　　　) (　　　　) (　　　　) (　　　　) a ...

異なるタイプの
組み合わせの攻略

例題で攻略していきます。

You should spend about 20 minutes on this task.

These charts provide information on marriage trends in two countries within the UK.

Summarise the information by selecting and reporting the main features, and make comparisons where relevant.

Write at least 150 words.

Marriage: England & Wales（%）, 1935 to 2016

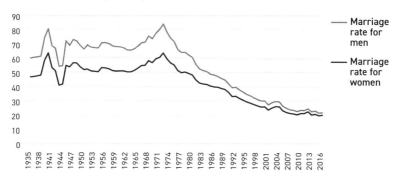

Wedding Days: England and Wales（%）, 2016

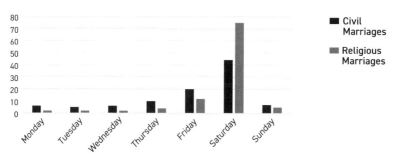

指示文とグラフを確認する

複数のグラフや図がある場合は、パラグラフを分けてそれぞれのグラフ・図の特徴を説明します。

タイプ	line & bar	数の単位	percentage (both charts)
テーマ	marriages & wedding days	期間	1935~2016 (82 years) & 2016
カテゴリー数	two & seven	場所	England & Wales (both charts)
全体の傾向・特徴	Line: figures & male-female gap declined Bar: Saturday = most popular wedding day		

エッセイの基本的な構成を決める

指示文とグラフから読み取れたことをもとに、本体1・2のおおまかな内容を決めます。本体1で折れ線グラフ、本体2で棒グラフについて書きます。

導入	タスク指示文をパラフレーズ。全体の傾向を書く
本体1	line chart (changes in proportions from 1935~2016)
本体2	bar chart (least popular → most popular days, 2016)
結論	この段階では未確定。時間があれば書く

指示文とグラフをもとに導入パラグラフを書く

第1文（＝[1]）は**タスク指示文をパラフレーズ**。それぞれのグラフについて、1文を別の語句で言い換えて、while（〜の一方）でつなぎます。

	①折れ線グラフ	②棒グラフ
These charts	*The line graph*	*(while) the bar chart*
provide	*reveals*	*shows*
information on marriage trends	*the marriage rates for males and females*	*the days and percentages of civil and religious marriages*

in two countries within the UK.		in England and Wales	
		from 1935 to 2016	in 2016.

[1] The line graph reveals the marriage rates for males and females in England and Wales from 1935 to 2016 while the bar chart shows the days and percentages of civil and religious marriages in 2016.

2文目（＝[2]）は全体の傾向や特徴を記述します。折れ線グラフからは男女とも結婚している人の割合が減っていて、棒グラフからは土曜日が結婚式に人気の曜日だとわかります。

[2] According to the information, the overall proportions and the gap between both genders declined, and Saturday was the most popular day for weddings.

本体パラグラフ用に情報を書き出し、整理する

2つの本体パラグラフ用に、**具体的な情報やデータ**を書き出します。

本体1 英文[3]〜[6]

[3] 1935: 47% women, 60% men = married

[4] 5 years later: both peaked at 20% higher, dropped 25% in 1944

[5] rates climbed → 2nd peak around 1972, % = nearly same as 1940

[6] both % steadily fell, finished with 20% each

本体2 英文[7]〜[9]

[7] Monday, Tuesday, Wednesday = least popular: civil = 5%, religious = 2%

[8] Thursday, Friday, Sunday = little popularity: civil = 20% on Fridays

[9] Saturday: 45% = civil, 75% = religious ceremonies

メモを使って実際の段落を書いていきます。

※下線はメモで書き出した語句です。

[3] In <u>1935</u>, <u>47%</u> of <u>women</u> and <u>60%</u> of <u>men married</u>. [4] <u>Five years later</u>, <u>both</u> figures <u>peaked at 20% higher</u> but then <u>dropped</u> by <u>25% in 1944</u>. [5] Thereafter, the <u>rates</u> gradually <u>climbed</u> and a <u>second peak</u> occurred <u>around 1972</u>, when the <u>percentages</u> almost mirrored those of <u>1940</u>. [6] Subsequently, though, <u>both</u> proportions <u>steadily fell</u> and <u>finished with</u> an equal figure of <u>20%</u>.

[7] Turning to the bar graph, <u>Monday</u>, <u>Tuesday</u> and <u>Wednesday</u> were the <u>least popular</u> days for holding either a <u>civil (5%)</u> or <u>religious</u> wedding <u>(2%)</u>. [8] <u>Thursday</u>, <u>Friday</u> and <u>Sunday</u> also had <u>little popularity</u> although the rates were higher, particularly for <u>civil</u> weddings held <u>on Fridays (20%)</u>. [9] Even so, the most striking statistics are for <u>Saturdays</u>, with <u>45%</u> for <u>civil</u> and <u>75%</u> for <u>religious ceremonies</u>.

結論も本体同様に情報をメモし、書く（任意）

[10] (line) marriage rates = high in first half of period, but declined by 2/3 in
　　　　second half

　　　(bar) in 2016, most couples chose Saturday for weddings

[10] To summarise, <u>marriage rates</u> remained <u>high</u> during the <u>first half of</u> the <u>period but declined by</u> roughly <u>two-thirds in</u> the <u>second half</u>, and <u>in 2016 most couples chose</u> to marry on a <u>Saturday</u>.

The line graph reveals the marriage rates for males and females in England and Wales from 1935 to 2016 while the bar chart shows the days and percentages of civil and religious marriages in 2016. According to the information, the overall proportions and the gap between both genders declined, and Saturday was the most popular day for weddings.

In 1935, 47% of women and 60% of men married. Five years later, both figures peaked at 20% higher but then dropped by 25% in 1944. Thereafter, the rates gradually climbed and a second peak occurred around 1972, when the percentages almost mirrored those of 1940. Subsequently, though, both proportions steadily fell and finished with an equal figure of 20%.

Turning to the bar graph, Monday, Tuesday and Wednesday were the least popular days for holding either a civil (5%) or religious wedding (2%). Thursday, Friday and Sunday also had little popularity although the rates were higher, particularly for civil weddings held on Fridays (20%). Even so, the most striking statistics are for Saturdays, with 45% for civil and 75% for religious ceremonies.

(181 words – 9 sentences)

To summarise, marriage rates remained high during the first half of the period but declined by roughly two-thirds in the second half, and in 2016 most couples chose to marry on a Saturday.

(214 words – 10 sentences)

折れ線グラフは、1935年から2016年までの、イングランドとウェールズの男女の婚姻率を、棒グラフは、2016年の民事婚と宗教婚の曜日と割合を明らかにしている。情報によると、全体の割合と性別間のギャップが減少し、結婚式に最も人気のある曜日は土曜だった。

1935年には、女性の47％、男性の60％が結婚していた。5年後には、両方の数字が20％上昇してピークに達し、その後1944年には25％低下した。それから、割合は徐々に上昇し、1972年頃に2度目のピークを迎え、1940年の割合とほぼ同じになった。しかしそれ以降、両者の割合は着実に低下し、等しく20％という数値で終了した。

棒グラフを見ると、月曜、火曜、そして水曜は、民事婚（5％）、宗教婚（2％）ともに、一番人気がない曜日だった。木曜、金曜、そして日曜もあまり人気がなかったものの、その割合はもう少し高く、特に金曜に行われた市民婚（20％）が高かった。それでも、最も顕著な統計値は土曜のもので、市民婚が45％、宗教婚が75％だった。

要約すると、既婚率は期間前半には高止まりしていたが、後半はざっと3分の2減少し、2016年は、ほとんどのカップルが土曜日に結婚することを選んだ。

エクササイズ

エッセイ中の重要語句と表現をエクササイズで確認します。

語句に当てはまる訳の番号を選んでください。

_____ rates		_____ an equal figure of	
_____ while		_____ Turning to	
_____ the gap between		_____ particularly for	
_____ genders		_____ Even so,	
_____ Five years later,		_____ the most striking	
_____ mirrored		_____ the first half of the period	
_____ Subsequently,		_____ by roughly two-thirds	

1. 5年後	5. 性別	ていた	12. …と等しい数値
2. …間のギャップ	6. …を見ると	9. それ以降	13. 期間前半
3. 率	7. それでも	10. 最も顕著な	14. 一方
4. 特に…で	8. 反映した、よく似	11. だいたい3分の2	

同じ意味の単語を記入してください。

• males　　　　 = 　m_ _
• females　　　 = 　w_ _ _ _
• percentages　 = 　p_ _ _ _ _ _ _ _ _ _ = f_ _ _ _ _ _ = r_ _ _ _

正しい単語を記入してください。

• Sunday, Monday, _____, _____, Thursday, Friday, _____

Self-Study!

折れ線グラフ①

タイプ別にモデルエッセイを分析・再構築することで、重要表現を身につけてライティング力を高めます。

You should spend about 20 minutes on this task.

This graph indicates how many cars were made in selected countries from 1991 to 2016.

Summarise the information by selecting and reporting the main features, and make comparisons where relevant.

Write at least 150 words.

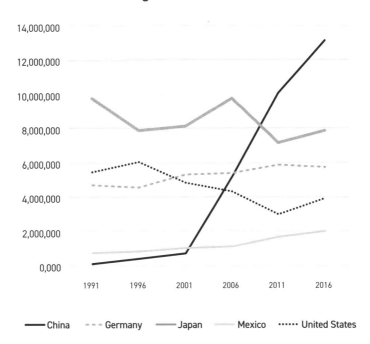

Passenger Car Production

— China   - - - Germany   — Japan   — Mexico   ······ United States

The multiple line chart illustrates the level of passenger car production in five nations between 1991 and 2016. According to the statistics, the numbers dropped for two countries and rose for three during the 26-year period.

In the initial year, Japan manufactured the highest number of cars, at 10 million. Then the figure contracted before peaking again with 10 million in 2006. Eventually, though, it finished at 8 million. Similarly, the US experienced a fluctuating and overall fall, from just under 6 million vehicles in 1991 to 4 million, twenty-five years on.

In terms of growth, Germany's car production began with roughly 4.5 million cars in 1991 and grew by 1.5 million during the entire term. Mexico had the second lowest starting figure, around 600,000, which slowly increased to 2 million in 2016. Despite building virtually no cars in 1991, China's production rate almost paralleled that of Mexico's until 2001, when the figure for each country reflected nearly a million. From then on, however, it climbed steadily to finish with the highest figure, 13 million cars. *(176 words – 10 sentences)*

To conclude, the graph reveals relatively minor changes in car production volumes for all the countries except China, which experienced rapid growth from 2001 onwards. *(201 words – 11 sentences)*

　この多角的な折れ線グラフは、1991年から2016年までの、5カ国の乗用車生産台数の水準を示している。統計によると、26年間で2カ国の数字が下がり、3カ国が上昇した。

　初年度は、日本が1000万と最も多い台数の自動車を生産した。その後数字は減少し、2006年に再び1000万の最高値をつけた。しかし、最終的には800万で終えた。同様に、アメリカは変動しながら全体的に減少していき、1991年の600万弱という台数から、25年後には400万となった。

　成長という意味では、ドイツの自動車生産台数は、1991年にざっと450万台で始まり、全期間で150万台増加した。メキシコは2番目に低い数字、60万台ほどから始まり、徐々に増加して、2016年には200万台となった。1991年には自動車をほとんど作っていなかったにもかかわらず、中国の生産率は2001年までメキシコと同じように推移し、両国の数字は100万台近くを示していた。しかし、その後は順調に増加し、最終的には1300万台という、最も高い数字で終了した。

　結論として、このグラフは、2001年以降急成長した中国を除くすべての国で、自動車生産台数の変化が比較的小さいことを表している。

Self-Study!

　モデルエッセイを分析していきます。エッセイの英文をもとに質問に**英語で**答えてください。回答がそのままエッセイを書く材料になります。

導入

Q1 タスク指示文は、どのように言い換えられている？

This graph
indicates
how many
cars were made
in selected countries
from 1991 to 2016.

Q2 全体的な傾向・要点は？

本体1 減った ↘

Q3 初年度に最も高い数字だったのはどの国で、その数字は？

Q4 その数字はどう変わり、最後にどうなった？

Q5 同様の傾向を示したのはどの国？

Q6 その最初と最後の数字は？

本体2 増えた ↗

Q7 最初の数字が3番目に低かった国は？

Q8 どの数字で始まり、どれくらい増加した？

Q9 最初の数字が2番目に低かった国は？

Q10 どの数字で始まり、どれくらい増加した？

Q11 最初の数字が最も低かった国は？

Q12 ほかの国とどの時点で似た傾向を示し、その後どう変化した？

結論 （任意）

Q13 具体的な傾向・要点は？

以下の回答例や自分が分析した結果をもとにエッセイを書きましょう。

導入

Q1 タスク指示文は、どのように言い換えられている？

This graph		*The multiple line chart*
indicates		*illustrates*
how many		*the level of*
cars were made		*passenger car production*
in selected countries		*in five nations*
from 1991 to 2016.		*between 1991 and 2016.*

Q2 全体的な傾向・要点は？

A. numbers dropped for two and rose for three countries

本体1 減った ↘

Q3 初年度に最も高い数字だったのはどの国で、その数字は？

A. Japan, 10 million

Q4 その数字はどう変わり、最後にどうなった？

A. contracted, peaked, finished with 8 million

Q5 同様の傾向を示したのはどの国？

A. the US, fluctuated and overall fall

Q6 その最初と最後の数字は？

A. 6 million, 4 million

本体2 増えた ↗

Q7 最初の数字が3番目に低かった国は？

A. Germany

Q8 どの数字で始まり、どれくらい増加した？

A. 4.5 million, and grew by 1.5 million

Q9 最初の数字が2番目に低かった国は？

A. Mexico

Q10 どの数字で始まり、どれくらい増加した？

A. 600,000, and increased to 2 million

Q11 最初の数字が最も低かった国は？

A. China (almost no cars)

Q12 ほかの国とどの時点で似た傾向を示し、その後どう変化した？

A. similar to Mexico until 2001, then climbed to 13 million

結論（任意）

Q13 具体的な傾向・要点は？

A. minor changes in production volumes, except China from 2001

エッセイ中の重要語句と表現をエクササイズで確認します。

語句に当てはまる訳の番号を選んでください。

_____ The multiple		_____ virtually	
_____ the level of		_____ almost paralleled	
_____ Eventually,		_____ From then on,	
_____ Similarly,		_____ minor changes	
_____ began with		_____ volumes	
_____ starting figure		_____ onwards	
_____ Despite			

1. …の水準	5. 最初の数字	9. その後は	13. 小さな変化
2. 分量	6. 最終的には	10. 先に、進んで	
3. ほぼ一致した	7. ほとんど	11. …で始まった	
4. 同様に	8. 多角的な、複合の	12. …にもかかわらず	

間違いを3箇所探してください。

• In the initial year, Japan manfactured the highest number of car, at 10 millions.

however を異なる場所に入れてください。

• From then on, it climbed steadily to finish with the highest figure, 13 million cars.

• From then on, it climbed steadily to finish with the highest figure, 13 million cars.

正解　8, 1, 6, 4, 11, 5, 12, 7, 3, 9, 13, 2, 10／manufactured, cars, million（sは不要）／
From then on, however, it climbed …　または　However, from then on, it climbed …

Task 1

Self-Study!
棒グラフ①

タイプ別にモデルエッセイを分析・再構築することで、重要表現を身につけてライティング力を高めます。

You should spend about 20 minutes on this task.

The bar chart indicates the number of companies according to their number of employees in Australia over a five-year period.

Summarise the information by selecting and reporting the main features, and make comparisons where relevant.

Write at least 150 words.

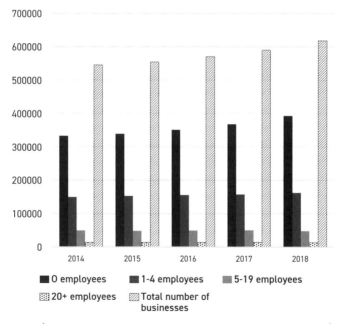

Small Business Employee Numbers

■ 0 employees ■ 1-4 employees ■ 5-19 employees
▓ 20+ employees ▨ Total number of businesses

（Companies with no employees employed part-time workers only.）

This vertical bar graph presents details on how many small businesses in Australia were employing different numbers of staff from 2014 to 2018. Overall, it is evident that while the total figure of companies grew over the five years, only those offering part-time jobs rose in number.

Three categories experienced no changes over the whole term. The number of companies with the most employees (20+) remained the lowest at around 10,000, and those which employed 5 to 19 workers stayed at roughly 40,000. Companies that employed the smallest number of full-time staff (1 to 4) also remained unchanged, with annual figures of about 150,000.

Conversely, a different trend can be seen among companies that employed no full-time workers. These companies, which hired only part-time staff, represented approximately 330,000 in 2014. Then, over the next four years, the figure climbed steadily to reach a peak of just under 400,000 in 2018. This climb mirrored the pattern for the total number of firms, which grew from 550,000 in the first year to around 620,000 in the last. *(175 words – 9 sentences)*

To conclude, the chart reveals that while the figures for companies with full-time positions were static, more companies were offering more part-time jobs year on year. *(201 words – 10 sentences)*

この縦棒グラフは2014年から2018年にかけて、どれだけのオーストラリアの中小企業が、それぞれ異なる数の従業員を雇用していたのかを詳細に示している。全体として、5年間で企業の総数は増加しているものの、増えているのはパートタイムの仕事を提供している企業だけであることは明らかだ。

全期間を通して、変化のなかったカテゴリーは3つある。従業員数が最も多い企業（20人以上）の数は、1万社ほどと最も少ないままで、5〜19人の労働者を雇っている企業は、ざっと4万社で推移した。フルタイムの社員の数が最も少ない企業（1〜4人）も、年間の数字は約15万社と、変化はなかった。

逆に、まったくフルタイムの労働者を雇っていない企業については、別の傾向が見られた。パートタイムの従業員しか雇っていないこれらの企業は、2014年にはおよそ33万社だった。その後、4年間で着実に数字が増え、2018年に最高値に達して40万社を少々下回った。この増え方は、最初の年の55万社から、最後の年の約62万社へと増加した総企業数の増え方によく似ている。

結論として、このグラフからは、常勤職がある企業の数字には動きがなかったものの、年々、より多くの企業がパートタイムの職を多く募集していることがわかる。

Self-Study!

　モデルエッセイを分析していきます。エッセイの英文をもとに質問に**英語で**答えてください。回答がそのままエッセイを書く材料になります。

導入

Q1 タスク指示文は、どのように言い換えられている？

> *The bar chart*
> *indicates*
> the number of companies according to their number of employees in Australia
> over a five-year period.

Q2 全体的な傾向・要点は？

本体1 数字に変化なし

Q3 5年間で変化がなかったカテゴリーはいくつあった？

Q4 フルタイムの従業員が最も多い企業の数は？

Q5 フルタイムの従業員が2番目に多い企業の数は？

Q6 フルタイムの従業員が最も少ない企業の数は？

本体2 数字が増加

Q7 異なる傾向が見られたカテゴリーは？

Q8 そのカテゴリーの最初の数値は？

Q9 そのカテゴリーの最後の数値は？

Q10 そのカテゴリーとほかのカテゴリーとの類似点は？　また、ほかのカテゴリーの最初と最後の数値は？

結論（任意）

Q11 具体的な傾向・要点は？

以下の回答例や自分が分析した結果をもとにエッセイを書きましょう。

導入

Q1 タスク指示文は、どのように言い換えられている？

The bar chart		*This vertical bar graph*
indicates		*presents details on*
the number of companies according to their number of employees in Australia		*how many small businesses in Australia were employing different numbers of staff*
over a five-year period.		*from 2014 to 2018.*

Q2 全体的な傾向・要点は？

A. total figure of companies grew, but only companies offering P/T jobs rose

本体1 数字に変化なし

Q3 5年間で変化がなかったカテゴリーはいくつあった？

A. three categories (companies with F/T workers)

Q4 フルタイムの従業員が最も多い企業の数は？

A. (20+) around 10,000

Q5 フルタイムの従業員が2番目に多い企業の数は？

A. (5-19) roughly 40,000

Q6 フルタイムの従業員が最も少ない企業の数は？

A. (1-4) about 150,000

本体2 数字が増加

Q7 異なる傾向が見られたカテゴリーは？

A. companies with no F/T staff (so only P/T staff)

Q8 そのカテゴリーの最初の数値は？

A. approximately 330,000 (2014)

Q9　そのカテゴリーの最後の数値は？

　　A. just under 400,000 (2018)

Q10　そのカテゴリーとほかのカテゴリーとの類似点は？　また、ほかのカテ
　　ゴリーの最初と最後の数値は？

　　A. their figures both grew, total number of firms = 550,000 ↗ 620,000

結論（任意）

Q11　具体的な傾向・要点は？

　　A. figures for companies with F/T positions = static,

　　　 more companies = offering more P/T jobs

エッセイ中の重要語句と表現をエクササイズで確認します。

語句に当てはまる訳の番号を選んでください。

_____ This vertical   _____ with annual figures of

_____ presents details on   _____ Conversely,

_____ the total figure   _____ mirrored the pattern for

_____ in number   _____ the total number of

_____ Three categories   _____ in the last (year)

_____ The number of ... with the   _____ static

       most ~   _____ year on year

1. 総数	5. 動きのない、変化しない	8. 年々	11. 逆に
2. …の詳細を示す	6. この縦の・垂直の	9. 最後の年の	12. ～が最も多い…の数
3. 3つのカテゴリー	7. 年間の数字は…で	10. …のパターンによく似ている	13. …の総数
4. 数のうえで			

同じ意味の単語を記入してください。

- companies = b_ _ _ _ _ _ _ _ _ = f _ _ _ _
- roughly = a_ _ _ _ _ _ _ _ _ _ _ _ = a _ _ _ _ _

カッコ内を正しい順序に並べ替えてください。

- Three [changes / no / categories / experienced] [whole / the / term / over].
- Conversely, [seen / different / among / be / a / can / trend] companies that employed no full-time workers.

正解   6, 2, 1, 4, 3, 12, 7, 11, 10, 13, 9, 5, 8 ／ businesses, firms, approximately, around ／ categories experienced no changes, over the whole term, a different trend can be seen among

74

Self-Study!

表①

タイプ別にモデルエッセイを分析・再構築することで、重要表現を身につけてライティング力を高めます。

You should spend about 20 minutes on this task.

The graph shows the number of international tourists to the six most popular cities in the world in 2020 and predictions by nation for 2040.

Summarise the information by selecting and reporting the main features, and make comparisons where relevant.

Write at least 150 words.

2020		2040	
CITY Ranking	No. of Tourists (million)	COUNTRY Ranking	No. of Tourists (million)
1. Bangkok (Thailand)	22.7	1. China	147
2. Paris (France)	19.1	2. France	146
3. London (England)	19	3. USA	136
4. Dubai (UAE)	15.9	4. Spain	130
5. Singapore	14.7	5. Thailand	99
6. Kuala Lumpur (Malaysia)	13.8	6. Italy	98

This table provides information on the top six cities visited by overseas holidaymakers in 2020 and predicts the six most popular countries in 2040. From the data, it is evident that destinations in Asia and Europe dominate in both years.

Regarding city rankings in 2020, Bangkok was the number one choice, with 22.7 million travellers. Next, two European cities, Paris and London, ranked second and third at 19.1 and 19 million tourists, respectively. Dubai followed with 15.9 million and Singapore with 14.7 million. Kuala Lumpur held the lowest position, with 13.8 million holidaymakers.

In terms of forecasts in visitor numbers to countries in 2040, the top spot is still likely to be occupied by an Asian country, but not Thailand. China is anticipated to attract 147 million tourists whereas Thailand will be in fifth position with nearly 100 million, which is marginally higher than Italy's figure. At 146 million, France will retain the second spot, almost matching the number for China. Finally, the USA is predicted to receive 136 million travellers while Spain can expect to welcome 130 million.

(179 words – 10 sentences)

Overall, the chart reveals the high popularity of Asia and Europe among holidaymakers, and indicates this trend will likely continue in the future.

(202 words – 11 sentences)

　この表は、2020年に海外からの行楽客が訪れた上位6都市の情報を提供し、2040年に人気が高くなると思われる6カ国を予測したものだ。データを見ると、どちらの年も、アジアとヨーロッパの都市が優位を占めていることがわかる。

　2020年の都市ランキングについては、1位がバンコクで、2270万人の旅行者が訪れた。次にヨーロッパの2都市、パリとロンドンが、それぞれ1910万人、1900万人の観光客数で2位と3位にランクインした。ドバイが1590万人、シンガポールが1470万人と続いている。最下位はクアラルンプールで、1380万人の行楽客が訪れた。

　2040年の各国への観光客数予測に関しては、第1位が引き続きアジアの国になると予想されているものの、それはタイではない。中国が1億4700万人の観光客を引きつけると見込まれており、一方タイは、イタリアの数字をわずかに上回る1億人近くで、5位となっている。フランスは、中国とほぼ同数の1億4600万人で、2位を維持する。最後に、アメリカは1億3600万人、スペインは1億3000万人の旅行者を迎えると予想されている。

　全体として、この表は行楽客の間でアジアとヨーロッパの人気が高いことを明らかにし、将来的にもこの傾向が続くであろうことを示している。

Self-Study!

　モデルエッセイを分析していきます。エッセイの英文をもとに質問に**英語**
で答えてください。回答がそのままエッセイを書く材料になります。

導入

Q1 タスク指示文は、どのように言い換えられている？

The graph
shows
the number of international tourists to the six most popular cities in the world in 2020
and predictions by nation for 2040.

Q2 全体的な傾向・要点は？

本体1　最も高い→最も低い――2020

Q3 2020年に最も高い数値だった都市とその数値は？

Q4 それに続くヨーロッパの2都市とそれらの数値は？

Q5 それに続く中東、アジアの2都市とそれらの数値は？

Q6 最も低い数値だった都市とその数値は？

本体2　最も高い→最も低い――2040

Q7 2040年に最高順位の国はどの地域にある？

Q8 最も高い数値の国と、その数値は？

Q9 タイの順位と数値は？　また、タイに似た数値の国は？

Q10 2番目に人気の国は？

Q11 そこと似たような残り2カ国とその数値は？

結論（任意）

Q12 具体的な傾向・要点は？

以下の回答例や自分が分析した結果をもとにエッセイを書きましょう。

導入

Q1 タスク指示文は、どのように言い換えられている？

The graph	*This table*
shows	*provides information on*
the number of international tourists to the six most popular cities in the world in 2020	*the top six cities visited by overseas holidaymakers in 2020*
and predictions by nation for 2040.	*and predicts the six most popular countries in 2040.*

Q2 全体的な傾向・要点は？

A. Asia and Europe dominate, both years

本体1 最も高い→最も低い── 2020

Q3 2020年に最も高い数値だった都市とその数値は？

A. Bangkok, 22.7 million travellers

Q4 それに続くヨーロッパの2都市とそれらの数値は？

A. Paris and London, 19.1 and 19 million

Q5 それに続く中東、アジアの2都市とそれらの数値は？

A. Dubai = 15.9 million, Singapore = 14.7 million

Q6 最も低い数値だった都市とその数値は？

A. Kuala Lumpur, 13.8 million

本体2 最も高い→最も低い── 2040

Q7 2040年に最高順位の国はどの地域にある？

A. Asia (but not Thailand)

Q8　最も高い数値の国と、その数値は？

　　A. China, 147 million

Q9　タイの順位と数値は？　また、タイに似た数値の国は？

　　A. Thailand = fifth, nearly 100 million, marginally higher than Italy

Q10　2番目に人気の国は？

　　A. France (almost matching China)

Q11　そこと似たような残り2カ国とその数値は？

　　A. USA = 136 million and Spain = 130 million

結論（任意）

Q12　具体的な傾向・要点は？

　　A. high popularity of Asia and Europe & will likely continue

エッセイ中の重要語句と表現をエクササイズで確認します。

語句に当てはまる訳の番号を選んでください。

_____ the top six

_____ predicts

_____ From the data,

_____ Regarding

_____ rankings

_____ followed with

_____ the lowest position

_____ forecasts

_____ the top spot

_____ still likely to be occupied by

_____ whereas

_____ in fifth position

_____ almost matching the number for

_____ will likely continue

1. 予測	5. 第1位	占められる見込みだ	12. …については
2. …とほぼ同数で	6. ランキング	9. 一方	13. 上位6つ
3. 予測する	7. 続きそうだ	10. 最下位	14. …で後に続いた
4. データからは	8. 変わらず…によって	11. 5位で	

同じ意味になるよう、単語を記入してください。

• number one choice　=　t_ _ s_ _ _

• predictions　=　f_ _ _ _ _ _ _

• is predicted to　=　is a_ _ _ _ _ _ _ _ _ to

以下の英文の正しい場所に ', respectively' を入れてください。

• Next, two European cities, Paris and London, ranked second and third at 19.1 and 19 million tourists.

正解　13, 3, 4, 12, 6, 14, 10, 1, 5, 8, 9, 11, 2, 7／top spot, forecasts, anticipated／
… tourists, respectively.

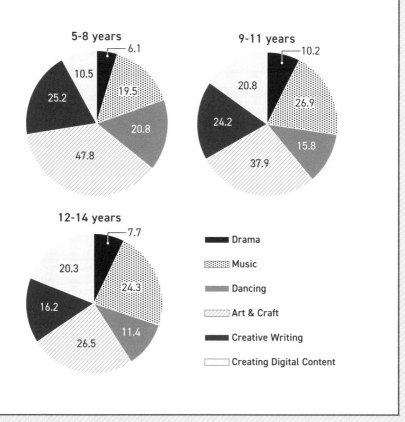

Self-Study!

円グラフ①

タイプ別にモデルエッセイを分析・再構築することで、重要表現を身につけてライティング力を高めます。

You should spend about 20 minutes on this task.

These charts indicate the results of a survey on the percentage of Australian children of different ages who enjoyed doing various activities in 2017-2018.

Summarise the information by selecting and reporting the main features, and make comparisons where relevant.

Write at least 150 words.

5-8 years
— 6.1
10.5
19.5
25.2
20.8
47.8

9-11 years
— 10.2
20.8
26.9
24.2
15.8
37.9

12-14 years
— 7.7
20.3
24.3
16.2
11.4
26.5

■ Drama
▨ Music
▨ Dancing
▨ Art & Craft
■ Creative Writing
□ Creating Digital Content

The three pie graphs reveal the outcome of a study on six activities among children aged 5 to 14 in Australia from 2017 to 2018. Looking at the data, the activities the children enjoyed changed as they grew older.

Among all ages, the most popular activity was art and craft. However, at 47.8% for children aged 5-8, the figure dropped to 37.9% for those aged 9-11 and shrank to 26.5% for 12- to 14-year-olds. Likewise, the proportion for creative writing declined from 25.2 to 24.2 and then 16.2%. There was also a consistent drop in the popularity of dancing, which virtually halved from 20.8% for the youngest to 11.4% for the oldest children. Drama was rated the least popular activity among all age groups. From the youngest to oldest, it was enjoyed by 6.1%, 10.2% and 7.7%, respectively.

In contrast, the proportion of children who enjoyed music jumped from around one-fifth for the younger children to approximately a quarter for both older groups. Finally, the rate for creating digital content had a more dramatic increase, doubling to around 20% for the middle and older age categories.

(186 words – 10 sentences)

In summary, the charts demonstrate that the children's interests altered with age.

(198 words – 11 sentences)

　3つの円グラフは、2017年から2018年にかけて、オーストラリアの5歳から14歳までの子どもを対象とした6つのアクティビティーに関する調査結果を示している。データを見ると、子どもたちが楽しむアクティビティーは年齢が上がるにつれて変化していた。

　すべての年齢で最も人気のあるアクティビティーは図面工作だった。しかし、5〜8歳の子どもでは47.8%だったのが、9〜11歳では37.9%に下がり、12〜14歳では26.5%へと縮小した。同様に、クリエイティブライティングの割合も、25.2%から24.2%、そして16.2%へと減少した。ダンスの人気も一貫して下がり続け、最年少の20.8%から、最年長の子どもたちの11.4%へと、ほぼ半減した。演劇はすべての年齢層で、最も人気のないアクティビティーだった。最年少から最年長まで、それぞれ6.1%、10.2%、7.7%の子どもが楽しんだ。

　対照的に、音楽を楽しんだ子どもたちは、年少者の約5分の1から、両方の年長グループでは約4分の1へと急増した。最後に、デジタル・コンテンツ作成の割合はより劇的な増加を示し、真ん中と最年長の年齢層では約20%と、2倍になった。

　要約すると、これらのグラフは子どもたちの興味が年齢とともに変化したことを示している。

Self-Study!

モデルエッセイを分析していきます。エッセイの英文をもとに質問に**英語で**答えてください。回答がそのままエッセイを書く材料になります。

導入

Q1 タスク指示文は、どのように言い換えられている？

These charts
indicate
the results of a survey on
the percentage of Australian children of different ages who enjoyed doing various activities
in 2017-2018.

Q2 全体的な傾向・要点は？

本体1 1～3番目に高い＆低い（＆人気がなくなった）

Q3 全年齢層で、最も人気のあったアクティビティーは？

Q4 各年齢層で、数値はどのように変わった（下がった）？

Q5 最も若い年齢層で、2番目に人気のあったアクティビティーはどれで、年齢が上がると数値はどのように変わった（下がった）？

Q6 最も若い年齢層で、3番目に人気のあったアクティビティーはどれで、最年長で数値はどのように変わった（下がった）？

Q7 全年齢層で、一番人気のなかったアクティビティーは？

Q8 数値はどのように変わった？

本体2 人気が出た

Q9 増加したアクティビティーとその数値は？

Q10 それ以上に増加したアクティビティーとその数値は？

結論（任意）

Q11 具体的な傾向・要点は？

以下の回答例や自分が分析した結果をもとにエッセイを書きましょう。

導入

Q1 タスク指示文は、どのように言い換えられている？

These charts	*The three pie graphs*
indicate	*reveal*
the results of a survey on	*the outcome of a study on*
the percentage of Australian children of different ages who enjoyed doing various activities	*six activities among children aged 5 to 14 in Australia*
in 2017-2018.	*from 2017 to 2018.*

Q2 全体的な傾向・要点は？

A. activities the children enjoyed changed as they grew older

本体1 1〜3番目に高い＆低い（＆人気がなくなった）

Q3 全年齢層で、最も人気のあったアクティビティーは？

A. art and craft

Q4 各年齢層で、数値はどのように変わった（下がった）？

A. 47.8% = age 5-8, 37.9% = age 9-11, 26.5% = 12- to 14-year-olds

Q5 最も若い年齢層で、2番目に人気のあったアクティビティーはどれで、年齢が上がると数値はどのように変わった（下がった）？

A. creative writing, 25.2 ↘ 24.2 ↘ 16.2%

Q6 最も若い年齢層で、3番目に人気のあったアクティビティーはどれで、最年長で数値はどのように変わった（下がった）？

A. dancing, halved from 20.8% for youngest to 11.4% for oldest children

Q7 全年齢層で、一番人気のなかったアクティビティーは？

A. drama

Q8 数値はどのように変わった?

　A. 6.1% ↗ 10.2% ↘ 7.7%

本体2 人気が出た

Q9 増加したアクティビティーとその数値は?

　A. music, one-fifth = younger group ↗ one-quarter = older groups

Q10 それ以上に増加したアクティビティーとその数値は?

　A. creating digital content, doubled to 20% for older ages

結論(任意)

Q11 具体的な傾向・要点は?

　A. children's interests altered with age

エッセイ中の重要語句と表現をエクササイズで確認します。

語句に当てはまる訳の番号を選んでください。

_____ The three		_____ virtually halved	
_____ the outcome of		_____ from around one-fifth	
_____ Looking at the data,		_____ a quarter	
_____ was rated		_____ Finally,	
_____ However,		_____ doubling to	
_____ Likewise,		_____ demonstrate	
_____ consistent			

1. 一貫して	5. 最後に	9. 約5分の1から	13. しかしながら
2. 4分の1	6. 評価された	10. その3つの	
3. …の結果	7. 2倍の…になって	11. 示す	
4. ほぼ半減した	8. データを見ると	12. 同様に	

正しい単語を選んでください。

• There was also a consistent drop in the [popular / popularity] of dancing,
[which / what] virtually [halved / doubled] from 20.8% for the youngest
to 11.4% for the oldest children.

導入の語句が結論でどう言い換えられていますか？　下線部に2語ずつ入れてください。

導入：... the activities the children enjoyed changed as they grew older

結論：... the _____ altered _____

正解 10, 3, 8, 6, 13, 12, 1, 4, 9, 2, 5, 7, 11／popularity, which, halved／
children's interests, with age

Self-Study!

プロセス図 ①

タイプ別にモデルエッセイを分析・再構築することで、重要表現を身につけてライティング力を高めます。

You should spend about 20 minutes on this task.

The chart below shows how peanuts and peanut products are made.

Summarise the information by selecting and reporting the main features, and make comparisons where relevant.

Write at least 150 words.

Products from Peanuts

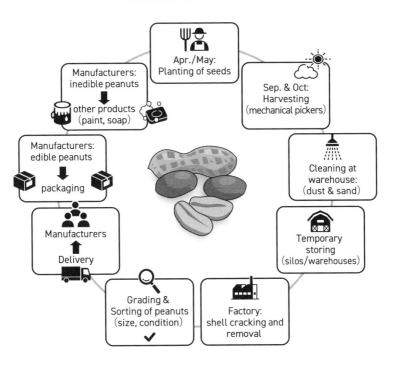

This flow chart indicates the basic method of producing peanuts and products made with the same ingredient. According to the diagram, there are nine steps in the whole process.

In order to grow peanuts, first, farmers plant peanut seeds in April or May. Then, around four to five months later, the ripe peanuts are harvested by machines called mechanical pickers. After being harvested, the peanuts are delivered to a warehouse where they are cleaned in order to remove dust and sand from their shells. Then, the clean peanuts, which still have their shells, are stored in silos or in the warehouse for a certain length of time.

In the next stage, the peanuts are transported to a factory. Here, the shells are cracked and removed, which leaves the actual peanuts. Then they are graded and sorted according to their size and condition. Following that, the peanuts are delivered to manufacturers, who use them in two ways. Namely, the edible peanuts are packaged for sale while the inedible ones are used to make different products such as paint and soap.

(179 words – 11 sentences)

In conclusion, the chart indicates that peanuts go through various processes resulting in food that may be eaten directly or in peanut-related products.

(202 words – 12 sentences)

　この工程図は、ピーナッツ、そして同じ原料を使用した製品の基本的な製造方法を示したものだ。この図によると、全工程には、9つの段階がある。

　ピーナッツを栽培するには、まず農業従事者が4月か5月にピーナッツの種を植える。そして、約4、5カ月後に、熟したピーナッツは、自動収穫機と呼ばれる機械で収穫される。収穫されたピーナッツは、倉庫に運ばれ、殻についたホコリや砂を取り除くためにきれいにされる。そして、まだ殻が残っているきれいなピーナッツは、サイロや倉庫に一定期間保存される。

　次の段階では、ピーナッツは工場に運ばれる。ここで、殻が割れて取り除かれ、ピーナッツの実が残る。そして、大きさや状態に応じて等級づけされ、選別される。その後、製造業社に出荷され、2つの用途で使用される。すなわち、食用に適するピーナッツは販売用に包装され、非食用のピーナッツは塗料や石けんなど、様々な製品を作るために使用される。

　結論として、この図は、ピーナッツが様々な工程を経て、直接食べることができる食品になるか、ピーナッツ関連製品で使用されることを示している。

Self-Study!

　モデルエッセイを分析していきます。エッセイの英文をもとに質問に**英語で**答えてください。回答がそのままエッセイを書く材料になります。

導入

Q1 タスク指示文は、どのように言い換えられている？

The chart below
shows
how peanuts and peanut products are made.

_____

Q2 全体的な傾向・要点は？

本体1 栽培から保存へ

Q3 最初に何が起こる？

Q4 次に何が起こり、それはどうやって行われる？

Q5 その後にピーナッツはどこに運ばれ、その理由は？

Q6 理由の詳細は？

Q7 ピーナッツは次にどうなる？

本体2 工場から製品へ

Q8 次にピーナッツはどこに運ばれ、その理由は？

Q9 次に何が起こる？

Q10 続いてピーナッツはどこに運ばれ、何通りの方法で使用される？

Q11 その方法は？

結論（任意）

Q12 具体的な傾向・要点は？

以下の回答例や自分が分析した結果をもとにエッセイを書きましょう。

導入

Q1 タスク指示文は、どのように言い換えられている？

The chart below	This flow chart
shows	indicates
how peanuts and peanut products are made.	the basic method of producing peanuts and products made with the same ingredient.

Q2 全体的な傾向・要点は？

A. nine steps in whole process

本体1 栽培から保存へ

Q3 最初に何が起こる？

A. peanut seeds = planted in Apr/May.

Q4 次に何が起こり、それはどうやって行われる？

A. harvested 4 ~ 5 months later by mechanical pickers

Q5 その後にピーナッツはどこに運ばれ、その理由は？

A. peanuts → warehouse → cleaned

Q6 理由の詳細は？

A. remove dust & sand from shells

Q7 ピーナッツは次にどうなる？

A. stored in silos or warehouse

本体2 工場から製品へ

Q8 次にピーナッツはどこに運ばれ、その理由は？

A. factory: shells = cracked and removed

Q9 次に何が起こる？

  A. graded & sorted: size, condition

Q10 続いてピーナッツはどこに運ばれ、何通りの方法で使用される？

  A. delivered to manufacturers: used in two ways

Q11 その方法は？

  A. edible = packaged for sale, inedible = used to make different products

結論（任意）

Q12 具体的な傾向・要点は？

  A. peanuts go through various processes, may be eaten or used for other products

エッセイ中の重要語句と表現をエクササイズで確認します。

語句に当てはまる訳の番号を選んでください。

_____ flow		_____ for a certain length of time	
_____ the basic method of		_____ In the next stage,	
_____ ingredient		_____ ... factory. Here,	
_____ nine steps in the whole process		_____ such as	
_____ In order to		_____ go through various processes	
_____ plant		_____ result in	
_____ called		_____ -related	

1. 様々な工程を経る	5. 植える	9. 次の段階では	13. 工場。ここで
2. …と呼ばれる	6. …になる	10. …するために	14. 全工程で9つの段階
3. 流れ	7. 一定期間	11. …など、…のような	
4. …の基本的な方法	8. …関連の	12. 原料	

正しい単語を選んでください。

• In order to grow peanuts, first, farmers plant peanut seeds [on / in / at] April or May.

空所に適切な動詞を入れてください。

• The ripe peanuts are (h_ _ _ _ _ _ed) by machines ...

• The peanuts are (d_ _ _ _ _ _ed) to a warehouse ...

• The clean peanuts ... are (s_ _ _ed) in silos ...

• The peanuts are (t_ _ _ _ _ _ _ed) to a factory ...

• The edible peanuts are (p_ _ _ _ _ed) for sale ...

正解 3, 4, 12, 14, 10, 5, 2, 7, 9, 13, 11, 1, 6, 8／in／harvested, delivered, stored, transported, packaged

Self-Study!

地図・図解①

タイプ別にモデルエッセイを分析・再構築することで、重要表現を身につけてライティング力を高めます。

You should spend about 20 minutes on this task.

The two maps below show changes to the Dunebay coastal area and Shore Island.

Summarise the information by selecting and reporting the main features, and make comparisons where relevant.

Write at least 150 words.

Shore Island (2000)

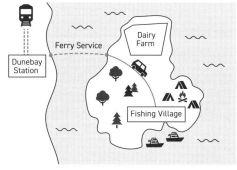

Shore Island (present~)

93

The upper map indicates features of Dunebay and Shore Island in 2000 while the lower one reveals later developments in the same locations. According to the content, major changes are evident, particularly on the island.

In 2000, close to the station, there was a ferry service to the west side of Shore Island. From there, one road ran directly to a fishing village in the south. A forest stood on the west side of the road and a campsite was located on its east side. The northern part of the island was primarily occupied by a dairy farm.

Today, there are some notable changes on the island. For instance, the ferry service has been replaced by a bridge, so vehicles can drive directly onto the island. In addition, the size of the forest has been reduced and a golf course built there. However, the fishing village and campsite remain as they were in 2000.

Two major developments are planned for 2035. First, an aquarium is going to be constructed south of the train station while the dairy farm will be turned into a resort hotel.

(185 words – 12 sentences)

Overall, it is clear that tourism is of growing importance to this area.

(198 words – 13 sentences)

　　上の地図は、2000年のデューンベイとショアー島の特徴を示し、下の地図は同じ場所での、その後の開発を明らかにしている。内容によると、特に島では大きな変化が見られる。

　　2000年当時、駅の近くにはショアー島の西側に行くフェリーの便があった。そこから南側の漁村へ直通の道が通っていた。道路の西側には森があり、東側にはキャンプ場があった。島の北部は、主に酪農場が占めていた。

　　現在、島にはいくつかの注目すべき変化がある。例えば、フェリーの代わりに橋が架けられたため、車が島に直接乗り入れられるようになった。さらに、森の面積が減り、ゴルフ場ができた。しかし、漁村やキャンプ場は、2000年当時と変わらず残っている。

　　2035年には2つの大きな開発が予定されている。まず、鉄道駅の南側に水族館が建設され、酪農場はリゾートホテルに変わる。

　　全体的に見て、この地域にとって観光の重要性が高まっていることは明らかだ。

Self-Study!

　モデルエッセイを分析していきます。エッセイの英文をもとに質問に**英語で**答えてください。回答がそのままエッセイを書く材料になります。

導入

Q1 タスク指示文は、どのように言い換えられている？

The two maps
show
changes to the Dunebay coastal area and Shore Island.

Q2 全体的な傾向・要点は？

本体1 2000年

Q3 2000年に島へと渡るための重要な設備は？

Q4 漁村へと向かう（続く）交通手段は？

Q5 道路の西側と東側に何があった？

Q6 島の北部には何があった？

本体2 現在

Q7 島に行く手段について、どのような変化があった？

Q8 島ではどんな変化があった？

Q9 島で変わらなかったものは？

本体3 未来

Q10 将来はどのような変化がある？

結論（任意）

Q11 具体的な傾向・要点は？

以下の回答例や自分が分析した結果をもとにエッセイを書きましょう。

導入

Q1 タスク指示文は、どのように言い換えられている？

The two maps		*The upper map*
show		*indicates*
changes to the Dunebay coastal area and Shore Island.		*features of Dunebay and Shore Island in 2000*
		while the lower one reveals later developments in the same location.

Q2 全体的な傾向・要点は？

A. major changes, particularly on island

本体1 2000年

Q3 2000年に島へと渡るための重要な設備は？

A. close to station: a ferry service to the island's west side

Q4 漁村へと向かう（続く）交通手段は？

A. a road running south

Q5 道路の西側と東側に何があった？

A. west side: a forest, east side: a campsite

Q6 島の北部には何があった？

A. a dairy farm

本体2 現在

Q7 島に行く手段について、どのような変化があった？

A. ferry service → bridge (vehicles can drive onto island)

Q8 島ではどんな変化があった？

 A. forest reduced & golf course built

Q9 島で変わらなかったものは？

 A. fishing village & campsite remain

本体3 未来

Q10 将来はどのような変化がある？

 A. (Dunebay) aquarium south of station

  (Shore Island) dairy farm → resort hotel

結論（任意）

Q11 具体的な傾向・要点は？

 A. tourism = growing importance to area

エッセイ中の重要語句と表現をエクササイズで確認します。

語句に当てはまる訳の番号を選んでください。

_____ features of

_____ close to

_____ to the west side of

_____ From there,

_____ directly to

_____ on the west side of the

_____ The northern part of the

_____ notable changes

_____ For instance,

_____ has been replaced by

_____ has been reduced

_____ remain as they were

_____ south of

_____ will be turned into

1. 例えば	5. 注目すべき変化	9. …の北部	13. …に直通の
2. …へと変更される	6. …の南	10. 減少させられた	14. そこから
3. …の西側への	7. …に取って代わられた	11. 変わらないままである	
4. …の近く	8. …の特徴	12. …の西側に	

正しい単語を選んでください。

• For instance, the ferry service has been replaced [for / by / to / over] a bridge, so vehicles can drive directly [into / at / onto / by] the island.

カッコ内を正しい順序に並べ替えてください。

• Today, [are / changes / some / notable / there] on the island.

• Two [planned / developments / major / are] for 2035.

正解 8, 4, 3, 14, 13, 12, 9, 5, 1, 7, 10, 11, 6, 2／by, onto／there are some notable changes, major developments are planned

Self-Study!

異なるタイプの組み合わせ①

タイプ別にモデルエッセイを分析・再構築することで、重要表現を身につけてライティング力を高めます。

You should spend about 20 minutes on this task.

The charts show a local library and reasons why people use it.

Summarise the information by selecting and reporting the main features, and make comparisons where relevant.

Write at least 150 words.

BALSHAW LIBRARY

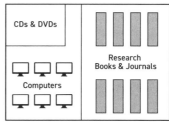

GROUND FLOOR

Reception	
Newspapers Magazines	Fiction
	Non-fiction
	Children's Books

1st. FLOOR

CDs & DVDs

Computers

Research Books & Journals

📋 SURVEY

What do you use the library for?	Teenagers	Adults	Pensioners
Borrowing books		✓	✓
Studying (school homework)	✓		
Personal research		✓	
Borrowing CDs/DVDs		✓	✓
Reading newspapers/magazines			✓

(✓ = most common responses)

While the floor plan depicts the sections of Balshaw Library, the table indicates the main reasons for teenagers, adults and pensioners to use the two-storey facility. Based on the information provided, the library can be used for various purposes, which differ according to age.

The library's reception is located on the ground floor. Also, books, which include fiction and non-fiction as well as those for children, can be found on this floor. In addition, there are magazines and newspapers for visitors to read. Turning to the first floor, there is a large area containing research books and journals. Moreover, people can use computers and borrow CDs and DVDs on this floor.

According to a survey on why people use the library, teenagers answered that they mostly use it to do their homework. As for adults, they responded with three reasons: borrowing books, doing personal research and borrowing CDs/ DVDs. The oldest group in the survey, pensioners, said they use the library for the same purposes as adults, with the exception of research. Instead, they like to read newspapers and magazines. *(179 words – 11 sentences)*

In conclusion, the library serves the interests and needs of its various users. Among them, teenagers mainly use it for doing homework while older people primarily use it to borrow books as well as music and films/documentaries, etc.

(217 words – 13 sentences)

　館内案内図にはバルショー図書館の各区域が描かれている一方、表には、10代、大人、年金生活者が、この2階建ての施設を利用する主な理由が示されている。提供された情報によると、図書館は年齢に応じて異なる様々な目的で使用することができる。

　図書館の受付は1階にある。この階には、フィクション、ノンフィクション、そして子ども向けのものを含めた書籍がある。また、訪れた人が読むことのできる雑誌や新聞も置いてある。2階を見ると、調査・研究用の書籍やジャーナルが置かれた広い場所がある。加えてこの階では、コンピューターを利用したり、CDやDVDを借りたりすることができる。

　図書館の利用理由に関する調査によると、10代の若者は、主に宿題をするために利用すると答えた。大人は、本を借りるため、個人的な調べ物をするため、そしてCD／DVDを借りるため、という3つの理由を答えた。今回の調査で最も高齢のグループである年金生活者も、調べ物を除いて大人と同じ目的で図書館を利用すると答えている。調べ物の代わりに、新聞や雑誌を読むのを好んでいる。

　結論として、図書館は様々な利用者の興味やニーズに応えている。その中でも、10代の若者は主に宿題をするために利用し、年長者は主として本、さらには音楽や映画、ドキュメンタリーなどを借りるために利用している。

Self-Study!

　モデルエッセイを分析していきます。エッセイの英文をもとに質問に**英語で**答えてください。回答がそのままエッセイを書く材料になります。

導入

Q1 タスク指示文は、どのように言い換えられている？

The charts
show
a local library
and reasons why
people use it.

_____

_____

_____

Q2 全体的な傾向・要点は？

本体1　建物の間取り：1階＆2階

Q3 図書館に入って、通例、最初に通る場所は？

Q4 この階にはどのような本が置いてある？

Q5 1階にはほかに何がある？

Q6 2階の半分を占めているものは？

Q7 2階にはほかに何がある？

本体2　調査結果

Q8 10代の若者は、主に何のために図書館を利用する？

Q9 大人は利用する理由をいくつ挙げていて、それは何？

Q10 年金生活者の傾向は？

結論（任意）

Q11 具体的な傾向・要点は？

以下の回答例や自分が分析した結果をもとにエッセイを書きましょう。

導入

Q1 タスク指示文は、どのように言い換えられている？

The charts	*While the floor plan*
show	*depicts*
a local library	*the sections of Balshaw Library,*
and reasons why people use it.	*the table indicates the main reasons for teenagers, adults and pensioners to use the two-storey facility.*

Q2 全体的な傾向・要点は？

A. library used for various purposes = differ according to age

本体1 建物の間取り：1階＆2階

Q3 図書館に入って、通例、最初に通る場所は？

A. reception

Q4 この階にはどのような本が置いてある？

A. fiction & non-fiction, children's books

Q5 1階にはほかに何がある？

A. magazines & newspapers

Q6 2階の半分を占めているものは？

A. large area with research books & journals

Q7 2階にはほかに何がある？

A. computers, CDs & DVDs

本体2 調査結果

Q8 10代の若者は、主に何のために図書館を利用する？

A. to do homework

Q9 大人は利用する理由をいくつ挙げていて、それは何？

   A. three: borrowing books, personal research, CDs/DVDs

Q10 年金生活者の傾向は？

   A. same purposes except research, instead = newspapers & magazines

結論（任意）

Q11 具体的な傾向・要点は？

   A. library serves various interests & needs of users:

     - teenagers = mainly homework

     - older people = primarily books, music, films

エッセイ中の重要語句と表現をエクササイズで確認します。

語句に当てはまる訳の番号を選んでください。

_____ floor plan

_____ the sections of

_____ the main reasons for ... to ~

_____ Based on the information
       provided,

_____ differ according to

_____ on the ground floor

_____ as well as

_____ According to a survey on

_____ answered

_____ responded with three reasons:

_____ in the survey

_____ purposes

_____ Instead,

1. …の区域	5. その調査で	9. …が～する主な理由	13. 答えた
2. 館内案内図	6. 提供された情報によると	10. その代わり	
3. 目的	7. …同様	11. 3つの理由を答えた	
4. …に関する調査によると	8. 1階に	12. …に応じて異なる	

同じ意味になるよう、単語を記入してください。

• is located　　=　　c_ _ b_ f_ _ _ _

• mostly　　　=　　m_ _ _ _ _　=　p_ _ _ _ _ _ _ _

下線部を1語に書き換えてください。

• Turning to the first floor, there is a large area <u>that contains</u> research books and
  journals.

Self-Study!
折れ線グラフ②

タイプ別にモデルエッセイを分析・再構築することで、重要表現を身につけてライティング力を高めます。

You should spend about 20 minutes on this task.

The chart shows the percentage of unemployment in selected nations in Europe from 2000 to 2018.

Summarise the information by selecting and reporting the main features, and make comparisons where relevant.

Write at least 150 words.

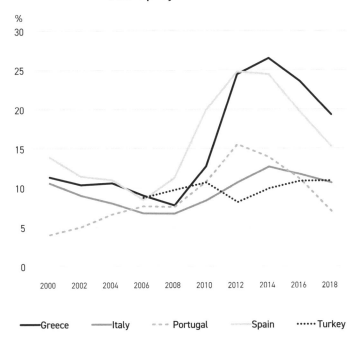

Unemployment Rates

This line graph provides data on the levels of unemployment in five European countries between the years 2000 and 2018. According to the information, the percentages fluctuated but mostly rose over the 19-year period.

In general, Spain and Greece experienced the highest rates of jobless individuals. In the first year, their figures stood at 14 and 12%, respectively. Thereafter, they dipped by around five per cent until 2006-8 before climbing and then peaking at around 25-27% in 2012-14. Even so, they fell in the remaining years, to finish with 19% for Greece and 15% for Spain.

In comparison, the other three nations maintained lower unemployment rates during the whole period. Although Italy's figure gently fluctuated, it started and ended with 11%. As for Turkey, its data begins from 2006, at 9%, and the figure grew marginally to finish with the same proportion as that of Italy. Portugal had the lowest rate in both the first and last years (4% and 7%). However, unemployment did peak at 15% in 2012, which was several percentage points above Italy and Turkey at the time. *(181 words – 11 sentences)*

Overall, the chart shows that unemployment rates went up marginally in all countries except Spain and Greece, who saw major increases.

(202 words – 12 sentences)

　この折れ線グラフは、2000年から2018年までの、欧州5カ国の失業率の水準に関するデータを提供している。情報によると、19年の間に割合は変動しながらも、ほとんどが上昇した。

　概して、スペインとギリシャの失業者の割合が最も高かった。最初の年の失業率は、それぞれ14％と12％だった。その後、2006年・2008年までは約5％減少したが、2012年・2014年にかけては上昇し、約25〜27％という最高値に達した。しかし、その後の数年間は低下し、ギリシャは19％、スペインは15％で終えた。

　それに比べて他の3カ国は、全期間で低い失業率を維持している。イタリアの数字はゆるやかに変動したものの、最初と最後は11％だった。トルコに関しては、2006年から9％で始まったデータはわずかに上昇して、イタリアと同じ割合で終わっている。ポルトガルは、最初の年も最後の年も、失業率が最も低かった（4％、7％）。しかし、失業率は2012年に15％と最高値に達し、当時のイタリアやトルコを数パーセント・ポイント上回っていた。

　全体的に見ると、このグラフはほぼすべての国で失業率がわずかに上昇し、例外は大幅に上昇したスペインとギリシャだったことを示している。

Self-Study!

モデルエッセイを分析していきます。エッセイの英文をもとに質問に**英語で**答えてください。回答がそのままエッセイを書く材料になります。

導入

Q1 タスク指示文は、どのように言い換えられている？

The chart shows the percentage of unemployment in selected nations in Europe from 2000 to 2018.

_____

_____

_____

_____

Q2 全体的な傾向・要点は？

本体1 より高い数字、似た傾向

Q3 ほかの国に比べて数字が高かった2カ国は？

Q4 同国の最初の年の割合は？

Q5 同国の2014年までの大きな変化は？

Q6 それらの国の割合はどのように終了した？

本体2 より低い数字

Q7 ほかの3カ国の概要は？

Q8 イタリアの傾向と数字は？

Q9 トルコの傾向と数字は？

Q10 最初と最後の年に最も低い失業率だった国と、その数字は？

Q11 全期間を通して、その国の目立った数字は？

結論（任意）

Q12 具体的な傾向・要点は？

以下の回答例や自分が分析した結果をもとにエッセイを書きましょう。

導入

Q1 タスク指示文は、どのように言い換えられている？

The chart		*This line graph*
shows		*provides data on*
the percentage of		*the levels of*
unemployment in selected nations in Europe		*unemployment in five European countries*
from 2000 to 2018.		*between the years 2000 and 2018.*

Q2 全体的な傾向・要点は？

A. percentages fluctuated, mostly rose

本体1 より高い数字、似た傾向

Q3 ほかの国に比べて数字が高かった2カ国は？

A. Spain and Greece

Q4 同国の最初の年の割合は？

A. 14%, 12%

Q5 同国の2014年までの大きな変化は？

A. both dipped 5% until 2006-8, climbed, peaked at 25-27% in 2012-14

Q6 それらの国の割合はどのように終了した？

A. 19% = Greece, 15% = Spain

本体2 より低い数字

Q7 ほかの3カ国の概要は？

A. lower unemployment during whole period

Q8 イタリアの傾向と数字は？

A. fluctuated, started & ended with 11%

Q9 トルコの傾向と数字は？

    A. began in 2006 (9%), finished with same % as Italy

Q10 最初と最後の年に最も低い失業率だった国と、その数字は？

    A. Portugal (4%, 7%)

Q11 全期間を通して、その国の目立った数字は？

    A. peaked at 15% in 2012

結論 (任意)

Q12 具体的な傾向・要点は？

    A. unemployment rates went up marginally in all countries except Spain
    and Greece

エッセイ中の重要語句と表現をエクササイズで確認します。

語句に当てはまる訳の番号を選んでください。

____ provides data on		____ unemployment rates	
____ the highest rates of		____ Although ..., it ~	
____ individuals		____ As for ..., its data begins from ~	
____ In the first year		____ in both the first and last years	
____ in the remaining years		____ several percentage points above	
____ In comparison,		____ at the time	
____ maintained			

1. …に関してデータは　　3. 残りの年では　　7. 個人、人　　10. 維持した
　 ～から始まっている　 4. 失業率　　　　 8. …に関するデータ　 11. …だけれども、それは~
2. …より数パーセント・　5. 当時　　　　　　 を提供する　　　 12. 最初の年も最後の年も
　 ポイント上回って　　 6. 比較すると　　 9. 最初の年には　 13. …の最も高い割合

同じ意味になるよう、空所に1語または2語を入れてください。

- 2000 ~ 2018　　=　over _____ period　（2語）
- 2000　　　　　 =　In _____ year　（2語）
- 2000 and 2018　=　the _____ and _____ years　（各1語）

下線部を1語に書き換えてください。

- … and the figure grew marginally to finish with the same proportion as <u>the proportion</u> of Italy.

棒グラフ②

タイプ別にモデルエッセイを分析・再構築することで、重要
表現を身につけてライティング力を高めます。

You should spend about 20 minutes on this task.

The graph reveals the value of exports from New Zealand to selected countries in the same month in different years.

Summarise the information by selecting and reporting the main features, and make comparisons where relevant.

Write at least 150 words.

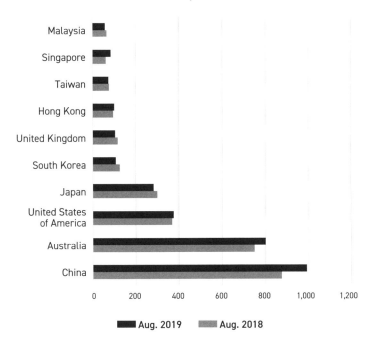

New Zealand Exports $(million)

This bar chart compares New Zealand's August exports in millions of dollars to ten countries in 2018 with those in 2019. According to the data, the value of exports can be divided into low, middle and high brackets, and all figures experienced relatively minimal change.

Exports to six countries were low in both years. For instance, the figures for Malaysia, Singapore and Taiwan ranged between 50 to 75 million dollars, while those for Hong Kong, the UK and South Korea were higher, at around $100 million each.

In the middle bracket, the value of exports to Japan stood at around $300 million in 2018 but dropped slightly the next year. With approximately $380 million, America's initial figure was higher, and it climbed slightly in 2019.

However, exports to Australia and China represented the largest income for New Zealand. In August 2018, their figures were roughly $750 million and $880 million, respectively. By the following year, the figures had risen by $50 million for Australia and $120 million for China, with the latter rise being the most notable one among all ten countries. *(182 words – 9 sentences)*

In conclusion, the graph reveals that the majority of New Zealand's exports went to countries with a large population or geographical size.

(204 words – 10 sentences)

　この棒グラフは、2018年と2019年の8月の、ニュージーランドから10カ国への輸出額を、100万ドル単位で比較している。このデータによると、輸出額は低位、中位、高位の区分に分けることができ、どの数字も比較的変化が少ない。

　6カ国への輸出額は両年とも低かった。例えば、マレーシア、シンガポール、そして台湾への額は、5000万ドルから7500万ドルの間で変動し、香港、英国、そして韓国はそれぞれ1億ドル前後と、少し高くなっている。

　中位の区分では、日本への輸出額が2018年は3億ドルほどだったが、翌年にはやや低下した。

アメリカの最初の数字は、およそ3億8000ドルともう少し高く、2019年にも少し増えている。

　しかし、オーストラリアと中国への輸出は、ニュージーランドにとって最大の収入となった。2018年8月のそれぞれの総額は、ざっと7億5000万ドルと8億8000万ドルだった。翌年になると、総額はオーストラリアで5000万ドル、そして中国で1億2000万ドル増加しており、後者の増加は全10カ国の中で最も顕著なものだった。

　結論として、このグラフは、ニュージーランドの輸出の大半が、人口や地理的規模の大きい国に向けられたことを示している。

Self-Study!

　モデルエッセイを分析していきます。エッセイの英文をもとに質問に**英語で**答えてください。回答がそのままエッセイを書く材料になります。

導入

Q1 タスク指示文は、どのように言い換えられている？

The graph
reveals
the value of exports
from New Zealand
to selected countries
in the same month in
different years.

_____

_____

_____

_____

_____

Q2 全体的な傾向・要点は？

本体1 低い数字

Q3 両年とも低い数字だった国はいくつある？

Q4 両年ともに、最も総額の低い3カ国の範囲は？

Q5 両年ともに、総額がやや高い3カ国の範囲は？

本体2 中間の数字

Q6 両年とも前述の6カ国よりも総額が高かった国とその数字は？

Q7 それ以上に総額が高かった国とその数字は？

本体3 一番高い数字

Q8 両年ともに最も総額が高かった2つの国は？

Q9 両国の2018年の数字は？

Q10 2019年にどのように数字が変わった？

結論（任意）

Q11 具体的な傾向・要点は？

以下の回答例や自分が分析した結果をもとにエッセイを書きましょう。

導入

Q1 タスク指示文は、どのように言い換えられている？

The graph		This bar chart
reveals		compares
the value of exports from New Zealand		New Zealand's August exports in millions of dollars
to selected countries		to ten countries
in the same month in different years.		in 2018 with those in 2019.

Q2 全体的な傾向・要点は？

A. low, medium and high brackets, all figures = minimal change

本体1 低い数字

Q3 両年とも低い数字だった国はいくつある？

A. six

Q4 両年ともに、最も総額の低い3カ国の範囲は？

A. Malaysia, Singapore and Taiwan: ranged 50 ~ 75 million dollars

Q5 両年ともに、総額がやや高い3カ国の範囲は？

A. Hong Kong, the UK and South Korea = higher: around $100 million

本体2 中間の数字

Q6 両年とも前述の6カ国よりも総額が高かった国とその数字は？

A. Japan: 300 million in 2018, dropped in 2019

Q7 それ以上に総額が高かった国とその数字は？

A. America: 380 million in 2018, climbed in 2019

本体3　**一番高い数字**

Q8　両年ともに最も総額が高かった2つの国は？

　　A.　Australia and China

Q9　両国の2018年の数字は？

　　A.　Australia = 750 million, China = 880 million

Q10　2019年にどのように数字が変わった？

　　A.　both rose; Australia by 50 million, China by 120 million

結論（任意）

Q11　具体的な傾向・要点は？

　　A.　majority of New Zealand's exports went to countries with large
　　　　population/land size

エッセイ中の重要語句と表現をエクササイズで確認します。

語句に当てはまる訳の番号を選んでください。

_____ in millions of dollars	_____ With approximately
_____ can be divided into	_____ represented the largest
_____ brackets	_____ the latter rise
_____ relatively	_____ the most notable
_____ ranged between	_____ among all
_____ In the middle bracket,	_____ the majority of

1. …の間で変動した　　4. 区分、階層　　8. 全…の中で　　12. …の大半・過半数
2. 比較的　　5. 最も顕著な　　9. 後者の増加
3. 最大の…となった・　6. 100万ドル単位で　　10. およそ…で
　を示した　　7. …に分けることができる　　11. 中位の区分では

下線部を1語に書き換えてください。

- This bar chart compares New Zealand's August exports in millions of dollars to ten countries in 2018 with exports in 2019.
- For instance, the figures for Malaysia, Singapore and Taiwan ranged between 50 to 75 million dollars, while the figures for Hong Kong ...

空所に 'By + Had' または 'In + were' の適切な方を入れてください。

- _____ August 2018, their figures _____ roughly $750 million and $880 million, respectively.
- _____ the following year, the figures _____ risen by $50 million for Australia and $120 million for China, ...

Self-Study!

表 ②

タイプ別にモデルエッセイを分析・再構築することで、重要表現を身につけてライティング力を高めます。

You should spend about 20 minutes on this task.

The following chart reveals the number of businesses in selected industries in Australia during five years.

Summarise the information by selecting and reporting the main features, and make comparisons where relevant.

Write at least 150 words.

Industry Type	2014	2015	2016	2017	2018
Agriculture, forestry & fishing	42,383	41,512	40,634	40,010	39,484
Manufacturing	23,333	23,302	23,370	23,431	23,673
Construction	89,441	91,729	95,298	99,343	104,024
Retail trade	36,098	35,583	35,435	35,206	35,247
Accommodation & food services	22,936	23,488	24,432	25,165	25,761
Information media & telecommunications	5,210	5,404	5,504	5,774	5,979

This table indicates how many companies existed in six industries in Australia from 2014 to 2018. Analysing the details, it is clear that two industries saw declines in numbers while the remainder experienced rises over the five-year period.

In terms of reduced numbers, there was a drop of around 850 companies in the retail trade industry, which finished at just over 35,200. The agriculture, forestry and fishing sector experienced an even larger fall, starting with roughly 42,400 and finishing with 39,500.

Conversely, there were increases in four industries. For instance, although information media and telecommunications had the lowest annual figure, which marked 5,210 in 2014, its total had climbed by approximately 750 four years later. Manufacturing also experienced modest growth (nearly 350 more companies) to reach 23,673 in 2018. Regarding the accommodation and food services industry, there was a more dramatic addition of around 2,800, bringing the total to 25,761 in the last year. However, the construction sector had the highest figure every year and the largest overall increase (just over 14,500) among all categories, ending with just over 104,000 companies.

(181 words – 9 sentences)

Overall, while the table reveals that both positive and negative changes occurred during the given period, the construction industry was particularly strong.

(203 words – 10 sentences)

この表は、2014年から2018年にかけて、オーストラリアの6つの産業にどれだけの企業が存在したかを示している。詳細を分析すると、5年間で2つの産業で数が減少し、残りの産業で増加したことは明らかだ。

減少数に関しては、小売業では約850社減少し、3万5200社強で終えた。農林水産業はさらに大幅に減少し、ざっと4万2400社で始まり、3万9500社で終了した。

逆に、4つの業界では増加した。例えば、情報メディア・通信業は、2014年は5210社と最も少なかったものの、4年後には総数がおよそ750社増えている。製造業もゆるやかな伸び（350社近い増加）を示し、2018年には2万3673社に達した。宿泊・飲食サービス業については、より劇的な約2800社の増加が見られ、最終年は合計2万5761社となった。しかし、建設業がすべてのカテゴリーの中で毎年最も高い数値と、全体的に最も大きな増加（1万4500社強）を示し、10万4000社強で終了している。

全体として、この表からは、所定の期間中に肯定的な変化と否定的な変化の両方が起きており、中でも建設業界が特に好調だったことがわかる。

Self-Study!

モデルエッセイを分析していきます。エッセイの英文をもとに質問に**英語で**答えてください。回答がそのままエッセイを書く材料になります。

導入

Q1 タスク指示文は、どのように言い換えられている？

The following chart
reveals
the number of businesses
in selected industries
in Australia
during five years.

_____
_____
_____
_____
_____

Q2 全体的な傾向・要点は？

本体1 減少（変化が大きい→さらに大きい）

Q3 企業数の減少が2番目に大きかった業種は？

Q4 その減少数と最後の数値は？

Q5 企業数の減少が最も大きかった業種は？

Q6 その業種の最初と最後の数値は？

本体2 増加（総数が少ない→多い）

Q7 企業数が最も少なかった業種は？

Q8 その最初の数値と増加数は？

Q9 2014年に企業数が3番目に少なかった業種は？

Q10 その増加数と最後の数値は？

Q11 2014年に企業数が2番目に少なかった業種は？

Q12 その増加数と最後の数値は？

Q13 企業数が最も多い業種は？

Q14 その増加数と最後の数値は？

結論（任意）

Q15 具体的な傾向・要点は？

以下の回答例や自分が分析した結果をもとにエッセイを書きましょう。

導入

Q1 タスク指示文は、どのように言い換えられている？

The following chart		This table
reveals		indicates
the number of businesses		how many companies
in selected industries		existed in six industries
in Australia		in Australia
during five years.		from 2014 to 2018.

Q2 全体的な傾向・要点は？

A. two industries saw declines, remainder experienced rises

本体1　減少（変化が大きい→さらに大きい）

Q3 企業数の減少が2番目に大きかった業種は？

A. retail trade

Q4 その減少数と最後の数値は？

A. 850 ↘ , final figure = 35,200

Q5 企業数の減少が最も大きかった業種は？

A. agriculture, forestry and fishing

Q6 その業種の最初と最後の数値は？

A. starting = 42,400, finishing = 39,500

本体2　増加（総数が少ない→多い）

Q7 企業数が最も少なかった業種は？

A. information media and telecommunications

Q8 その最初の数値と増加数は？

A. 2014 = 5,210, four years later = ↗ by 750

Q9 2014年に企業数が3番目に少なかった業種は？

   A. manufacturing

Q10 その増加数と最後の数値は？

   A. (+350), 2018 = 23,673

Q11 2014年に企業数が2番目に少なかった業種は？

   A. accommodation and food services

Q12 その増加数と最後の数値は？

   A. ↗ 2,800 to 25,761 in last year

Q13 企業数が最も多い業種は？

   A. construction

Q14 その増加数と最後の数値は？

   A. ↗ 14,500 to 104,000 companies

結論（任意）

Q15 具体的な傾向・要点は？

   A. both positive and negative changes, construction was particularly

     strong

エッセイ中の重要語句と表現をエクササイズで確認します。

語句に当てはまる訳の番号を選んでください。

_____ Analysing the details, it is clear that

_____ the remainder

_____ In terms of

_____ an even larger fall

_____ starting and finishing with

_____ experienced modest growth

_____ a more dramatic addition

_____ the highest figure every year

_____ the largest overall increase

_____ ending with

_____ both positive and negative changes occurred

_____ was particularly strong

1. 特に好調だった
2. 詳細を分析すると…は明らかだ
3. 残り（のもの）
4. …で終了して
5. …に関しては
6. 肯定的と否定的両方の変化が起きた
7. より劇的な増加
8. 毎年最も高い数値
9. 最初と最後は…で
10. さらに大幅な減少
11. 全体的に最も大きな増加
12. ゆるやかな伸びを示した

正しいつづりを選んでください。

• aguriculture / agriculture

• telecommunications / telecomunications

• accomodation / accommodation

• construction / constraction

必要なものは、数字にコンマを入れてください。

• 850

• 42400

• 5210

• 104000

正解 2, 3, 5, 10, 9, 12, 7, 8, 11, 4, 6, 1 ／ agriculture, telecommunications, accommodation, construction ／ 850（コンマ不要）, 42,400, 5,210, 104,000

You should spend about 20 minutes on this task.

The two graphs reveal the proportion of people in various age groups in the UK who used the internet in different years.

Summarise the information by selecting and reporting the main features, and make comparisons where relevant.

Write at least 150 words.

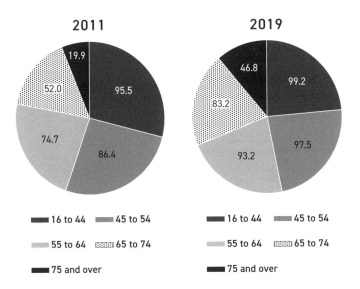

Percentages for Each Age Group

2011

95.5
19.9
52.0
74.7
86.4

■■■ 16 to 44   ■■■ 45 to 54
■■■ 55 to 64   ▦▦▦ 65 to 74
■■■ 75 and over

2019

99.2
46.8
83.2
97.5
93.2

■■■ 16 to 44   ■■■ 45 to 54
■■■ 55 to 64   ▦▦▦ 65 to 74
■■■ 75 and over

(Each figure is a percentage for that particular age group.
E.g. 19.9% = out of 100% of people aged 75+.)

This set of pie charts compares the percentage of internet users according to five age categories in Britain in 2011 and 2019. In general, it is evident that the proportions for all age groups rose over the nine-year period.

In 2011, the highest rate was for the youngest internet users (16 to 44 years-old), at 95.5%. This situation remained unchanged eight years later with an even higher figure of 99.2%. Users aged between 45 and 54 reflected the second largest proportion in both years, with 86.4 and 97.5%, respectively. The next highest age category, 55 to 64, registered a figure of 74.7% in 2011, and by 2019 it had gone up significantly, to 93.2%.

Users over the age of 75, which was the oldest age category, had by far the lowest rate in both years. Only 19.9% used the internet in 2011, but there was a remarkable increase, as the figure more than doubled to 46.8%. Yet, the most dramatic rise can be seen amongst individuals between the ages of 65 and 74, whose rate surged by around 30% to 83.2%. *(181 words – 9 sentences)*

To conclude, the comparative graphs reveal that the proportion of internet users increased among all age groups, and especially older generations.

(202 words – 10 sentences)

　この1組の円グラフは、2011年と2019年の英国で、5つの年齢区分別にインターネット利用者の割合を比較したものだ。概して、9年間ですべての年齢層の割合が増加していることがわかる。

　2011年に最も割合が高かったのは、最も若いインターネット利用者（16歳から44歳）の95.5%だった。この状況は8年後も変わらず、99.2%とさらに高い数値を示している。45歳から54歳までの利用者は、両年ともそれぞれ86.4%と97.5%と、2番目に高い割合を示した。次に多い55〜64歳の年齢区分は、2011年には74.7%という数値を記録し、2019年には大幅に増加して、93.2%となっ

ている。

　最高齢の年齢区分である75歳以上の利用者は、両年とも圧倒的に低い割合だった。2011年のインターネット利用率はわずか19.9%だったが、目覚ましい伸びを見せ、46.8%と2倍以上に増加した。しかし、最も劇的に増えたのが、65歳から74歳までの人々で、約30%増の83.2%に達している。

　結論として、比較グラフでは、すべての年齢層、特に高年齢層でインターネット利用者の割合が増加していることがわかる。

Self-Study!

　エッセイの英文をもとに質問に**英語で**答えてください。グラフ全体に対する割合ではなく、数値が**セグメントごとの割合**を示すタイプの円グラフです。

導入

[Q1] タスク指示文は、どのように言い換えられている？

| *The two graphs* |
| *reveal* |
| *the proportion of* |
| *people in various age* |
| *groups in the UK who* |
| *used the internet* |
| *in different years.* |

_____

_____

_____

_____

_____

_____

[Q2] 全体的な傾向・要点は？

本体1　トップ3──2011年＆2019年

[Q3] 2011年に最も高い数値だった年齢層と、その数値は？

[Q4] 2019年にその数値はどうなった？

[Q5] 両方の年で2番目に高い数値だった層と、その数値は？

[Q6] 2011年に3番目に高い数値だった層と、その数値は？

[Q7] 2019年にその数値はどうなった？

本体2　最も低い層＆最も大きい増加

[Q8] 2011年と2019年に最も低い数値だった層は？

[Q9] 2011年の数値は何で、どのように変わった？

[Q10] 最も増えたのはどの層だった？

[Q11] その増加率は？

結論（任意）

[Q12] 具体的な傾向・要点は？

以下の回答例や自分が分析した結果をもとにエッセイを書きましょう。

導入

Q1 タスク指示文は、どのように言い換えられている？

The two graphs	*This set of pie charts*
reveal	*compares*
the proportion of	*the percentage of*
people in various age groups in the UK who used the internet	*internet users according to five age categories in Britain*
in different years.	*in 2011 and 2019.*

Q2 全体的な傾向・要点は？

A. proportions for all age groups rose

本体1 トップ3——2011年&2019年

Q3 2011年に最も高い数値だった年齢層と、その数値は？

A. (16 to 44 yrs.) 95.5%

Q4 2019年にその数値はどうなった？

A. ↗ to 99.2%

Q5 両方の年で2番目に高い数値だった層と、その数値は？

A. 45 to 54 yrs., 86.4 & 97.5%

Q6 2011年に3番目に高い数値だった層と、その数値は？

A. 55 to 64 yrs., 74.7%

Q7 2019年にその数値はどうなった？

A. ↗ to 93.2%

本体2 最も低い層&最も大きい増加

Q8 2011年と2019年に最も低い数値だった層は？

A. over 75 yrs.

Q9 2011年の数値は何で、どのように変わった？

 A. 19.9%, and ↗ to 46.8%

Q10 最も増えたのはどの層だった？

 A. ages 65 ～ 74

Q11 その増加率は？

 A. ↗ by around 30% (83.2%)

結論 (任意)

Q12 具体的な傾向・要点は？

 A. proportions increased among all groups, esp. older generations

エッセイ中の重要語句と表現をエクササイズで確認します。

語句に当てはまる訳の番号を選んでください。 ※訳は同じものが2つあります。

＿＿＿ set of	＿＿＿ registered a figure of
＿＿＿ In general,	＿＿＿ over the age of
＿＿＿ This situation remained unchanged	＿＿＿ in both years
	＿＿＿ there was a remarkable increase
＿＿＿ aged between ... and ~	＿＿＿ the figure more than doubled to
＿＿＿ , respectively	＿＿＿ between the ages of ... and ~
＿＿＿ The next highest	＿＿＿ the comparative graphs

1. …の数値を記録した
2. 比較グラフ
3. …歳超の
4. 目覚ましい伸びを見せた
5. (1) 組の
6. 次に多い
7. この状況は変わらないままだった
8. それぞれ
9. 概して
10. …から~歳の
11. …から~歳の
12. 両年で
13. …となる2倍以上の数値

間違いをそれぞれ2箇所探してください。

- This set of pie chart compares the percentage of internet user according to ...
- In 2011, a highest rate was in the youngest internet users ...

以下の英文の正しい場所に ', *which was the oldest age category,*' を入れてください。

- Users over the age of 75 had by far the lowest rate in both years.

正解 5, 9, 7, 10 [11], 8, 6, 1, 3, 12, 4, 13, 11 [10], 2 ／ chart → charts, user → users, a → the, in → for ／ ... 75, *which was the oldest age category,* had ...

プロセス図②

タイプ別にモデルエッセイを分析・再構築することで、重要表現を身につけてライティング力を高めます。

You should spend about 20 minutes on this task.

This flow chart shows how a wine barrel is made.

Summarise the information by selecting and reporting the main features, and make comparisons where relevant.

Write at least 150 words.

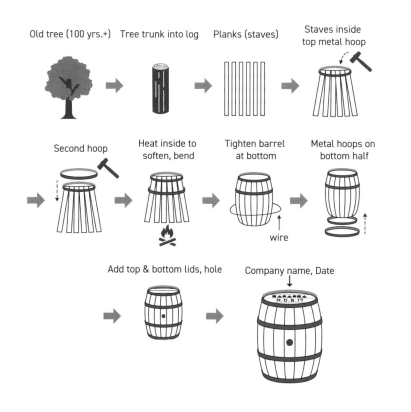

The given diagram illustrates the method of producing a barrel for holding wine. According to the details, production basically requires two materials and includes ten stages.

To make a wine barrel, first, a tree that is at least a hundred years old must be selected and its trunk cut into a log. Then the log is cut into planks, or staves. After that, the staves are aligned around the inside of a metal hoop, and the hoop is hammered downwards. Next, a second hoop is put on the barrel and hammered further down its body. Following that, the barrel is placed over a fire to heat the inside so that the wood softens and bends. Then a wire is put around the bottom part of the barrel and tightened in order to bring the staves together. After that, two metal hoops are put on the bottom half of the barrel. Next, lids are put on the top and bottom, and a hole is drilled in the middle of the barrel. Finally, the maker's name and the date are stamped on the top lid.

(183 words – 11 sentences)

In summary, the flow chart indicates that the process is relatively simple and requires few materials.

(199 words – 12 sentences)

　　この図は、ワインを入れる樽の製造方法を描いている。その詳細によると、製造には基本的に2つの材料が必要で、10の段階がある。

　　ワイン樽を作るには、まず、樹齢100年以上の木を選別し、その幹を丸太に切る必要がある。そして、その丸太を厚板（樽板）に切り出す。その後、金属製の輪っかの内側に樽板を並べ、下に向かって輪っかを打ち込む。次に、2つ目の輪っかを樽に乗せ、さらに樽本体に沿って打ち込んでいく。続いて、樽を火にかけ、木が柔らかくなって曲げられるように、内側を加熱する。その後、樽板をまとめるために、樽の底部に針金を巻き付けて、締め付ける。それから、樽の下半分に2つの金属製の輪っかをつける。次に、上下に蓋を取り付け、樽の真ん中に穴を開ける。最後に、上蓋に製作者の名前と日付を刻印する。

　　要約すると、この工程図は、この過程が比較的簡単で、必要な材料が少ないことを示している。

Self-Study!

　モデルエッセイを分析していきます。エッセイの英文をもとに質問に**英語で**答えてください。回答がそのままエッセイを書く材料になります。

導入

Q1 タスク指示文は、どのように言い換えられている？

This flow chart
shows
how a wine barrel is made.

Q2 全体的な傾向・要点は？

本体1　全工程：最初から最後

Q3 まず何が必要で、どのように変化させる？

Q4 そこからより小さな、どんな部品が作られる？

Q5 その部品と使用される、2つ目の部品は？

Q6 どのような動作が繰り返される？

Q7 次に樽に何をする？

Q8 樽の底部は、どのように締め付けられる？

Q9 工程初期のどのような動作が繰り返される？

Q10 ほかにどのようなことを樽に行う？

Q11 最後に樽に何をする？

結論（任意）

Q12 具体的な傾向・要点は？

以下の回答例や自分が分析した結果をもとにエッセイを書きましょう。

導入

Q1 タスク指示文は、どのように言い換えられている？

This flow chart
shows
how a wine barrel is made.

➡

The given diagram
illustrates
the method of producing
a barrel for holding wine.

Q2 全体的な傾向・要点は？

A. requires two materials & includes ten stages

本体1 全工程：最初から最後

Q3 まず何が必要で、どのように変化させる？

A. tree (at least 100 yrs. old) → trunk cut → log

Q4 そこからより小さな、どんな部品が作られる？

A. log cut into planks (staves)

Q5 その部品と使用される、2つ目の部品は？

A. staves aligned inside metal hoop, & hoop hammered downwards

Q6 どのような動作が繰り返される？

A. second hoop put on barrel & hammered further down body

Q7 次に樽に何をする？

A. barrel placed over fire & heated to soften & bend wood

Q8 樽の底部は、どのように締め付けられる？

A. wire put around bottom of barrel & tightened

Q9 工程初期のどのような動作が繰り返される？

A. two metal hoops put on bottom half of barrel

Q10 ほかにどのようなことを樽に行う？

A. lids put on top & bottom, hole drilled in middle of barrel

Q11 最後に樽に何をする？

    A.　maker's name & date stamped on top lid

結論（任意）

Q12 具体的な傾向・要点は？

    A.　process = simple, requires few materials

エッセイ中の重要語句と表現をエクササイズで確認します。

語句に当てはまる訳の番号を選んでください。

＿＿＿ The given diagram	＿＿＿ further down
＿＿＿ materials	＿＿＿ the inside
＿＿＿ includes ten stages	＿＿＿ so that
＿＿＿ To make	＿＿＿ the bottom part of
＿＿＿ cut into	＿＿＿ on the bottom half of
＿＿＿ around the inside of	＿＿＿ in the middle of

1. 内側　　　　　　4. …の内側 (の周囲) に　　7. …の底部　　　10. …するために
2. 材料　　　　　　5. …の真ん中に　　　　　8. 10の段階がある　11. 提供された図
3. 作るためには　　6. …の下半分に　　　　　9. …に切る　　　　12. …のさらに下方に

空所に 'is' または 'are' を入れてください。

- Then the log ＿＿＿＿ cut ...

- After that, the staves ＿＿＿＿ aligned ...

- Next, a second hoop ＿＿＿＿ put ...

- Following that, the barrel ＿＿＿＿ placed ...

- Then a wire ＿＿＿＿ put ...

- After that, two metal hoops ＿＿＿＿ put ...

- Next, lids ＿＿＿＿ put ...

- Finally, the maker's name and the date ＿＿＿＿ stamped ...

正解 11, 2, 8, 3, 9, 4, 12, 1, 10, 7, 6, 5／is, are, is, is, is, are, are, are

Self-Study!

地図・図解②

タイプ別にモデルエッセイを分析・再構築することで、重要表現を身につけてライティング力を高めます。

You should spend about 20 minutes on this task.

These plans show different proposals for the layout of a new office.

Summarise the information by selecting and reporting the main features, and make comparisons where relevant.

Write at least 150 words.

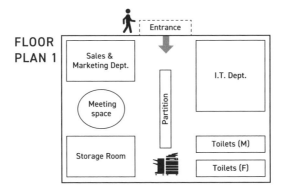

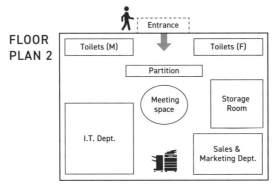

The two diagrams illustrate proposed layouts for a new work location. Overall, it is clear that the designs differ in various ways.

According to Floor Plan 1, the office has a partition in the middle with a photocopier placed at the far end. When you enter the office, the I.T. department is situated on the left side, and the male and female toilets are in the far left corner. In the near, right-hand corner is the sales and marketing department, and next to it is a space for holding meetings. A storage room sits in the far-right corner.

In the second plan, as you enter the office, the partition is horizontal and blocks the view into the office. Moreover, the toilets are separated and located in the corners near the entrance. The storage room is situated on the left and the sales and marketing department is in the far left-hand corner while the I.T. department sits in the opposite corner. Lastly, the photocopier is positioned in the same place as in Plan 1, but the meeting space is in the centre of the whole floor, behind the partition.

(188 words – 10 sentences)

In conclusion, the proposals have different layouts and the positioning of the partition is a key factor in each design.

(208 words – 11 sentences)

　この2つの図は、新しい仕事場の配置案を描いたものだ。全体的に見て、それぞれのデザインが様々な点で異なっていることは明らかだ。
　間取り図案1によると、オフィスは真ん中にパーティションがあり、一番奥にコピー機が置かれている。オフィスに入ると、左側にはIT部門があり、左奥の隅には男女のトイレがある。手前の右隅には販売・マーケティング部門があり、その隣には会議を行うスペースがある。右奥の隅には、倉庫部屋がある。
　2つ目の図案では、オフィスに入るとパーティションが横向きにあり、オフィス内への視界をさえぎっている。さらにトイレは分かれていて、入り口付近の両隅に配置されている。倉庫部屋は左側にあり、左奥の隅には販売・マーケティング部門がある一方、向かい側の隅にはIT部門が配置されている。最後に、コピー機は図案1と同じ場所に配置されているが、会議スペースはフロアの中央、パーティションの後ろにある。
　結論から言うと、両提案の配置は異なり、パーティションの位置がそれぞれのデザインの重要な要素となっている。

Self-Study!

　モデルエッセイを分析していきます。エッセイの英文をもとに質問に**英語で**答えてください。回答がそのままエッセイを書く材料になります。

導入

Q1 タスク指示文は、どのように言い換えられている？

*These plans
show
different proposals for
the layout of
a new office.*

➡️ _____

Q2 全体的な傾向・要点は？

本体1 間取り図案1

Q3 図案1では、オフィスに入ってまず何を目にする？
Q4 （入って）左側と、左奥の隅に何がある？
Q5 手前の右隅と、その隣には何がある？
Q6 右奥の隅には何がある？

本体2 間取り図案2

Q7 図案2では、オフィスに入るとどんな違いがある？
Q8 手前の両隅については、どんな違いがある？
Q9 （入って）左側、左奥の隅、そしてその向かい側には何がある？
Q10 図案1との類似点と相違点は？

結論（任意）

Q11 具体的な傾向・要点は？

以下の回答例や自分が分析した結果をもとにエッセイを書きましょう。

導入

Q1 タスク指示文は、どのように言い換えられている?

These plans		*The two diagrams*
show		*illustrate*
different proposals for the layout of		*proposed layouts for*
a new office.		*a new work location.*

Q2 全体的な傾向・要点は?

　A. designs differ in various ways

本体1　間取り図案1

Q3 図案1では、オフィスに入ってまず何を目にする?

　A. partition in middle, photocopier at far end

Q4 (入って) 左側と、左奥の隅に何がある?

　A. I.T. dept., male & female toilets

Q5 手前の右隅と、その隣には何がある?

　A. sales & marketing dept., space for meetings

Q6 右奥の隅には何がある?

　A. storage room

本体2　間取り図案2

Q7 図案2では、オフィスに入るとどんな違いがある?

　A. partition = horizontal (blocks view into office)

Q8 手前の両隅については、どんな違いがある?

　A. toilets separated & located in corners

Q9　(入って) 左側、左奥の隅、そしてその向かい側には何がある？

　　A. storage room, sales & marketing, I.T. dept.

Q10　図案1との類似点と相違点は？

　　A. photocopier position = same place, but meeting place is in centre of

　　　floor

結論 (任意)

Q11　具体的な傾向・要点は？

　　A. proposals = different layouts, partition = key factor

エッセイ中の重要語句と表現をエクササイズで確認します。

語句に当てはまる訳の番号を選んでください。 ※訳は同じものが2つあります。

_____ proposed layouts		_____ a space for
_____ differ in various ways		_____ as you
_____ partition		_____ horizontal
_____ at the far end		_____ in the same place as
_____ When you		_____ proposals
_____ in the far-left corner		_____ the positioning of
_____ In the near, right-hand corner		_____ a key factor

1. 左奥の隅に	5. …の位置	9. 様々な点で異なっ	12. …のスペース
2. 手前の右隅に	6. (人が) …する時	ている	13. 一番奥に
3. 横向きの、水平の	7. 提案	10. 重要な要素	14. 配置案
4. パーティション	8. (人が) …する時	11. …と同じ場所に	

カッコ内の動詞を正しい形に直してください。

• ... the I.T. department is (situate) on the left side ...

• ... the male and female toilets (be) in the far-left corner ...

• A storage room (sit) in the far-right corner.

• Moreover, the toilets are (separate) and (locate) in the corners ...

• ... the photocopier is (position) in the same place ...

• ... the meeting space (be) in the centre ...

正解 14, 9, 4, 13, 6 [8], 1, 2, 12, 8 [6], 3, 11, 7, 5, 10／situated, are, sits, separated, located, positioned, is

Self-Study!

異なるタイプの 組み合わせ②

タイプ別にモデルエッセイを分析・再構築することで、重要表現を身につけてライティング力を高めます。

You should spend about 20 minutes on this task.

These graphs show the percentage of cigarette and e-cigarette smokers in the United Kingdom over a five-year period.

Summarise the information by selecting and reporting the main features, and make comparisons where relevant.

Write at least 150 words.

Cigarette Smokers by Country (%)					
	2014	2015	2016	2017	2018
England	17.8	16.9	15.5	14.9	14.4
Scotland	20.3	19.1	17.7	16.3	16.3
Wales	19.4	18.1	16.9	16.1	15.9
Northern Ireland	18	19	18.1	16.5	15.5

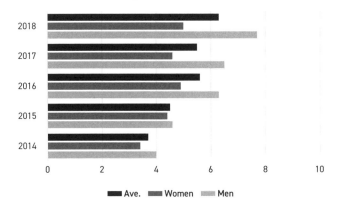

UK: E-cigarette Smokers (%)

■ Ave.　■ Women　▨ Men

The table and the bar chart compare British smoking trends concerning regular cigarettes and e-cigarettes between 2014 and 2018. According to the statistics, opposing tendencies are evident in the given period.

In 2014, Scotland marked the highest rate of cigarette smokers, at 20.3%. However, the figure dropped in consecutive years and then remained at 16.3% in 2017-18. The pattern in Wales was similar, starting with 19.4% and shrinking to 15.9% in 2018. As for Northern Ireland, despite experiencing a one per cent rise in 2015, the rate also fell over the five years, from 18 to 15.5%. Annually, the lowest figure was in England, where the proportion declined from 17.8 to 14.4% in 2014 and 2018, respectively.

By contrast, over the same period, the percentage of males and females who smoked e-cigarettes steadily climbed. In fact, their combined average rate reflected just under 4% in the initial year but exceeded 6% in the final one. Furthermore, throughout the period, the figure was consistently higher for men, and the gap widened from approximately 0.5% to nearly 3% higher than the rate for women. *(182 words – 10 sentences)*

In summary, the two charts reveal that while cigarettes decreased in popularity in every country in the UK, e-cigarettes became more popular year by year, especially among the male population. *(212 words – 11 sentences)*

表と棒グラフは、2014年から2018年の間に、通常のタバコと電子タバコに関する英国の喫煙傾向を比較したものだ。この統計データによると、この期間中、相反する傾向がはっきり見られる。

2014年、スコットランドはタバコを吸う人の割合が20.3％で最も高かった。しかし、その後の年は連続して数値が下がり、2017-18年には、16.3％にとどまった。ウェールズの傾向も似ていて、19.4％から始まり、2018年には15.9％にまで縮小した。北アイルランドについては、2015年に1％上昇したが、5年間で18％から15.5％へと低下した。毎年最も低い数値を示したのはイングランドで、2014年と2018年では、それぞれ17.8％から14.4％まで割合が減少している。

対照的に、同じ期間に電子タバコを吸っていた男性と女性の割合は、着実に増加した。実際、男性と女性を合わせた平均値は、最初の1年はわずか4％弱だったが、最終年には6％を超えた。さらに、この期間を通して、男性の方が一貫して高い数値を示しており、女性の割合との差は、約0.5％から約3％にまで拡大している。

要約すると、2つのグラフからは、英国のどこでもタバコの人気が低下したのに対し、電子タバコは年々、特に男性の間で人気が高まったことがわかる。

Self-Study!

　モデルエッセイを分析していきます。エッセイの英文をもとに質問に**英語で**答えてください。回答がそのままエッセイを書く材料になります。

導入

Q1 タスク指示文は、どのように言い換えられている？

> *These graphs*
> *show*
> *the percentage of cigarette and e-cigarette smokers in the United Kingdom*
> *over a five-year period.*

Q2 全体的な傾向・要点は？

本体1　表：タバコ

Q3 最初の年に最も高い割合だった国とその数値は？

Q4 その後の4年間でどうなった？

Q5 最初の年に2番目に高かった国は？　最初と最後の年の数値は？

Q6 割合が上昇した国、上昇率と時期は？　最初と最後の年の数値は？

Q7 最も低い割合だった国と、最初と最後の年の数値は？

本体2　棒グラフ：電子タバコ

Q8 タバコの喫煙者と比べて、全体的な違いは？

Q9 最初と最後の年の平均値は？

Q10 男性と女性との違いはどれくらいで、どう変化した？

結論（任意）

Q11 具体的な傾向・要点は？

以下の回答例や自分が分析した結果をもとにエッセイを書きましょう。

導入

Q1 タスク指示文は、どのように言い換えられている？

These graphs	The table and the bar chart
show	*compare*
the percentage of cigarette and e-cigarette smokers in the United Kingdom	*British smoking trends concerning regular cigarettes and e-cigarettes*
over a five-year period.	*between 2014 and 2018.*

Q2 全体的な傾向・要点は？

　　A. opposing tendencies are evident

本体1 表：タバコ

Q3 最初の年に最も高い割合だった国とその数値は？

　　A. Scotland: 20.3%

Q4 その後の4年間でどうなった？

　　A. dropped & remained at 16.3% in 2017-18

Q5 最初の年に2番目に高かった国は？　最初と最後の年の数値は？

　　A. Wales: 2014 = 19.4% ↘ to 15.9% in 2018

Q6 割合が上昇した国、上昇率と時期は？　最初と最後の年の数値は？

　　A. Northern Ireland: 1% ↗ in 2015, five years = 18% ↘ 15.5%

Q7 最も低い割合だった国と、最初と最後の年の数値は？

　　A. England: 17.8% ↘ 14.4% in 2014 & 2018

本体2 棒グラフ：電子タバコ

Q8 タバコの喫煙者と比べて、全体的な違いは？

　　A. % of males & females who smoked e-cigarettes climbed

Q9　最初と最後の年の平均値は？

　　A.　initial = under 4%, final = exceeded 6%

Q10　男性と女性との違いはどれくらいで、どう変化した？

　　A.　figure consistently higher for men, gap widened: 0.5% ↗ nearly 3%

結論（任意）

Q11　具体的な傾向・要点は？

　　A.　(table) cigarettes = less popular

　　　　(bar) e-cigarettes = more popular, esp. among male population

エクササイズ

エッセイ中の重要語句と表現をエクササイズで確認します。

語句に当てはまる訳の番号を選んでください。

_____ trends concerning		_____ In fact,	
_____ statistics		_____ combined average rate	
_____ opposing tendencies		_____ throughout	
_____ marked		_____ consistently	
_____ consecutive		_____ the gap widened	
_____ Annually,		_____ year by year	
_____ By contrast,		_____ especially among	

1. 相反する傾向　　5. …に関する傾向　　9. 毎年　　13. 差が拡大した
2. 統計データ　　6. 対照的に　　10. 合わせた平均値　　14. 年々
3. …を通して　　7. 実際　　11. 特に…の間で
4. 示した　　8. 一貫して　　12. 連続した

エッセイの英文を確認し、空所に時を表すフレーズを入れてください。

- However, the figure dropped ( ) and then ...

- By contrast, ( ), the percentage of ...

- Furthermore, ( ), the figure was ...

空所に前置詞を入れてください。

- The pattern ( ) Wales was similar, starting ( ) 19.4% and shrinking ( ) 15.9% ( ) 2018.

- As ( ) Northern Ireland, despite experiencing a one per cent rise in 2015, the rate also fell ( ) the five years, ( ) 18 ( ) 15.5%.

正解 5, 2, 1, 4, 12, 9, 6, 7, 10, 3, 8, 13, 14, 11／in consecutive years, over the same period, throughout the period／in[for], with[at], to, in, for[to], over[during], from, to

Self-Study!

折れ線グラフ③

タイプ別にモデルエッセイを分析・再構築することで、重要表現を身につけてライティング力を高めます。

You should spend about 20 minutes on this task.

This graph reveals government debt as a percentage of gross domestic product (GDP) for the G7 countries in 2010-2015.

Summarise the information by selecting and reporting the main features, and make comparisons where relevant.

Write at least 150 words.

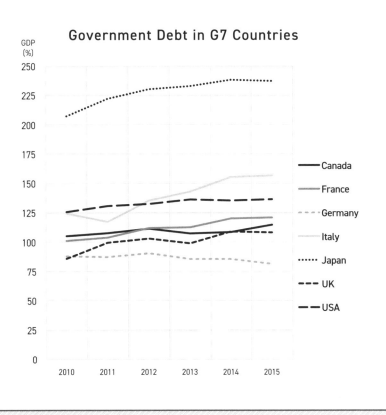

The given line chart indicates the approximate levels of government debt in terms of proportion of GDP for the G7 nations between 2010 and 2015. According to the information, over the six-year period the figures rose for all countries except one.

Japan had by far the highest rate in all years, starting at 205% and rising to 235% by 2015. Italy, however, experienced the largest increase, from 125% to 160%, and finished with the second highest figure. The US also started with the same figure as Italy but experienced a 10% increase, and therefore ended with the third highest rate.

France and Canada had similar trends, beginning with figures of just over 100%, which climbed moderately to end with 120 and 115%, respectively. As for the UK, although it started with the lowest proportion (just under 85%), it saw a major rise, reaching 110% in 2015. However, in clear contrast to the preceding six nations, Germany posted a modest decline in its rate. Specifically, it dropped from 85% in the first year to roughly 80% in the final one.

(179 words – 10 sentences)

In summary, government debt as a percentage of GDP dipped for Germany but grew for all other countries, especially Japan, whose figure was extremely high throughout the entire term.

(208 words – 11 sentences)

　　ここにある折れ線グラフは、G7諸国の2010年から2015年までにおけるGDP比で見た政府債務残高のおおよその水準を示している。この情報によると、6年間で1カ国を除くすべての国で、数値が上昇している。

　　日本はすべての年で飛び抜けて最も高い比率を示し、205％で始まって2015年までに235％に上昇した。一方イタリアは125％から160％と最も大きな増加となり、2番目に高い数値で終了した。アメリカはイタリアと同じ数値で始まったが、上昇率は10％だったため、3番目に高い比率で終わった。

　　フランスとカナダは似た傾向を示し、100％をわずかに上回る数値で始まり、少しずつ上昇して最後はそれぞれ120％と115％となった。英国に関しては、最も低い割合（85％弱）で開始したものの高い上昇率を示し、2015年には110％に達した。一方、前述の6カ国とは対照的に、ドイツは債務残高の減少を示した。具体的には、初年度の85％から、最終年度はざっと80％に減少した。

　　要約すると、政府債務の対GDP比は、ドイツでは低下したが、ほかのすべての国で上昇し、特に日本は、全期間を通して極めて高い数値を示した。

Self-Study!

　モデルエッセイを分析していきます。エッセイの英文をもとに質問に**英語で**答えてください。回答がそのままエッセイを書く材料になります。

導入

Q1 タスク指示文は、どのように言い換えられている?

| This graph |
| reveals |
| government debt |
| as a percentage of gross domestic product (GDP) for the G7 countries |
| in 2010-2015. |

_____
_____
_____
_____
_____

Q2 全体的な傾向・要点は?

本体1 125%以上の国

Q3 全期間を通して最も高い比率の国と、その開始・終了時の数値は?

Q4 最も高い上昇率を示して2番目に高い比率で終わった国は? その開始・終了時の数値は?

Q5 3番目に高い比率で終わった国と、その開始時の数値と上昇率は?

本体2 125%未満の国

Q6 似た傾向を示した2つの国と、その開始・終了時の数値は?

Q7 最も低い比率で始まったが高い上昇率を示した国は? その開始・終了時の数値は?

Q8 唯一減少した国と、その開始・終了時の数値は?

結論 (任意)

Q9 具体的な傾向・要点は?

以下の回答例や自分が分析した結果をもとにエッセイを書きましょう。

導入

Q1 タスク指示文は、どのように言い換えられている？

This graph		*The given line chart*
reveals		*indicates*
government debt		*the approximate levels of government debt*
as a percentage of gross domestic product (GDP) for the G7 countries		*in terms of proportion of GDP for the G7 nations*
in 2010-2015.		*between 2010 and 2015.*

Q2 全体的な傾向・要点は？

A. figures rose for all countries except one

本体1　125%以上の国

Q3 全期間を通して最も高い比率の国と、その開始・終了時の数値は？

A. Japan: 2010 = 205%, ↗ 235% by 2015

Q4 最も高い上昇率を示して2番目に高い比率で終わった国は？　その開始・終了時の数値は？

A. Italy: 125% ↗ 160%

Q5 3番目に高い比率で終わった国と、その開始時の数値と上昇率は？

A. US: 125% ↗ +10%

本体2　125%未満の国

Q6 似た傾向を示した2つの国と、その開始・終了時の数値は？

A. France & Canada: beginning = just over 100%,

ended with 120% & 115%

Q7 最も低い比率で始まったが高い上昇率を示した国は？　その開始・終了
時の数値は？

A. UK: lowest proportion (under 85%), reached 110%

Q8 唯一減少した国と、その開始・終了時の数値は？

A. Germany: 85% ↘ 80%

結論（任意）

Q9 具体的な傾向・要点は？

A. debt as a percentage of GDP dipped for Germany, grew for all other

countries, esp. Japan

エッセイ中の重要語句と表現をエクササイズで確認します。

語句に当てはまる訳の番号を選んでください。

____ approximate		____ preceding	
____ for all ... except ~		____ from ... in the first year to ~ in	
____ by far		the final one	
____ in all years		____ as a percentage of	
____ therefore		____ extremely	
____ moderately		____ the entire term	
____ In clear contrast to			

1. …とは明確に対照的に	4. 初年度の…から最終年度の〜へ	7. …の比率として、対…比で	10. 前述の
2. すべての年で	5. その結果	8. 概算の	11. 〜を除くすべての…で
3. 全期間	6. ゆるやかに	9. 断然、飛び抜けて	12. 極めて

動詞を過去形にしてください。

- rise   → _____
- experience → _____
- finish   → _____
- end   → _____
- start   → _____

- see   → _____
- post   → _____
- dip   → _____
- grow   → _____

that, which, where, whose から正しいものを入れてください。

- ... figures of just over 100%, (   ) climbed ...

- ... especially Japan, (   ) figure was extremely high ...

正解 8, 11, 9, 2, 5, 6, 1, 10, 4, 7, 12, 3／rose, experienced, finished, ended, started, saw, posted, dipped, grew／which, whose

Self-Study!

棒グラフ③

タイプ別にモデルエッセイを分析・再構築することで、重要表現を身につけてライティング力を高めます。

You should spend about 20 minutes on this task.

This bar graph indicates the percentage of tax money spent on roads in Northern Ireland in five different years.

Summarise the information by selecting and reporting the main features, and make comparisons where relevant.

Write at least 150 words.

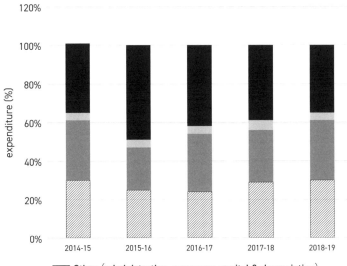

Expenditure on NI Roads: 2014–15 to 2018-19

- ■ Other (administration, resources, capital & depreciation)
- Public lighting
- Maintenance (structural, routine, winter)
- New construction & improvement

The vertical bar chart illustrates what proportion of public taxes were used for four categories of road-related work in Northern Ireland from 2014 to 2019. With the exception of 2015-16, in general, the figures for each category changed relatively little over the five-year period.

The largest amount of annual expenditure was for administration, resources, capital and depreciation. In 2014-15, the proportion stood at around 36% of the total. Then, the following year it grew by around fifteen per cent before slightly dipping in the remaining years to end with the original figure. In stark contrast, lighting for roads received the smallest amount of funding from public funds, at approximately 4% every year.

The two remaining categories showed almost identical figures over the entire period. Spending on structural, routine and winter maintenance and on new construction and improvement each measured 30% in the first year. In 2015-16, however, the amount shrank to approximately 24% each. Afterwards, the figures for both categories exhibited a similar, rising pattern and finished at the same level as in the initial year.　　　　　　　　　　　　　　*(176 words – 10 sentences)*

In conclusion, the graph reveals that there was minimal fluctuation over the whole period and the proportions for all categories in the first and final years were identical.　　　　　　　　　　　　　　　　　　*(204 words – 11 sentences)*

　この縦棒グラフは、2014年から2019年にかけて、北アイルランドで4つのカテゴリーの道路関連作業に、どのような割合で公租が使われたのかを説明している。2015-16年を除くと、概して各カテゴリーの数字は、5年間で比較的変化が少なかった。

　年間支出の中で最も多かったのは、管理費、資源費、資本金および減価償却費だった。2014-15年度には、その割合は全体の36%を占めていた。それが、翌年には約15%増加し、その後は残りの数年をかけて少しずつ減少して、最終的には元の数字で終わっている。著しく対照的に、道路照明が公的資金から受ける金額が最も少なく、毎年およそ4%だった。

　残りの2つのカテゴリーは、全期間を通してほぼ同じ数字を示した。初年度の、構造物、定期および冬季保守と、新規建設および改良への支出は、それぞれ30%だった。しかし2015-16年には、それぞれおよそ24%に縮小した。それ以降、両カテゴリーの数値は同様の上昇パターンを見せ、初年度と同じ水準で終わった。

　結論として、このグラフからは、全期間にわたってほぼ変動がなく、初年度と最終年度の全カテゴリーの比率が同じだったことがわかる。

Self-Study!

　モデルエッセイを分析していきます。エッセイの英文をもとに質問に**英語**で答えてください。回答がそのままエッセイを書く材料になります。

導入

Q1 タスク指示文は、どのように言い換えられている？

| *This bar graph* |
| *indicates* |
| *the percentage of* |
| *tax money spent on roads in Northern Ireland* |
| *in five different years.* |

Q2 全体的な傾向・要点は？

本体1 最も大きい＆最も小さい

Q3 どの年も最も大きい割合を占めたカテゴリーは？

Q4 その初年度の数字は？

Q5 その翌年度の数字は？　最終的にどのように変化した？

Q6 どの年も最も小さい割合を占めたカテゴリーとその数字は？

本体2 その他──類似

Q7 似たような傾向があったカテゴリーはいくつ？

Q8 それはどのカテゴリーで、初年度の数字は？

Q9 数字は次の年度にどのように変化した？

Q10 その後数字はどのように変化し、終了した？

結論（任意）

Q11 具体的な傾向・要点は？

以下の回答例や自分が分析した結果をもとにエッセイを書きましょう。

導入

Q1 タスク指示文は、どのように言い換えられている？

This bar graph		The vertical bar chart
indicates		illustrates
the percentage of		what proportion of
tax money spent on roads in Northern Ireland		public taxes were used for four categories of road-related work in Northern Ireland
in five different years.		from 2014 to 2019.

Q2 全体的な傾向・要点は？

A. except 2015-16, the figures changed relatively little

本体1 最も大きい＆最も小さい

Q3 どの年も最も大きい割合を占めたカテゴリーは？

A. administration, resources, capital and depreciation

Q4 その初年度の数字は？

A. 2014-2015 = 36%

Q5 その翌年度の数字は？　最終的にどのように変化した？

A. 2015-2016 = grew by 15%, dipped & ended with original figure

Q6 どの年も最も小さい割合を占めたカテゴリーとその数字は？

A. lighting for roads = 4% every year

本体2 その他──類似

Q7 似たような傾向があったカテゴリーはいくつあった？

A. two categories

Q8 それはどのカテゴリーで、初年度の数字は？

    A. 2014-2015: structural, routine and winter maintenance, 30%

                     new construction and improvement, 30%

Q9 数字は次の年度にどのように変化した？

    A. 2015-2016: shrank to 24%

Q10 その後数字はどのように変化し、終了した？

    A. similar, rising pattern, finished with 30%

結論（任意）

Q11 具体的な傾向・要点は？

    A. minimal fluctuation over whole period, % for all categories in first &
last years = identical

エッセイ中の重要語句と表現をエクササイズで確認します。

語句に当てはまる訳の番号を選んでください。

_____ With the exception of   _____ In stark contrast,

_____ The largest amount of   _____ almost identical figures

_____ annual expenditure   _____ measured

_____ grew by around fifteen per cent   _____ Afterwards,

_____ end with   _____ the same level as

_____ the original figure   _____ minimal fluctuation

1. …で終わる	5. 約15％増加した	8. (測定値が)～だった	12. 著しく対照的に
2. 元の数字	6. それ以降は	9. …の最大量・最高額	
3. 年間支出	7. ごくわずかな・	10. …と同じ水準	
4. ほぼ同じ数字	最小量の変動	11. …を除くと	

下線部と同じ意味の単語を記入してください。

- the <u>next</u> year   =   _____

- to <u>finish</u> with   =   _____

- The two <u>other</u> categories   =   _____

- in the <u>first</u> year   =   _____

- in the first and <u>last</u> years   =   _____

間違いを2箇所探してください。

- In 2015-16, however, the number shrank to aproximately 24% each.

正解　11, 9, 3, 5, 1, 2, 12, 4, 8, 6, 10, 7／following, end, remaining, initial, final／
number → amount[percentage/proportion/figure], aproximately → approximately

Self-Study!

表 ③

タイプ別にモデルエッセイを分析・再構築することで、重要表現を身につけてライティング力を高めます。

You should spend about 20 minutes on this task.

The table below illustrates past and future life expectancy predictions for people in a number of countries between 2005 and 2060.

Summarise the information by selecting and reporting the main features, and make comparisons where relevant.

Write at least 150 words.

	2005 - 2010		2025 - 2030		2055 - 2060	
	Males	Females	Males	Females	Males	Females
China	73.2	75.8	76.2	78.8	79.8	82.4
Germany	77.1	82.3	80.5	85.1	84.3	88.9
India	63.3	66.7	67.7	71.5	72.4	76.5
Japan	79.2	86.0	82.3	89.2	86.2	93.0
Sweden	79.0	83.1	81.7	85.8	85.3	89.3
USA	75.6	80.6	79.0	83.1	82.7	86.5

This data reveals predicted lifespans in six countries for three, six-year terms up to 2060. Overall, it is clear that in future years people will live longer and women will continue to outlive men.

Japan shows the highest figures in all years for both genders. There, life expectancy in the first period stood at 79.2 (males) and 86 years (females), and both sexes can expect to live a further six or seven years in 2055-2060. In all years, Sweden and Germany follow Japan with figures of around one to four years lower.

In the USA and China, men and women are anticipated to live an extra three to four years by 2025-2030. Then, this pattern is predicted to repeat itself in 2055-2060, when the figures are assumed to be 82.7 and 86.5 in America, and 79.8 and 82.4 in China.

Finally, India has the lowest figures in all periods, starting at 63.3 for males, and 66.7 for females. Despite this, life expectancy is forecast to see the most significant overall rise (roughly 10 years) among all six countries by 2055-2060.

(180 words – 9 sentences)

To conclude, the chart reveals that lifespans are estimated to increase by at least six years during the first half of the 21st century. *(204 words – 10 sentences)*

　このデータは6カ国において、2060年までの、6年ごとの3期間で予測される寿命を示している。全体として、将来的に人々はより長生きし、女性は引き続き男性よりも長く生きることが明らかだ。

　日本は、男女ともにすべての期間で最も高い数値を示している。同国では第1期の平均寿命は79.2歳（男性）と86歳（女性）で、2055年から2060年には、さらに6、7年長生きすることが期待できる。すべての年において、スウェーデンとドイツは、1年から4年低い数字で、日本に続いている。

　アメリカと中国では、2025年から2030年までに男女ともに3、4年寿命が延びることが予測される。その後、この傾向が2055年から2060年にも繰り返され、アメリカでは82.7歳と86.5歳、中国では79.8歳と82.4歳になると推測される。

　最後に、インドはすべての期間で最も低い数値を示しており、男性は63.3歳、女性は66.7歳で始まっている。それにもかかわらず、同国の平均寿命は6カ国の中で、2055年から2060年までに全体的に最も顕著な伸び（ざっと10年）を見ることになると予想されている。

　結論として、この図表は21世紀の前半に、寿命が少なくとも6年延びるであろうことを示している。

Self-Study!

　モデルエッセイを分析していきます。エッセイの英文をもとに質問に**英語で**答えてください。回答がそのままエッセイを書く材料になります。

導入

Q1 タスク指示文は、どのように言い換えられている？

The table below
illustrates
past and future life expectancy predictions for people
in a number of countries
between 2005 and 2060.

_____

_____

_____

_____

_____

Q2 全体的な傾向・要点は？

本体1 上位3カ国

Q3 全期間で男女ともに最も高い数値だった国は？

Q4 その国の第1期の数値は？

Q5 最終期までに何が起こることが予想される？

Q6 すべての年で最も高い国に続く2カ国はどこで、その国と比べて両国の数字はどれくらい低い？

本体2 続く2カ国

Q7 続く2カ国で、第2期に予想される傾向は？

Q8 最終期に予想される傾向は？

本体3 最下位国

Q9 第1期に最も低い数値なのはどの国で、その数字は？

Q10 最終期に予想される傾向は？

結論（任意）

Q11 具体的な傾向・要点は？

以下の回答例や自分が分析した結果をもとにエッセイを書きましょう。

導入

Q1 タスク指示文は、どのように言い換えられている？

The table below		This data
illustrates		reveals
past and future life expectancy predictions for people		predicted lifespans
in a number of countries		in six countries
between 2005 and 2060.		for three, six-year terms up to 2060.

Q2 全体的な傾向・要点は？

A. people will live longer, women continue to outlive men

本体1　上位3カ国

Q3 全期間で男女ともに最も高い数値だった国は？

A. Japan

Q4 その国の第1期の数値は？

A. 2005~2010: males = 79.2, females = 86

Q5 最終期までに何が起こることが予想される？

A. 2055~2060: live a further 6 ~ 7 years

Q6 すべての年で最も高い国に続く2カ国はどこで、その国と比べて両国の数字はどれくらい低い？

A. Sweden & Germany, around 1 ~ 4 years lower

本体2　続く2カ国

Q7 続く2カ国で、第2期に予想される傾向は？

A. USA & China: 2025-2030 = live an extra 3 ~ 4 years

Q8 最終期に予想される傾向は？

A. repeated pattern (2055-2065): USA = 82.7 + 86.5 yrs., China = 79.8 + 82.4 yrs.

本体3 最下位国

Q9 第1期に最も低い数値なのはどの国で、その数字は？

A. India, 2005~2010: males: 63.3, females: 66.7

Q10 最終期に予想される傾向は？

A. the most significant rises, roughly 10 yrs. by 2055-2060

結論（任意）

Q11 具体的な傾向・要点は？

A. lifespans estimated to increase at least 6 years in first half of 21st century

エッセイ中の重要語句と表現をエクササイズで確認します。

語句に当てはまる訳の番号を選んでください。

____ predicted	____ this pattern is predicted to
____ for three, six-year terms	repeat itself in
____ in future years	____ in all periods
____ for both genders	____ is forecast to see
____ in the first period	____ overall
____ with figures of around	____ at least
____ by 2025-2030	

1. 少なくとも
2. 男女ともに
3. 2025年から2030年までに
4. 6年ごとの3期間
5. 第1期には
6. この傾向は…に繰り返すと推測される
7. 将来的に
8. 見ると予想される
9. おおよそ…の数字で
10. 予測される
11. 全体的な
12. 全期間で

下線部と同じ意味の単語を記入してください。

- it is <u>evident</u> that　　　　　=　_____
- an <u>additional</u> three to four years　=　_____
- the most <u>dramatic</u> overall rise　=　_____

エッセイと最初と最後の2文字を参考にして、空所の動詞を完成させてください。

- ... men and women are an_____ed to live ...
- Then, this pattern is pr_____ed to repeat ...
- ..., when the figures are as_____ed to be ...
- ... life expectancy is fo_____st to see ...

正解 10, 4, 7, 2, 5, 9, 3, 6, 12, 8, 11, 1／clear, extra, significant／anticipated, predicted, assumed, forecast

Self-Study!

円グラフ③

タイプ別にモデルエッセイを分析・再構築することで、重要表現を身につけてライティング力を高めます。

You should spend about 20 minutes on this task.

These graphs show the percentage of gas emissions by industrial sector in Canada in 2015 and gives forecasts for 2035.

Summarise the information by selecting and reporting the main features, and make comparisons where relevant.

Write at least 150 words.

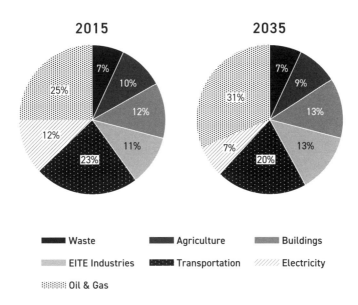

Emissions

2015

2035

- ■ Waste
- ■ Agriculture
- ■ Buildings
- ▨ EITE Industries
- ▨ Transportation
- ▨ Electricity
- ▨ Oil & Gas

The left pie chart presents data on the proportions of gas emitted in Canada by seven sectors of industry in 2015 while the right one speculates on the rates in 2035. According to the statistics, most areas are anticipated to experience changes ranging from -5% to +6% during the given time scale.

As the only exception, the rate of gas emissions from waste is anticipated to remain unchanged, at 7%. However, the amount from agriculture is expected to decline by 1% to 9%. Similarly, emissions from transportation are forecast to fall from 23 to 20%. The largest drop (5%), however, is likely to be from electricity, whose figure will represent 7% in 2035.

Turning to increases in emissions, the proportion produced by buildings is predicted to grow 1%, to 13%. A slightly larger increase (2%) is probably going to come from the EITE industries sector, also to 13%. However, the oil and gas category dominates the statistics in both years, standing at 25% in 2015, and the figure is expected to surge to 31% twenty years on. *(177 words – 9 sentences)*

In general, the comparison indicates that emissions from one sector will likely stay the same while those from three will rise and three will fall.

(202 words – 10 sentences)

左の円グラフは、2015年にカナダで7つの産業部門によって排出されたガスの割合を示したもので、右の円グラフは、2035年の割合を推測したものだ。統計データによると、ほとんどの分野で、この期間中に-5から+6％の変化があると見込まれている。

唯一の例外として、廃棄物からのガス排出量は、7％で変わらない見込みだ。しかし、農業からの排出量は、1％減少し、9％になると予想される。同様に交通機関からの排出量も、23％から20％に減少すると予想される。だが、最も大きな減少 (5%) は電力からのもので、2035年には7％になると思われる。

排出量の増加については、建物からの排出量が1％増加して、13％になると予測されている。EITE (エネルギー集約型の輸出入が多い) 産業部門では、増加率がやや大きくなり (2%)、同じく13％になると思われる。しかし、いずれの年も、石油・ガス部門が統計の最上位を占めており、2015年には25％、20年後には31％にまで急増すると予期されている。

概して、この比較は、1部門の排出量は変わらない可能性が高く、3部門からの排出量は増加し、3部門の排出量は減少するであろうことを示している。

Self-Study!

モデルエッセイを分析していきます。エッセイの英文をもとに質問に**英語で**答えてください。回答がそのままエッセイを書く材料になります。

導入

Q1 タスク指示文は、どのように言い換えられている？

These graphs
show
the percentage of
gas emissions by industrial
sector in Canada in 2015
and gives forecasts for 2035.

Q2 全体的な傾向・要点は？

本体1 変化なし＆減少

Q3 変化がない部門とその数値は？

Q4 減少が最も少ない部門はどれで、どのくらい減る？

Q5 次に大きく減少する部門とその数値は？

Q6 最も大きく減少する部門とその数値は？

本体2 増加

Q7 増加が最も少ない部門とその数値は？

Q8 それよりやや大きく増加する部門とその数値は？

Q9 どちらの年も最も数値が大きい部門とその数値は？

結論（任意）

Q10 具体的な傾向・要点は？

以下の回答例や自分が分析した結果をもとにエッセイを書きましょう。

導入

Q1 タスク指示文は、どのように言い換えられている？

These graphs		The left pie chart
show		presents data on
the percentage of		the proportions of
gas emissions by industrial sector in Canada in 2015		gas emitted in Canada by seven sectors of industry in 2015
and gives forecasts for 2035.		while the right one speculates on the rates in 2035.

Q2 全体的な傾向・要点は？

A. most areas anticipated to experience changes ranging from -5% to +6%

本体1 変化なし＆減少

Q3 変化がない部門とその数値は？

A. waste, 7%

Q4 減少が最も少ない部門はどれで、どのくらい減る？

A. agriculture: by 1% to 9%

Q5 次に大きく減少する部門とその数値は？

A. transportation: 23% ↘ 20%

Q6 最も大きく減少する部門とその数値は？

A. electricity (↘ 5%): 7% in 2035

本体2 増加

Q7 増加が最も少ない部門とその数値は？

A. buildings (↗ 1%): 13%

Q8 それよりやや大きく増加する部門とその数値は？

A. EITE industries (↗ 2%): also 13%

Q9 どちらの年も最も数値が大きい部門とその数値は？

A. oil and gas: 25% = 2015, 31% = twenty years on

結論（任意）

Q10 具体的な傾向・要点は？

A. emissions from one sector = likely stay the same, three = rise, three = fall

エッセイ中の重要語句と表現をエクササイズで確認します。

語句に当てはまる訳の番号を選んでください。

____ The left	____ is probably going to come from
____ the right	____ sector
____ most areas	____ dominates
____ ranging from ... to ~	____ twenty years on
____ time scale	____ the comparison
____ As the only exception,	____ those from

1. 部門	4. 左の	7. …からのもの	10. ほとんどの分野
2. ～からになりそうだ	5. 20年後	8. 右の	11. 期間
3. 最上位を占める	6. 比較	9. …から～にわたる	12. 唯一の例外として

下線部が何を指すかを答えてください。

- The left pie chart presents data on the proportions of gas emitted in Canada by seven sectors of industry in 2015 while the right <u>one</u> speculates on the rates in 2035.

- As the only exception, the rate of gas emissions from waste is anticipated to remain unchanged, at 7%. However, the <u>amount</u> from agriculture is expected to decline by 1% to 9%.

- In general, the comparison indicates that emissions from one sector will likely stay the same while <u>those</u> from three will rise and three will fall.

Self-Study!

プロセス図③

タイプ別にモデルエッセイを分析・再構築することで、重要表現を身につけてライティング力を高めます。

You should spend about 20 minutes on this task.

These diagrams reveal how a narrowboat goes through a lock to move up and down waterways.

Summarise the information by selecting and reporting the main features, and make comparisons where relevant.

Write at least 150 words.

NARROWBOAT LOCK SYSTEM

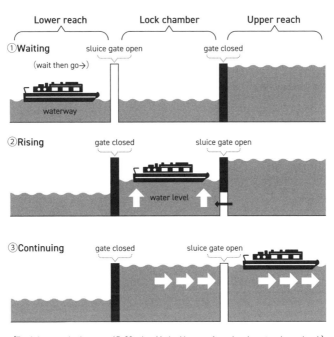

(Total time required approx. 15~20 mins. Method is same for going down to a lower level.)

The three illustrations depict the way a narrowboat progresses through a lock system in order to travel along a canal. According to the content, there are three stages and the total time takes around 15 to 20 minutes.

In the first stage, the narrowboat must wait in the lower reach of the waterway. Then a sluice gate is opened and the boat can move into the lock chamber. There, the water level behind a closed, second gate is higher than in the lock chamber.

Next, the first sluice gate is closed, and the second one is opened so that water from the upper reach can enter the lock chamber. As the water enters the chamber, the water level rises and so does the narrowboat.

Finally, when the second gate is fully open and the water in the chamber is at the same height as that of the upper reach, the boat can pass and continue its journey along the waterway. If a boat wants to travel from a higher to a lower part of the river, the whole process is reversed. *(181 words – 9 sentences)*

To conclude, narrowboats can easily navigate canals with different land levels by using the lock system. *(197 words – 10 sentences)*

3枚のイラストは、ナローボート（運河用の細長い船）が運河を航行するために、ロックシステムを通過する方法を描いたものだ。内容によると、3つの段階があり、全体で15〜20分程度かかる。

最初の段階では、ナローボートは、水路の低水位側で待機しなくてはならない。その後、水門が開かれ、ボートは隔室に移動することができる。そこでは、閉じられた2つ目の門の向こう側の水位が隔室よりも高くなっている。

次に、第1の水門が閉じられ、高水位側からの水が隔室に流れ込むように、第2の水門が開かれる。隔室に水が入ると水位が上がり、ナローボートも上昇する。

最後に、第2の門が完全に開き、隔室内の水位が高水位側と同じ高さになると、ボートは通過することができ、水路に沿って旅を続けることができる。ボートが川の高い部分から低い部分に航行したい場合は、すべての工程が逆に行われる。

結論として、ナローボートはロックシステムを利用することで、土地の高さが異なる運河を、容易に航行することができる。

Self-Study!

　モデルエッセイを分析していきます。エッセイの英文をもとに質問に**英語**
で答えてください。回答がそのままエッセイを書く材料になります。

導入

Q1 タスク指示文は、どのように言い換えられている？

These diagrams	
reveal	
how	
a narrowboat goes through a lock	
to move up and down waterways.	

Q2 全体的な傾向・要点は？

本体1　待機

Q3 第1段階の初めに何が起こる？

Q4 次に何が起こる？

Q5 2つ目の門の状況は？

本体2　上昇

Q6 第2段階の始めに何が起こる？

Q7 次に何が起こる？

本体3　運航再開

Q8 2つ目の門が完全に開いたら何が起こる？

Q9 ボートが高い水位から低い水位に航行したい場合はどうする？

結論（任意）

Q10 具体的な傾向・要点は？

以下の回答例や自分が分析した結果をもとにエッセイを書きましょう。

導入

Q1 タスク指示文は、どのように言い換えられている?

These diagrams		*The three illustrations*
reveal		*depict*
how	➡	*the way*
a narrowboat goes through a lock		*a narrowboat progresses through a lock system*
to move up and down waterways.		*in order to travel along a canal.*

Q2 全体的な傾向・要点は?

A. there are three stages, time takes around 15~20 mins.

本体1 待機

Q3 第1段階の初めに何が起こる?

A. narrowboat must wait in lower reach

Q4 次に何が起こる?

A. 1st sluice gate opened, boat → lock chamber

Q5 2つ目の門の状況は?

A. water level behind closed 2nd gate = higher than in lock chamber

本体2 上昇

Q6 第2段階の始めに何が起こる?

A. 1st sluice gate is closed, 2nd is opened so water from upper reach enters

Q7 次に何が起こる?

A. water in chamber rises, so narrowboat rises

本体3 運航再開

Q8 2つ目の門が完全に開いたら何が起こる?

　A. water becomes same height as in upper reach, boat can pass and continue journey

Q9 ボートが高い水位から低い水位に航行したい場合はどうする?

　A. whole process is reversed

結論 (任意)

Q10 具体的な傾向・要点は?

　A. narrowboats can easily navigate canals by using lock system

エッセイ中の重要語句と表現をエクササイズで確認します。

語句に当てはまる訳の番号を選んでください。

____ progresses through	____ Next,
____ content	____ that of (= the height of)
____ there are three stages	____ can pass
____ In the first stage	____ the whole process
____ ... lock chamber. There,	____ is reversed
____ is higher than	____ by using

1. すべての工程　　5. 3つの段階がある　　9. 次に　　　　　　12. …のそれ
2. 利用することで　6. …より高い　　　　10. 逆にする、逆行する　　（…の高さ）
3. 内容　　　　　　7. 通過する　　　　　11. …隔室。そこでは
4. 通過できる　　　8. 最初の段階では

正しい方を選んでください。

- In the first stage, the narrowboat [must / can] wait in the lower reach of the waterway.
- Then a sluice gate is opened and the boat [can / must] move into the lock chamber.
- To conclude, narrowboats [can / must] easily navigate canals with different land levels ...

to, along, of, into, from から正しいものを入れてください。

- ... in order to travel (　　　　) a canal ...
- ... the boat can move (　　　　) the lock chamber ...
- If a boat wants to travel (　　　　) a higher (　　　　) a lower part (　　　　) the river ...

地図・図解③

タイプ別にモデルエッセイを分析・再構築することで、重要表現を身につけてライティング力を高めます。

You should spend about 20 minutes on this task.

The maps below show a university's facilities in two different years.

Summarise the information by selecting and reporting the main features, and make comparisons where relevant.

Write at least 150 words.

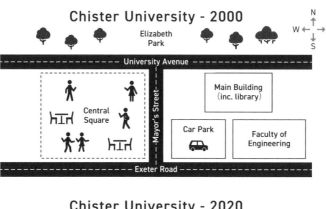

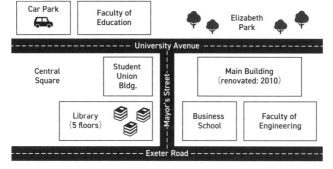

These two illustrations detail the facilities at Chister University in 2000 and 2020. Looking at the differences, it is evident that the university experienced significant changes over the twenty-year period.

In 2000, one key feature of the campus was Elizabeth Park, which was located on the north side of the university. Opposite the park, Central Square occupied land stretching from University Avenue to Exeter Road. Main Building, which housed the library, was situated to the east of Mayor's Street. South of the building there was a car park on the left and the Faculty of Engineering on the right, both of which faced Exeter Road.

By 2020, the park had been reduced in size and the new space was occupied by the Faculty of Education. Moreover, the car park relocated adjacent to this faculty, and the Business School occupied the original car park area. Other major developments were the construction of the Student Union building and a five-storey library in Central Square. Finally, the Faculty of Engineering and Main Building remained, although the latter was renovated in 2010.

(178 words – 10 sentences)

In summary, it is apparent that the university expanded during the two decades in order to offer a wider range of options for students.

(202 words – 11 sentences)

この2枚のイラストは、2000年と2020年の、チスター大学の施設を詳述している。その違いを見ると、20年の間に大学が大きく変化したことは明白だ。

2000年は、大学の北側にあるエリザベス公園が、キャンパスの重要な特徴の1つだった。公園の向かい側は、セントラル広場がユニバーシティー大通りからエクセター道にかけての土地を占めていた。図書館も入っていた本館は、メイヤーズ通りの東側に位置していた。その本館の南側には、左に駐車場、右に工学部があり、どちらもエクセター道に面していた。

2020年までには、公園は縮小され、新たなスペースは教育学部が占有した。さらに、駐車場は教育学部の隣に移設され、駐車場があった場所は現在ビジネススクールとなった。その他の主な開発としては、セントラル広場に学生会館と5階建ての図書館が建設された。最後に、工学部と本館は残ったが、本館は2010年に改装されている。

要約すると、この大学は20年間で、学生により幅広い選択肢を提供するために拡大していったことがわかる。

Self-Study!

　モデルエッセイを分析していきます。エッセイの英文をもとに質問に**英語で**答えてください。回答がそのままエッセイを書く材料になります。

導入

Q1　タスク指示文は、どのように言い換えられている？

The maps below		
show		
a university's facilities		
in two different years.		

_____

_____

_____

_____

Q2　全体的な傾向・要点は？

本体1　2000年の施設

Q3　2000年のキャンパスマップ上部にあった重要な特徴は？

Q4　公園の向かい側にあるもう1つの広い場所は？

Q5　地図の真ん中を通る道路の東側にあるのは？

Q6　その下にあって、南側の道路に面していたのは？

本体2　2020年の施設

Q7　2020年に公園に起きた変化は？

Q8　公園の場所でほかにどんな変化があった？

Q9　それ以外に大学で起こった2つの大きな変化は？

Q10　基本的に変わらなかった2つの施設は？

結論（任意）

Q11　具体的な傾向・要点は？

以下の回答例や自分が分析した結果をもとにエッセイを書きましょう。

導入

Q1　タスク指示文は、どのように言い換えられている？

The maps below		These two illustrations
show		detail
a university's facilities		the facilities at Chister University
in two different years.		in 2000 and 2020.

Q2　全体的な傾向・要点は？

A. significant changes over twenty-year period

本体1　2000年の施設

Q3　2000年のキャンパスマップ上部にあった重要な特徴は？

A. Elizabeth Park, north of university

Q4　公園の向かい側にあるもう１つの広い場所は？

A. Central Square (University Ave. ⇔ Exeter Rd.)

Q5　図の真ん中を通る道路の東側にあるのは？

A. Main Building (housed library)

Q6　その下にあって、南側の道路に面していたのは？

A. car park = left, Faculty of Engineering = right (faced Exeter Rd.)

本体2　2020年の施設

Q7　2020年に公園に起きた変化は？

A. park: reduced in size, new Faculty of Education

Q8　公園の場所でほかにどんな変化があった？

A. car park: relocated adjacent to this faculty ←→ Business School = original car park area

Q9 それ以外に大学で起こった2つの大きな変化は？

A. Student Union building & 5-flr. library built in Central Square

Q10 基本的に変わらなかった2つの施設は？

A. Faculty of Engineering, Main Building (but renovated, 2010)

結論（任意）

Q11 具体的な傾向・要点は？

A. university expanded to offer wider options for students

Task 1

4. タイプ別セルフスタディ3

エッセイ中の重要語句と表現をエクササイズで確認します。

語句に当てはまる訳の番号を選んでください。

_____ detail   _____ faced

_____ Looking at the differences,   _____ in size

_____ one key feature of   _____ adjacent to

_____ occupied   _____ Other major developments

_____ housed   _____ renovated

_____ to the east of   _____ range of options

1. 違いを見ると   4. 選択肢、選択の範囲   7. 詳述する   10. …の東側に向かって
2. 占めていた   5. …の重要な特徴の1つ   8. 面していた、対面した   11. 改装した
3. 規模において   6. その他の主な開発   9. …に隣接して   12. 収容した

空所に2語を入れて、「2000年〜2020年」に関するエッセイの表現を完成させてください。

- over the _____

- during the _____

下線部はエッセイでどう表現されていますか？

- South of the building there was a car park on the left and the Faculty of Engineering on the right, which both faced Exeter Road.

- Finally, the Faculty of Engineering and Main Building remained, although Main Building was renovated in 2010.

正解 7, 1, 5, 2, 12, 10, 8, 3, 9, 6, 11, 4／twenty-year period, two decades／both of which, the latter

Self-Study!

異なるタイプの 組み合わせ③

タイプ別にモデルエッセイを分析・再構築することで、重要表現を身につけてライティング力を高めます。

You should spend about 20 minutes on this task.

The charts reveal how breakfast cereal is made and how the cost of a box of cereal is divided up.

Summarise the information by selecting and reporting the main features, and make comparisons where relevant.

Write at least 150 words.

How Breakfast Cereal Is Made

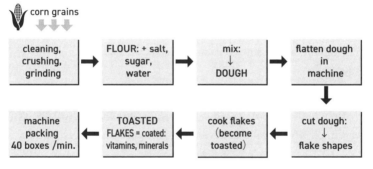

Cost Distribution Each Box

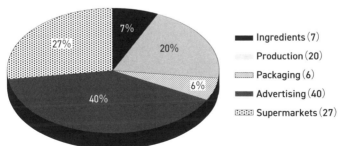

These two diagrams illustrate the process of making breakfast cereal from corn grains and the cost breakdown for each box produced. According to the information, the process has eight stages and the cost is divided in five ways.

The method of producing breakfast cereal begins with the cleaning of corn grains. After being cleaned, the grains are crushed and ground to produce flour. Then, salt, sugar and water are added to the flour, and mixed to produce dough. Next, the dough is flattened in a machine before being cut into flake shapes, and the flakes are cooked. After this, the toasted flakes are coated with vitamins and minerals. Finally, the flakes are packaged by a machine that packs forty boxes per minute.

Turning to the cost breakdown per box, the lowest proportion (6%) is spent on packaging. This is followed by ingredients, whose amount is marginally higher, at 7%. A larger figure of 20% covers the cost of production while supermarkets take 27%. Finally, advertising constitutes the largest share, with 40% of the cost of each box.

(177 words – 12 sentences)

Overall, the charts suggest that the method of producing breakfast cereal is relatively simple and reveal that advertising consumes the biggest portion of the cost of the product.

(204 words – 13 sentences)

この2つの図は、トウモロコシの粒から朝食用シリアルを作る工程と、製造される1箱あたりの費用の内訳を示している。情報によると、この工程には8つの段階があり、費用は5通りに分割されている。

朝食用シリアルの製造方法は、トウモロコシの粒を洗浄することから始まる。洗浄した後、粒を砕き、ひいて粉にする。それから、粉に塩、砂糖、水を加えて混ぜ合わせ、生地を作る。次に、機械で生地を平らにしてからフレーク状に切り、フレークを焼く。この後、焼いたフレークに、ビタミンやミネラルをまぶす。最後に、1分間に40箱詰めることができる機械でフレークを箱詰めする。

1箱あたりの費用内訳を見ると、最も低い割合（6％）が、包装に使われる。続いて、原材料が7％と、わずかに多い。製造費用が20％という大きな数値を占め、スーパーは、27％を取る。最後に広告費が、1箱あたりのコストの40％という、最も大きな割合を占めている。

全体的に見ると、これらの図表は、朝食用シリアルの製造方法が比較的シンプルであることを示し、また広告費が製品コストで最も大きな割合を占めていることを明らかにしている。

Self-Study!

　モデルエッセイを分析していきます。エッセイの英文をもとに質問に**英語で**答えてください。回答がそのままエッセイを書く材料になります。

導入

Q1 タスク指示文は、どのように言い換えられている？

The charts
reveal
how breakfast cereal is made
and how the cost of a box of
cereal is divided up.

＿＿＿＿＿＿＿＿＿＿＿＿＿＿
＿＿＿＿＿＿＿＿＿＿＿＿＿＿
＿＿＿＿＿＿＿＿＿＿＿＿＿＿

Q2 全体的な傾向・要点は？

本体1　製造方法

Q3 工程の最初に3つ起こることは？　何が作られる？

Q4 それに何が加えられ、何が行われ、何が作られる？

Q5 生地はどのように変えられ、次に何が起こる？

Q6 加熱後は何が起こる？

本体2　費用配分

Q7 シリアル1箱にかかる費用のうち、最も低い割合の数値と対象は？

Q8 2番目に低い割合の数値と対象は？

Q9 その次に高い2つの割合の数値と対象は？

Q10 最も高い割合の数値と対象は？

結論（任意）

Q11 具体的な傾向・要点は？

Task 1

4.
タイプ別セルフスタディ3

以下の回答例や自分が分析した結果をもとにエッセイを書きましょう。

導入

Q1 タスク指示文は、どのように言い換えられている?

The charts		*These two diagrams*
reveal		*illustrate*
how breakfast cereal is made		*the process of making breakfast cereal from corn grains*
and how the cost of a box of cereal is divided up.		*and the cost breakdown for each box produced.*

Q2 全体的な傾向・要点は?

A. eight stages, cost = divided in five ways

本体1 製造方法

Q3 工程の最初に3つ起こることは? 何が作られる?

A. cleaning of corn grains, crushed & ground → flour

Q4 それに何が加えられ、何が行われ、何が作られる?

A. salt, sugar & water = added & mixed → dough

Q5 生地はどのように変えられ、次に何が起こる?

A. flattened, cut into flake shapes & cooked

Q6 加熱後は何が起こる?

A. toasted flakes coated with vitamins & minerals

本体2 費用配分

Q7 シリアル1箱にかかる費用のうち、最も低い割合の数値と対象は?

A. 6%, packaging

Q8 2番目に低い割合の数値と対象は?

A. 7%, ingredients

[Q9] その次に高い2つの割合の数値と対象は？

    A. 20% = production, 27% = supermarkets

[Q10] 最も高い割合の数値と対象は？

    A. advertising = 40%

結論（任意）

[Q11] 具体的な傾向・要点は？

    A. (process) method is relatively simple

       (pie) advertising consumes biggest portion of cost of breakfast cereal

エッセイ中の重要語句と表現をエクササイズで確認します。

語句に当てはまる訳の番号を選んでください。

_____ the cost breakdown		_____ A larger figure of	
_____ is divided in five ways		_____ constitutes the largest share	
_____ After being ...		_____ suggest	
_____ After this,		_____ consumes	
_____ per box		_____ the biggest portion of	
_____ This is followed by		_____ product	

1. 1箱あたり	4. 最も大きな割合を	7. 使う	11. これに続いて
2. …というもっと	占める	8. 5通りに分割される	…がある
大きな数値	5. 費用の内訳	9. …された後	12. 示す
3. 製品	6. …の最も大きな割合	10. この後、次に	

エッセイと最初の1文字を参考にして、空所に正しい語句を入れてください。

• These t_____ diagrams illustrate the p_____ of m_____
breakfast cereal f_____ corn grains.

• The m_____ of p_____ breakfast cereal b_____ with
t_____ cleaning o_____ corn grains.

that または whose を入れてください。

• *that*: Finally, the flakes are packaged by a machine, packs forty boxes per
minute.

• *whose*: This is followed by ingredients, amount is marginally higher, at 7%.

正解 5, 8, 9, 10, 1, 11, 2, 4, 12, 7, 6, 3 ／ two, process, making, from, method, producing, begins,
the, of ／ ... machine that packs ..., ... ingredients, whose rate ...

Task 2

本番のエッセイの書き方

🔍 タスクを理解し、トピックについて考える　　5分

Step 1　タスク説明文を注意深く読む

Step 2　エッセイの基本構造とトピックについて考える

- ●「賛成か反対か」を述べる問題は、どちらの立場で書くかを決める。
- ● 自分から遠すぎる内容ではなく、身近な日常生活にまつわることを考える と書きやすい。

Step 3　導入パラグラフを書く（通例3文）

1文目：トピックをおおまかに紹介する。
2文目：トピックの具体的な側面に言及する。
3文目：自分の立場＝エッセイの主張を記述する。

📚 アイデアを膨らませ、整理する　　5分

Step 4　本体パラグラフのアイデアを書き出す

- ● アイデアのまとめ方。
  ① 各本体パラグラフで扱う内容を決め、関連するアイデア（具体例や理由） をノートにいくつか書く。
  ② その中から良いアイデアを各パラグラフで3つ程度選ぶ。
  ③ どの順番で提示するかを整理する。

✏ 本体エッセイを書く　　　　　　　　　　25分

Step 5　本体パラグラフ①を書く（通例3〜5文）
Step 6　本体パラグラフ②を書く（通例3〜5文）
Step 7　本体パラグラフ③を書く（通例3〜5文）＊エッセイによる

● まず、そのパラグラフのトピック・センテンス（そのパラグラフで何を扱うか）を書き、次の文で具体的な考えや理由を示し、具体例で説明する。
● 必要があれば、本体パラグラフ③を書く。

注意　紙ではなくパソコンで受験する場合
導入パラグラフを書いたら、まず各本体パラグラフの第1文（トピック・センテンス）をすべて書く。その後で各パラグラフを完成させる。

Step 8　結論を書く（通例2〜3文）

● 自分の立場＝エッセイの主張を再び述べて、各本体パラグラフの重要な点に言及する。
● 最後はエッセイを締めくくる1文にする。

🔍 ミスをチェック　　　　　　　　　　　　5分

Step 9　優先順位をつけてミスを確認する

● 事前に「自分が行いがちなミス」を把握しておき、それを中心にチェック。
● タスク説明文の語句を使う場合は特にスペリングミスに注意。
● 時間があれば、「ミスの種類別※」にエッセイ全体を何度かチェックする。

※冠詞と複数形、動詞の3人称・時制、スペリング、判別困難な書き文字。

それでは、Task 2をエッセイのタイプ別に攻略していきましょう。

賛成・反対を述べる

例題で「賛成または反対の表明」を攻略していきます。

You should spend about 40 minutes on this task.

Some people believe that it is better to stay with one company during a career. Do you agree or disagree with this point of view?

Give reasons for your answer and include any relevant examples from your own knowledge or experience.

Write at least 250 words.

エッセイの基本構成

このタイプの場合、賛成または反対いずれかの立場でエッセイを展開します。

パターン1	導入	▶	賛成	▶	賛成	▶	(賛成)	▶	結論
パターン2	導入	▶	反対	▶	反対	▶	(反対)	▶	結論

タスク説明文を確認する

説明文を注意深く読んで内容を確認します。

トピック	employment during career / working life
論点	better to stay with one company?
タスク	agree or disagree

エッセイ・プランニング

本体パラグラフの数と方向性を決めます。

導入	トピック・論点・タスク→主張を要約する
本体1〜3	reason 1〜3
結論	メインの考えを再提示し、自分の意見を書く

導入パラグラフを書く

トピック・論点・主張を自分の言葉で書き、必要に応じてそれらをまとめます。ここでは導入を2文にします。

トピック	[1] in the past, employees worked for same company throughout life
論点	[2-1] some people still prefer this today
主張	[2-2] more beneficial not to stay with same company (= *disagree*)

[1] In the past, there was a tendency for employees to work for the same employer throughout their working life. [2-1] Although some individuals still prefer this option today, [2-2] I believe it is more beneficial not to remain with the same company for an entire career.

本体パラグラフ用にアイデアを書き出し、整理する

アイデアを練り、英文ごとに書き出します。各パラグラフは、そのパラグラフで何を扱うかを述べるトピック・センテンスで始めます。次の文からは、より具体的な考えや理由を書き、情報や例を加えます。
※太字はパラグラフ内のメイン・アイデア

本体1　英文 [3]〜[5]

[3] **one company = may lose interest in your job**
[4] completely familiar with content, people & atmosphere = become bored
[5-1] **changing jobs = can stay motivated**
[5-2] will meet new co-workers, situations & challenges

本体2　英文 [6]〜[8]

[6] **moving to another company = can develop existing skills & knowledge & gain opportunities in new areas**
[7] beneficial in today's changing world → industries fade, others appear
[8] if possess knowledge & skills → easier to switch industries & remain employed

本体3　英文 [9]〜[11]

[9] **same company = miss chance to discover better positions**

[10] researching other companies & attending interviews = may find
    something more rewarding and fulfilling
[11] if companies retain CV, might receive job offers later

メモを使って実際の段落を書いていきます。
※下線はメモで書き出した語句です。

[3] Firstly, if you continually work for only <u>one company</u>, over time you <u>may lose interest in your job</u>. [4] Being <u>completely familiar with</u> your job <u>content</u>, co-workers and your company's <u>atmosphere</u>, you could <u>become bored</u>. [5-1] Yet, by <u>changing jobs</u> every so often, people <u>can stay motivated</u> [5-2] as they <u>will meet new co-workers, situations and challenges</u>.

[6] Secondly, by <u>moving to another company</u>, it is possible to <u>develop</u> your <u>existing skills and knowledge</u> as well as <u>gain opportunities</u> to work <u>in new areas</u> of business. [7] This can be <u>beneficial in today's</u> quickly <u>changing world</u> where some <u>industries fade</u> away while <u>others appear</u>, thrive and evolve. [8] Therefore, <u>if</u> a person <u>possesses</u> an array of <u>knowledge and skills</u>, it will be <u>easier to switch</u> to different <u>industries and</u> thus <u>remain employed</u>.

[9] Finally, when people stay with the <u>same company</u> for a whole career, they <u>miss</u> the <u>chance to discover positions</u> with <u>better</u> salaries and work conditions. [10] However, by <u>researching</u> jobs with <u>other companies and attending interviews</u> they <u>may find something more</u> financially <u>rewarding and</u> personally <u>fulfilling</u>. [11] Furthermore, <u>if companies retain</u> their <u>CV</u>, those individuals <u>might receive</u> unexpected <u>job offers</u> at <u>later</u> dates.

結論は本体を要約し、主張を再び述べる

[12] more advantageous to work for different companies
[13] can retain interest in work, develop knowledge & abilities, find ideal job
[14] though, important not to change companies too frequently

[12] To summarise, rather than have lifetime employment with a single company, I think it is <u>more advantageous to work for different companies</u> during a career. [13] You <u>can retain</u> an <u>interest in</u> your <u>work</u>, <u>develop</u> your <u>knowledge and abilities</u> and <u>find</u> your <u>ideal job</u>. [14] At the same time, <u>though</u>, it is <u>important not to change companies too frequently</u>.

モデルエッセイ　　　　　　　　　　　　　　　　　◀))29

In the past, there was a tendency for employees to work for the same employer throughout their working life. Although some individuals still prefer this option today, I believe it is more beneficial not to remain with the same company for an entire career.

Firstly, if you continually work for only one company, over time you may lose interest in your job. Being completely familiar with your job content, co-workers and your company's atmosphere, you could become bored. Yet, by changing jobs every so often, people can stay motivated as they will meet new co-workers, situations and challenges.

Secondly, by moving to another company, it is possible to develop your existing skills and knowledge as well as gain opportunities to work in new areas of business. This can be beneficial in today's quickly changing world where some industries fade away while others appear, thrive and evolve. Therefore, if a person possesses an array of knowledge and skills, it will be easier to switch to different industries and thus remain employed.

Finally, when people stay with the same company for a whole career, they miss the chance to discover positions with better salaries and work conditions. However, by researching jobs with other companies and attending interviews they may find something more financially rewarding and personally fulfilling. Furthermore, if companies retain their CV, those individuals might receive unexpected job offers at later dates.

To summarise, rather than have lifetime employment with a single company, I think it is more advantageous to work for different companies during a career. You can retain an interest in your work, develop your knowledge and abilities and find your ideal job. At the same time, though, it is important not to change companies too frequently. *(287 words – 14 sentences)*

従業員はかつて、職業人生を通して同じ雇用主のもとで働く風潮があった。今でもこの選択肢を好む人もいるが、私は同じ会社で職業人生すべてを過ごさない方が、より有益だと考えている。

まず、1つの会社で働き続けると、仕事への興味がなくなってしまうことがある。仕事内容や同僚、会社の雰囲気にすっかり慣れてしまい、飽きてしまう可能性がある。しかし、転職を繰り返すことで、新しい同僚、状況、そして課題に出合うことができ、モチベーションを維持することができる。

第2に、会社を移ることで、今までのスキルや知識を向上させるだけでなく、新しいビジネス分野で働く機会を得ることも可能になる。これは、ある産業が衰退する一方で、別の産業が出現し、繁栄して進化する、変化の激しい今日の世界では有益なことだ。したがって、数々の知識やスキルを持っている人は、異業種への転職が容易となり、働き続けることができる。

最後に、キャリアを通じて同じ会社にずっといると、より良い給与や労働条件の職務を見つける機会を逃してしまう。しかし、他社の求人情報を調べ、面接を受けることで、より金銭的に報われ、個人的にも充足感を得られる何かを見つけるかもしれない。さらには、企業が履歴書を保管することで、その人は後日、思いがけない仕事の依頼を受ける可能性もある。

まとめると、1社で終身雇用されるよりも、キャリアを通じていろいろな会社で働いた方が有益だと思う。仕事への興味を持ち続け、知識や能力を高め、理想の仕事を見つけることができる。ただそれと同時に、あまり頻繁に会社を変えないことも重要だ。

エクササイズ

エッセイ中の重要語句と表現をエクササイズで確認します。

語句に当てはまる訳の番号を選んでください。

_____ employer

_____ beneficial

_____ career

_____ lose interest in

_____ (be) familiar with

_____ job content

_____ co-workers

_____ knowledge

_____ thrive

_____ evolve

_____ an array of

_____ remain employed

_____ positions

_____ salaries

_____ CV

1. 知識
2. 働き続ける、雇用され続ける
3. …に慣れる
4. 有益な
5. 雇用主
6. 給与
7. 数々の
8. 職業人生、経歴
9. 仕事内容
10. 繁栄する
11. …への興味がなくなる
12. 職
13. 履歴書
14. 同僚
15. 進化する

日本語訳とエッセイを参考に残りの文字を入れてください。

- financially rew_____ （金銭的に報われて）

- personally ful_____ （個人的に充実感のある）

- lifetime emp_____ （終身雇用）

カッコ内を正しい順序に並べ替えてください。

- In the past, [tendency / there / a / for / was] employees to work for the same employer …

- At [time / same / the], though, [not / is / change / it / to / important] companies too frequently.

正解　5, 4, 8, 11, 3, 9, 14, 1, 10, 15, 7, 2, 12, 6, 13／rewarding, fulfilling, employment／there was a tendency for, the same time, it is important not to change

物事の両面と意見を述べる

例題で「両面の提示」を攻略していきます。

You should spend about 40 minutes on this task.

Some people think it is better to live in the city while others say the countryside is better.
Discuss both attitudes and give your own opinion.

Give reasons for your answer and include any relevant examples from your own knowledge or experience.

Write at least 250 words.

エッセイの基本構成

このタイプの場合、各パラグラフでそれぞれの面について述べます。

パターン	導入 ▶ A面の主張 ▶ B面の主張 ▶ 結論

タスク説明文を確認する

説明文を注意深く読んで内容を確認します。

トピック	places for living
論点	preference of city vs countryside
タスク	discuss, and write own opinion

エッセイ・プランニング

本体パラグラフの数と方向性を決めます。

導入	トピック・論点・タスク→主張を要約する
本体1	why some people prefer city
本体2	why others prefer countryside
結論	メインの考えを再提示し、自分の意見を書く

導入パラグラフを書く

トピック・論点・主張を自分の言葉で書き、必要に応じてそれらをまとめます。ここでは導入を3文にします。

トピック	[1] people have two choices about where to reside
論点	[2] certain individuals favour urban areas, others prefer rural settings
主張	[3] why such personal preferences

[1] In general, <u>people have two choices</u> regarding <u>where to reside</u>. [2] While <u>certain individuals favour</u> living in <u>urban areas, others prefer rural settings</u>. [3] This leads to the question of <u>why</u> each side has <u>such personal preferences</u>.

本体パラグラフ用にアイデアを書き出し、整理する

アイデアを練り、英文ごとに書き出します。各パラグラフは、そのパラグラフで何を扱うかを述べるトピック・センテンスで始めます。次の文からは、より具体的な考えや理由を書き、情報や例を加えます。
※太字はパラグラフ内のメイン・アイデア

本体1　英文 [4]〜[9]

[4] city has particular attractions

[5] **various options to enjoy daily lives**

[6] shops, restaurants, cinemas, theatres, museums

[7] **excellent health services** (best hospitals & medical care in urban centres)

[8] **greater opportunities to obtain employment** (high concentration of companies)

[9] higher salaries & better fringe benefits

本体2　英文 [10]〜[15]

[10] residing in countryside is a popular choice

[11] **lifestyle is more relaxed and less stressful**

[12] residents rarely experience crowded situations (rush-hour trains &

tend not to worry about time
[13] **little pollution = life is healthier** (water and air quality = better)
[14] **lower cost of living** (esp. price of land and housing)
[15] **rural properties are more spacious** = more comfortable

メモを使って実際の段落を書いていきます。
※下線はメモで書き出した語句です。

[4] There is no doubt that living in the <u>city has particular attractions</u>. [5] First, it provides <u>various options</u> that enable people <u>to enjoy</u> their <u>daily lives</u>. [6] These include numerous <u>shops, restaurants, cinemas, theatres</u> and <u>museums</u>, to name a few. [7] In addition, there is the <u>prevalence of excellent health services</u>, as the <u>best hospitals and medical care</u> are often located <u>in urban centres</u>. [8] Thirdly, cities provide <u>greater opportunities to obtain employment</u> due to their <u>higher concentration of companies</u>. [9] Moreover, positions in cities tend to have <u>higher salaries and better fringe benefits</u>.

[10] Nevertheless, <u>residing in</u> the <u>countryside is a popular choice</u> for many people. [11] Without a doubt, the <u>lifestyle is</u> much <u>more relaxed and</u> far <u>less stressful</u> than city life. [12] For instance, countryside <u>residents rarely experience crowded situations</u> such as <u>rush-hour trains and tend not to worry about time</u>. [13] Furthermore, with <u>little pollution</u>, rural <u>life is healthier</u> since the <u>water and air quality</u> are <u>better</u>. [14] A final benefit is the <u>lower cost of living</u>, <u>especially</u> the <u>price of land and housing</u>. [15] Also, <u>rural properties are</u> generally <u>more spacious</u>, and therefore, <u>more comfortable</u>.

結論は本体を要約し、主張を再び述べる

[16] city = better when young
[17] urban areas = greater opportunities: education, suitable & rewarding career
[18] however, countryside = more desirable when older → tranquillity & quality of life

[16] From a personal perspective, I believe it is <u>better</u> to live in the <u>city when</u> you are <u>young</u> and have energy. [17] This is due to the fact that <u>urban areas</u> tend to provide <u>greater opportunities</u> for <u>education</u> and better chances of finding a <u>suitable and rewarding career</u>. [18] <u>However</u>, as you get <u>older</u>, the <u>countryside</u> is <u>more desirable</u> due to its <u>tranquillity</u> and the <u>quality of life</u> it offers.

モデルエッセイ　　　　　　　　　　　　　　　　　　　🔊30

In general, people have two choices regarding where to reside. While certain individuals favour living in urban areas, others prefer rural settings. This leads to the question of why each side has such personal preferences.

There is no doubt that living in the city has particular attractions. First, it provides various options that enable people to enjoy their daily lives. These include numerous shops, restaurants, cinemas, theatres and museums, to name a few. In addition, there is the prevalence of excellent health services, as the best hospitals and medical care are often located in urban centres. Thirdly, cities provide greater opportunities to obtain employment due to their higher concentration of companies. Moreover, positions in cities tend to have higher salaries and better fringe benefits.

Nevertheless, residing in the countryside is a popular choice for many people. Without a doubt, the lifestyle is much more relaxed and far less stressful than city life. For instance, countryside residents rarely experience crowded situations such as rush-hour trains and tend not to worry about time. Furthermore, with little pollution, rural life is healthier since the water and air quality are better. A final benefit is the lower cost of living, especially the price of land and housing. Also, rural properties are generally more spacious, and therefore, more comfortable.

From a personal perspective, I believe it is better to live in the city when you are young and have energy. This is due to the fact that urban areas tend to provide greater opportunities for education and better chances of finding a suitable and rewarding career. However, as you get older, the countryside is more desirable due to its tranquillity and the quality of life it offers. *(282 words – 18 sentences)*

一般的に、人はどこに居住するかについて2つの選択肢がある。都市部に住むことを好む人もいれば、田舎の環境を好む人もいる。これは、なぜそれぞれの側がそのような個人的な好みを持っているのか、という疑問につながる。

都会に住むことに特別な魅力があるのは間違いない。第1に、都会は人々が日常生活を楽しむことができるような、様々な選択肢を提供している。その中には、少し挙げるだけでも、数多くの店、レストラン、映画館、劇場、美術館などが含まれる。さらに、最高の病院や医療機関は都心にあることが多いため、優れた医療サービスが普及している。第3に、都市にはより多くの企業が集中しているため、就職の機会が増える。さらに、都市部の職の方が給料が高く、福利厚生も充実している傾向がある。

そうは言っても、田舎暮らしも多くの人にとって人気のある選択肢だ。都会生活に比べて生活様式は間違いなくのんびりしていて、ストレスもはるかに少ない。例えば、田舎に住んでいる人は、ラッシュ時の電車のような混雑状態を経験することはほとんどなく、あまり時間を気にしない傾向がある。さらに、汚染も少ないので、水や空気の質も良く、田舎暮らしはより健康的だ。最後の利点は、生活費の安さ、特に土地や住宅の価格である。また、田舎の物件は一般的にもっと広々としているため、より快適に過ごすことができる。

個人的な視点から言うと、若くてエネルギーがあるうちは都会に住んだ方がいいと思う。これは都市部にいた方が、教育を受ける機会が広がったり、自分に合った、やりがいのある仕事を見つける可能性が高まったりするからだ。しかし、田舎は静けさがあり、質の高い生活を提供してくれるため、年齢を重ねるにつれてそちらの方が魅力的になってくる。

エクササイズ

エッセイ中の重要語句と表現をエクササイズで確認します。

語句に当てはまる訳の番号を選んでください。

_____ reside

_____ urban

_____ rural settings

_____ attractions

_____ prevalence of

_____ health services

_____ fringe benefits

_____ Nevertheless,

_____ Without a doubt,

_____ pollution

_____ cost of living

_____ properties

_____ spacious

_____ tranquillity

_____ quality of life

1. そうは言っても	4. 汚染	8. 医療サービス	12. 間違いなく
2. 福利厚生、賃金外給付	5. 田舎の環境	9. 生活の質	13. 静けさ
	6. 住む	10. 魅力	14. 広々とした
3. 物件、不動産	7. …の普及	11. 都市の	15. 生活費

同じ意味になるよう単語を記入してください。

• the city/cities　=　u_____ a_____

　　　　　　　　　=　u_____ c_____

• the countryside　=　r_____ s_____

カッコ内を正しい順序に並べ替えてください。

• There [no / that / doubt / is] living in the city has particular attractions.

• From [perspective / personal / a], [it / better / to / believe/ is / I] live in the city ...

• This [is / the / fact / to / that / due] urban areas tend to provide ...

問題と解決策を提示する

例題で「問題と解決策の提示」を攻略していきます。

You should spend about 40 minutes on this task.

Stress is now a major problem in many countries around the world.
What are some of the factors in modern society that cause stress, and how can we reduce it?

Give reasons for your answer and include any relevant examples from your own knowledge or experience.

Write at least 250 words.

エッセイの基本構成

このタイプの場合、問題と解決策を以下のように提示します。

パターン1	導入 ▶	問題 (2、3個)	▶	解決案 (2、3個)	▶	結論
パターン2	導入 ▶ 問題1&解決案 ▶	問題2&解決案 ▶	(問題3&解決案) ▶	結論		

タスク説明文を確認する

説明文を注意深く読んで内容を確認します。

トピック	stress
論点	problem around world, in modern society
タスク	causes of stress & how to reduce it

エッセイ・プランニング

本体パラグラフの数と方向性を決めます。

導入	トピック・論点・タスク→主張を要約する
本体1	causes of stress
本体2	ways to reduce stress

結論	メインの考えを再提示し、自分の意見を書く

導入パラグラフを書く

トピック・論点・主張を自分の言葉で書き、必要に応じてそれらをまとめます。ここでは導入を3文にします。

トピック	[1] quality of live has improved for people in numerous countries
論点	[2] yet, the number who suffer from stress is on rise
主張	[3] leads to question of why an increase & how to minimize stress

[1] In recent decades, the quality of life has greatly improved for people in numerous countries around the planet. [2] Yet, despite this positive trend, the number who suffer from stress is on the rise. [3] This leads to the question of why there is such an increase and how to minimize it.

本体パラグラフ用にアイデアを書き出し、整理する

アイデアを練り、英文ごとに書き出します。各パラグラフは、そのパラグラフで何を扱うかを述べるトピック・センテンスで始めます。次の文からは、より具体的な考えや理由を書き、情報や例を加えます。
※太字はパラグラフ内のメイン・アイデア

本体1　英文 [4]〜[8]

[4] **concerns about money**
[5] rises in cost of living → worry about paying for accommodation, food, & education, healthcare
[6] work harder & longer hours → little time to relax physically/mentally
[7] **spread of computers & smartphones**
[8] although wonderful devices, consume attention → little time to enjoy other activities

本体2　英文 [9]〜[12]

[9] to reduce stress, three measures
[10] **governments control price rises → match rises in workers' pay**

メモを使って実際の段落を書いていきます。
※下線はメモで書き出した語句です。

[4] For the vast majority of people, the main source of stress stems from <u>concerns about money</u>. [5] Owing to continuous <u>rises in</u> the <u>cost of living</u>, people constantly <u>worry about paying for</u> everything from <u>accommodation</u> to <u>food and education</u> to <u>healthcare</u>. [6] As a result, we tend to <u>work harder and longer hours</u> and have <u>little time to relax</u> both <u>physically and mentally</u>. [7] Another major factor is the rapid <u>spread of computers and smartphones</u>. [8] <u>Although</u> they are <u>wonderful devices</u>, they <u>consume</u> far too much of our <u>attention</u> and leave us with <u>little time to enjoy</u> a variety of <u>other activities</u>.

[9] In order <u>to reduce</u> levels of <u>stress</u>, <u>three measures</u> ought to be taken. [10] Firstly, <u>governments</u> should carefully <u>control price rises</u> so that they <u>match rises in workers' pay</u>. [11] Secondly, <u>companies</u> ought to <u>prohibit employees from taking</u> their <u>work home</u> after they leave their workplace <u>and not allow</u> them to <u>work on</u> their <u>days off</u>. [12] Thirdly, <u>people</u> should <u>turn off</u> their <u>home computers and smartphones</u> for a specific amount of time every day and <u>do different activities</u>, such as reading or exercising, during that time.

結論は本体を要約し、主張を再び述べる

[13] two causes of stress: money worries & technology that deprives time for other pursuits

[14-1] if measures outlined = implemented

[14-2] workers = better work-life balance & reduce levels of stress

[13] In conclusion, <u>two causes of stress</u> in modern society are <u>money worries and technology that deprives</u> us of <u>time for other pursuits</u>. [14-1] However, <u>if</u> the <u>measures outlined</u> above were actually <u>implemented</u>, [14-2] it would result in <u>workers</u> having a <u>better work-life balance and</u> would <u>reduce</u> their <u>levels of stress</u>.

モデルエッセイ　　　🔊31

In recent decades, the quality of life has greatly improved for people in numerous countries around the planet. Yet, despite this positive trend, the number who suffer from stress is on the rise. This leads to the question of why there is such an increase and how to minimize it.

For the vast majority of people, the main source of stress stems from concerns about money. Owing to continuous rises in the cost of living, people constantly worry about paying for everything from accommodation to food and education to healthcare. As a result, we tend to work harder and longer hours and have little time to relax both physically and mentally. Another major factor is the rapid spread of computers and smartphones. Although they are wonderful devices, they consume far too much of our attention and leave us with little time to enjoy a variety of other activities.

In order to reduce levels of stress, three measures ought to be taken. Firstly, governments should carefully control price rises so that they match rises in workers' pay. Secondly, companies ought to prohibit employees from taking their work home after they leave their workplace and not allow them to work on their days off. Thirdly, people should turn off their home computers and smartphones for a specific amount of time every day and do different activities, such as reading or exercising, during that time.

In conclusion, two causes of stress in modern society are money worries and technology that deprives us of time for other pursuits. However, if the measures outlined above were actually implemented, it would result in workers having a better work-life balance and would reduce their levels of stress.

(280 words – 14 sentences)

ここ数十年、地球上の多くの国で、人々の生活の質は大きく向上した。だが、このような肯定的な傾向にもかかわらず、ストレスに悩む人の数は増加の一途をたどっている。このことは、なぜそのような増加があり、それを最小限に抑えるにはどうすればいいか、という疑問へとつながる。

多くの人にとって、ストレスの主な原因はお金の悩みから生じる。生活費の上昇が続き、人々は常に住居費、食費、教育費、医療費など、あらゆる面でお金の心配が絶えない。その結果、私たちは長時間労働を強いられ、心身ともにリラックスする時間が少なくなりがちだ。別の主要な要因として、パソコンやスマートフォンの急速な普及がある。素晴らしい機器ではあるが、私たちの関心をあまりにも奪い、ほかの様々な活動を楽しむ時間が少なくなっている。

ストレス解消のためには、3つの対策が必要だ。第1に、政府は物価の上昇を、労働者の給与の上昇に見合うように注意深く管理すべきである。第2に、会社は社員が退社後に仕事を持ち帰ることを禁止し、休日出勤をさせないようにするべきだ。第3に、人々は毎日一定時間、自宅のパソコンやスマートフォンの電源を切り、その間に読書や運動など別の活動をするべきだ。

結論として、現代社会におけるストレスの2つの原因は、お金の心配と、テクノロジーによってほかの趣味のための時間が奪われることだ。しかし上記のような対策が実施されれば、労働者のワークライフバランスが向上し、ストレスの度合いも軽減されることにつながるだろう。

エクササイズ

エッセイ中の重要語句と表現をエクササイズで確認します。

語句に当てはまる訳の番号を選んでください。

_____ planet

_____ suffer from

_____ minimize

_____ stems from

_____ concerns

_____ worry about

_____ healthcare

_____ physically and mentally

_____ our attention

_____ reduce

_____ prohibit

_____ workplace

_____ deprives

_____ pursuits

_____ work-life balance

1. 禁止する
2. …から生じる
3. 心身ともに
4. 最小限にする

5. 減らす
6. 惑星、(the ~) 地球
7. ワークライフバランス
8. 奪う

9. 気晴らし、趣味
10. …について心配する
11. 事柄、心配事
12. 健康管理、医療

13. …に苦しむ
14. 職場
15. 私たちの関心

source, majority, spread を適切な空所に入れてください。

• the vast _____ of ...

• the main _____ of ...

• the rapid _____ of ...

カッコ内を正しい順序に並べ替えてください。

• This [of / the / to / why / there / question / leads / is] such an increase and how to minimize it.

• However, if the measures [implemented / above / actually / outlined / were], it [result / in / would] ...

議論を評価する

例題で「議論の評価」を攻略していきます。

You should spend about 40 minutes on this task.

Tourism is growing in many parts of the world, particularly in developing countries.
To what extent does this trend benefit the countries and their people?

Give reasons for your answer and include any relevant examples from your own knowledge or experience.

Write at least 250 words.

エッセイの基本構成

このタイプの場合、両方の立場に触れる必要があります。

パターン1	導入 ▶	評価できる ▶	（評価できる） ▶	異論あり ▶	結論
パターン2	導入 ▶	異論あり ▶	（異論あり） ▶	評価できる ▶	結論

タスク説明文を確認する

説明文を注意深く読んで内容を確認します。

トピック	tourism is growing, esp. in developing countries
論点	benefits for the countries and people
タスク	how much?

エッセイ・プランニング

本体パラグラフの数と方向性を決めます。

導入	トピック・論点・タスク→主張を要約する
本体1	benefits = some
本体2	disadvantages = more

| 結論 | メインの考えを再提示し、自分の意見を書く |

導入パラグラフを書く

トピック・論点・主張を自分の言葉で書き、必要に応じてそれらをまとめます。ここでは導入を2文にします。

トピック	[1] dramatic rise in people taking holidays abroad, esp. to developing nations
論点	[2-1] countries & citizens experience merits
主張	[2-2] they (merits) are outweighed by demerits

[1] The travel industry is witnessing a <u>dramatic rise in</u> the number of <u>people taking holidays abroad, especially to developing nations</u>. [2-1] Although such <u>countries and</u> their <u>citizens experience</u> various <u>merits</u> as a result of this ongoing trend, [2-2] I believe <u>they are outweighed by demerits</u>.

本体パラグラフ用にアイデアを書き出し、整理する

アイデアを練り、英文ごとに書き出します。各パラグラフは、そのパラグラフで何を扱うかを述べるトピック・センテンスで始めます。次の文からは、より具体的な考えや理由を書き、情報や例を加えます。

※太字はパラグラフ内のメイン・アイデア

本体1　英文 [3]〜[5]

[3] benefits: one is **creation of jobs**

[4] new airports, hotels, restaurants = employment rates go up, and salaries raise local standard of living

[5-1] **government receives more tax money**

[5-2] allows to construct/improve schools, hospitals, transportation systems

本体2　英文 [6]〜[11]

[6] numerous disadvantages: first is **increased pollution**

[7] more coaches and cars, extra rubbish generated by services for visitors

Task 2

1. タイプ別エッセイの攻略

[8] negative impacts on native animal and plant species

[9] multi-national companies build resorts → species lose habitat & food

[10] local culture is replaced by imported culture

[11] instead of streets with local shops & restaurants, tend to see foreign brands

メモを使って実際の段落を書いていきます。
※下線はメモで書き出した語句です。

[3] On the one hand, I do accept that nations receive certain benefits from increased tourism, and one is the creation of jobs. [4] When new airports, hotels and restaurants are built, employment rates go up and salaries enable local residents to raise their standard of living. [5-1] In addition, governments receive more tax money from businesses involved in tourism and [5-2] this additional income allows them to construct or improve schools, hospitals and transportation systems.

[6] However, despite the positive aspects outlined above, there are numerous disadvantages, the first of which is increased pollution. [7] This comes not only from having more coaches and cars on the roads but also from the extra rubbish generated by providing services for visitors. [8] Secondly, there are negative impacts on native animal and plant species. [9] When multi-national companies purchase beautiful, local land and coastal areas in order to build hotel resorts, many species lose their precious habitat and food sources. [10] A final drawback is that local culture is often replaced by imported culture. [11] Instead of seeing streets lined with local shops and restaurants selling traditional food and goods, we tend to see foreign brands such as McDonald's, Nike and Louis Vuitton, to name a few.

結論は本体を要約し、主張を再び述べる

[12-1] increased tourism = creates jobs & extra funds for public facilities

[12-2] also pollution, loss of nature, demise of local culture

[13] therefore, by and large trend does not benefit countries and people

[12-1] To conclude, while <u>increased tourism creates jobs and</u> brings <u>extra funds for</u> building <u>public facilities</u>, [12-2] it <u>also</u> leads to <u>pollution</u>, a <u>loss of nature</u> and the <u>demise of local culture</u>. [13] <u>Therefore,</u> I believe that <u>by and large</u> the <u>trend does not benefit countries and</u> their <u>people</u>.

モデルエッセイ　　　　　　　　　　　　　　　　　　　　◀))32

The travel industry is witnessing a dramatic rise in the number of people taking holidays abroad, especially to developing nations. Although such countries and their citizens experience various merits as a result of this ongoing trend, I believe they are outweighed by demerits.

On the one hand, I do accept that nations receive certain benefits from increased tourism, and one is the creation of jobs. When new airports, hotels and restaurants are built, employment rates go up and salaries enable local residents to raise their standard of living. In addition, governments receive more tax money from businesses involved in tourism and this additional income allows them to construct or improve schools, hospitals and transportation systems.

However, despite the positive aspects outlined above, there are numerous disadvantages, the first of which is increased pollution. This comes not only from having more coaches and cars on the roads but also from the extra rubbish generated by providing services for visitors. Secondly, there are negative impacts on native animal and plant species. When multi-national companies purchase beautiful, local land and coastal areas in order to build hotel resorts, many species lose their precious habitat and food sources. A final drawback is that local culture is often replaced by imported culture. Instead of seeing streets lined with local shops and restaurants selling traditional food and goods, we tend to see foreign brands such as McDonald's, Nike and Louis Vuitton, to name a few.

To conclude, while increased tourism creates jobs and brings extra funds for building public facilities, it also leads to pollution, a loss of nature and the demise of local culture. Therefore, I believe that by and large the trend does not benefit countries and their people. *(286 words – 13 sentences)*

旅行業界では、海外、特に発展途上国で休暇を過ごす人が劇的に増えている。このような傾向が続いている結果、その国や国民は様々なメリットを得られるものの、私はデメリットがそれを上回ると考えている。

一方では、観光客の増加によって国家が受ける恩恵もあり、その1つが雇用の創出であることは認める。空港やホテル、レストランが新しくできれば、雇用率が上がり、給料によって地域住民の生活水準が上がる。加えて、政府は観光に関わる事業者からの税金が増えるので、この追加収入によって、学校、病院、そして交通機関などの建設、もしくは整備が可能になる。

しかし、上記のような良い面ばかりでなく、多くの欠点もあって、第1に、公害の増加だ。これは、道路を走るバスや車が増えるだけでなく、観光客へのサービスの提供によって発生する、余分なゴミのせいでもある。第2に、在来の動植物種への悪影響がある。多国籍企業がホテルリゾートを建設するために、地元の美しい土地や海岸地域を購入すると、多くの種は貴重な生息地や食料源を失うことになる。最後の欠点は、地元の文化がしばしば輸入文化に取って代わられることだ。伝統的な食べ物や商品を売る地元の店やレストランが並ぶ通りではなく、いくつか例に挙げると、マクドナルド、ナイキ、ルイ・ヴィトンなどの外国ブランドを目にすることが多くなる。

結論として、観光客の増加は雇用を創出し、また公共施設を建設する余剰資金をもたらすが、公害や自然の喪失、そして地域文化の衰退を招く。したがって、この傾向は概して、国や人々のためにならないと思う。

エクササイズ

エッセイ中の重要語句と表現をエクササイズで確認します。

語句に当てはまる訳の番号を選んでください。

_____ travel industry   _____ animal and plant species

_____ witnessing   _____ multi-national companies

_____ ongoing trend   _____ habitat and food sources

_____ employment rates   _____ Instead of ...ing

_____ involved in   _____ , to name a few

_____ construct or improve   _____ the demise of

_____ rubbish   _____ by and large

_____ generated

1. 多国籍企業
2. …の衰退・消滅
3. 動植物種
4. ゴミ
5. いくつか例を挙げると
6. 継続している傾向
7. 発生した
8. …する代わりに
9. 建設・整備する
10. 旅行業界
11. 雇用率
12. 概して
13. 目撃している、(場所などで) 起こっている
14. 生息地や食料源
15. …に関わる

Task 2

1. タイプ別エッセイの攻略

同じ意味の単語を答えてください。

• merits　　=　b_____　=　p_____ a_____

• demerits　=　d_____　=　n_____ i_____　=　d_____

カッコ内を正しい順序に並べ替えてください。

• On [do / hand, / I / that / one / the / accept] nations receive certain benefits from ...

• However, [positive / the / aspects / despite] outlined above, [disadvantages / are / numerous / there].

原因とその影響を述べる

例題でこのタイプを攻略していきます。

You should spend about 40 minutes on this task.

In today's society people tend to buy many things and throw them away even though they can still be used.
What are some causes of this behaviour? What are some effects?

Give reasons for your answer and include any relevant examples from your own knowledge or experience.

Write at least 250 words.

エッセイの基本構成

このタイプの場合、各パラグラフで原因と影響を述べます。

パターン1	導入 ▶	原因 (2、3個) ▶	影響 (2、3個) ▶	結論
パターン2	導入 ▶	原因1＆影響 ▶	原因2＆影響 ▶ (原因3＆影響) ▶	結論

タスク説明文を確認する

説明文を注意深く読んで内容を確認します。

トピック	people buy many things
論点	throw them away even though can still use them
タスク	causes & effects of this behaviour

エッセイ・プランニング

本体パラグラフの数と方向性を決めます。

導入	トピック・論点・タスク→主張を要約する
本体1	causes of buying & throwing things away
本体2	effects of this trend

結論	メインの考えを再提示し、自分の意見を書く

導入パラグラフを書く

トピック・論点・主張を自分の言葉で書き、必要に応じてそれらをまとめます。ここでは導入を3文にします。

トピック	[1] majority of consumers enjoy shopping
論点	[2] often purchase and discard items even when still usable
主張	[3] why we behave this way & how it affects society?

[1] Without a doubt, the majority of consumers enjoy shopping for new products. [2] Unfortunately, though, we often purchase more than we need and then discard the items even when they are still usable. [3] This leads to the question of why we behave in this way and how it affects our society.

本体パラグラフ用にアイデアを書き出し、整理する

アイデアを練り、英文ごとに書き出します。各パラグラフは、そのパラグラフで何を扱うかを述べるトピック・センテンスで始めます。次の文からは、より具体的な考えや理由を書き、情報や例を加えます。
※太字はパラグラフ内のメイン・アイデア

本体1 英文 [4]〜[9]

[4] **low prices for certain products**
[5] inexpensive clothes = abundant, so buy though do not need them
[6] **troublesome to replace broken parts**
[7] rather than replace a part, throw away appliance & buy new one
[8] **constant stream of advertising** (TV, magazines, internet)
[9] sophisticated techniques encourage us to buy products

本体2 英文 [10]〜[13]

[10] result of aforementioned causes = various effects
[11] **people feel happy** when purchase products but (generates large sales

& profits for companies) **drains our finances**
[12] **do not use products for long, throw away & replace more frequently**
[13] **accelerates depletion of natural resources & destruction of environment**

メモを使って実際の段落を書いていきます。
※下線はメモで書き出した語句です。

[4] A first reason for unnecessary purchases is due to <u>low prices for certain products</u>. [5] For instance, <u>inexpensive clothes</u> are <u>abundant, so</u> we frequently <u>buy</u> them even <u>though</u> we <u>do not</u> actually <u>need them</u>. [6] A further cause is that consumers find it <u>troublesome to replace parts</u> when they break. [7] For instance, <u>rather than replace a</u> small broken <u>part</u> of an electrical appliance, we generally <u>throw</u> the <u>appliance away and buy</u> a <u>new one</u>. [8] A third reason is the <u>constant stream of advertising</u> we receive on <u>television</u>, in <u>magazines</u> and on the <u>internet</u>. [9] These clever adverts use <u>sophisticated techniques</u> to strongly <u>encourage us to buy</u> their <u>products</u>.

[10] As a <u>result of</u> the <u>aforementioned causes</u>, there are <u>various effects</u>. [11] First of all, while most <u>people feel happy when</u> they <u>purchase</u> new <u>products</u>, it <u>generates large sales and profits for companies</u> but unnecessarily <u>drains our</u> personal <u>finances</u>. [12] Moreover, after buying the products, since we <u>do not use</u> them <u>for</u> as <u>long</u> as possible and <u>throw</u> them <u>away</u>, we <u>replace</u> them <u>more frequently</u>. [13] Subsequently, this <u>accelerates</u> the <u>depletion of natural resources</u> used to make the products <u>and</u> the <u>destruction of</u> the <u>environment</u>.

結論は本体を要約し、主張を再び述べる

[14] three causes of excessive consumption: low prices, not replacing broken parts, constant advertising
[15] mainly negative impacts, so consumers ought to think about what they need rather than want

[14] To conclude, in my opinion <u>three causes of excessive consumption</u> are <u>low prices, not replacing broken parts</u> and <u>constant advertising</u>. [15] Since they have <u>mainly negative impacts</u> on society, before purchasing products, <u>consumers ought to think about what they need rather than</u> what they <u>want</u>.

モデルエッセイ ◀))33

Without a doubt, the majority of consumers enjoy shopping for new products. Unfortunately, though, we often purchase more than we need and then discard the items even when they are still usable. This leads to the question of why we behave in this way and how it affects our society.

A first reason for unnecessary purchases is due to low prices for certain products. For instance, inexpensive clothes are abundant, so we frequently buy them even though we do not actually need them. A further cause is that consumers find it troublesome to replace parts when they break. For instance, rather than replace a small broken part of an electrical appliance, we generally throw the appliance away and buy a new one. A third reason is the constant stream of advertising we receive on television, in magazines and on the internet. These clever adverts use sophisticated techniques to strongly encourage us to buy their products.

As a result of the aforementioned causes, there are various effects. First of all, while most people feel happy when they purchase new products, it generates large sales and profits for companies but unnecessarily drains our personal finances. Moreover, after buying the products, since we do not use them for as long as possible and throw them away, we replace them more frequently. Subsequently, this accelerates the depletion of natural resources used to make the products and the destruction of the environment.

To conclude, in my opinion three causes of excessive consumption are low prices, not replacing broken parts and constant advertising. Since they have mainly negative impacts on society, before purchasing products, consumers ought to think about what they need rather than what they want.

(281 words – 15 sentences)

Task 2

1. タイプ別エッセイの攻略

大多数の消費者が、新しい商品を買うことを楽しんでいるのは間違いない。しかし、残念なことに、私たちは必要以上に商品を購入し、まだ使えるにもかかわらず、その商品を廃棄してしまうことがよくある。このことは、なぜ私たちがこのような行動をとるのか、そしてそれが社会にどのような影響を与えるのか、という疑問へとつながる。

無駄な買い物をする第1の理由は、特定の商品が低価格であることだ。例えば、安価な洋服が豊富にあるため、実際には必要でないにもかかわらず、頻繁に買ってしまう。さらなる理由としては、消費者は物が壊れた時に部品を交換するのが面倒に思ってしまうということがある。例えば、電化製品の壊れた小さな部品を交換するよりも、たいてい、その電化製品を捨てて、新しいものを買う。第3の理由は、テレビ、雑誌、インターネットなどで、絶え間なく流される広告だ。これらの巧妙な広告には、私たちに自社製品を購入するよう強く促す、高度な技術が使われている。

上記のような要因の結果、様々な影響が生じる。まず、多くの人は新製品を購入することで幸せを感じるが、それは企業にとって大きな売上と利益を生む一方で、私たち個人の家計を不必要に疲弊させる。また、買った後、できる限り長く使おうとはせずに捨ててしまうため、買い替えの頻度が高くなる。結果的に、製品の材料となる天然資源の枯渇と環境破壊を加速させることになる。

結論として、私の考えでは、過剰な買い物の3つの原因は価格の安さ、壊れた部品の交換をしないこと、そして絶え間ない広告だ。これらは主に社会に悪影響を与えるので、消費者は商品を購入する前に、何が欲しいかではなく、何が必要かを考えるべきだと思う。

エクササイズ

エッセイ中の重要語句と表現をエクササイズで確認します。

語句に当てはまる訳の番号を選んでください。

____ consumers

____ Unfortunately,

____ unnecessary

____ abundant

____ replace

____ electrical appliance

____ sophisticated techniques

____ sales and profits

____ drains

____ personal finances

____ accelerates

____ depletion

____ natural resources

____ destruction

____ excessive

1. 消費者	5. 残念なことに	9. 不要な、必要以上の	13. 電化製品
2. 豊富な	6. 加速させる	10. 売上と利益	14. 交換する
3. 天然資源	7. 枯渇させる	11. 高度な技術	15. 破壊
4. 家計、個人財務	8. 過剰な	12. 枯渇	

同じ意味の単語を答えてください。

- buy　　　　=　p_____
- throw away　=　d_____

effects, conclude, doubt, result を適切な空所に入れてください。

- Without a (　　　　), the majority of consumers ....
- As a (　　　) of the aforementioned causes, there are various (　　　　).
- To (　　　), in my opinion, three causes of ...

Task 2

1. タイプ別エッセイの攻略

賛成・反対を述べる①

タイプ別にモデルエッセイを分析・再構築することで、重要
表現を身につけてライティング力を高めます。

All mothers and fathers should be made to take childcare courses.
Do you agree with this point of view?

モデルエッセイ ◀))34

The majority of young adults become parents at some point in their lives. In relation to this, couples who already have children often talk about the difficulty of raising them. As such, it has been suggested that all mothers and fathers be required to attend courses to learn about childcare, which is an idea I completely agree with.

To begin with, parents are not experts at raising children, especially those having their first child. They have limited knowledge regarding how babies and infants develop physically and mentally, so they face many challenges. However, if parents take courses from qualified teachers who understand child development, child-rearing will be easier and more enjoyable.

Even after having a child, parents ought to continue attending courses periodically. This will encourage them to reflect on the experience of raising their first child, and improve their parenting skills even further. Moreover, research into how children develop is constantly progressing and new data regularly appears. Therefore, it is beneficial for parents to have access to the latest findings from teachers in childcare courses.

A final reason in favour of parents joining childcare courses is that they can receive advice and support from other parents. During the courses, they will talk about their experiences and ideas, discuss their worries and even pass on their existing knowledge of raising a first or subsequent child. Such communication will enable them to overcome parenting problems more easily than trying to do it by themselves.

To summarise my position, I strongly feel that every mother and father should be required by law to attend childcare courses. In doing so, it will benefit them and their children, and result in happier families. *(281 words – 15 sentences)*

Self-Study!

モデルエッセイを分析していきます。エッセイの英文をもとに質問に**英語で**答えてください。回答がそのままエッセイを書く材料になります。

導入

Q1 エッセイのトピックは？　　　Q3 エッセイの全体的な主張は？
Q2 エッセイの論点は？

本体1 賛成する理由1

Q4 最初の理由は？　　　Q6 ほかの例・詳細は？
Q5 その具体例・詳細は？

本体2 賛成する理由2

Q7 2つ目の理由は？　　　Q9 ほかの例・詳細は？
Q8 その具体例・詳細は？

本体3 賛成する理由3

Q10 3つ目の理由は？　　　Q12 ほかの例・詳細は？
Q11 その具体例・詳細は？

結論

Q13 主張はどのように言い換えられている？
Q14 主張を裏づける総括的な理由は？

以下の回答例や自分の分析した結果をもとにエッセイを書きましょう。

導入

Q1 エッセイのトピックは？

  A. majority of young adults become parents

Q2 エッセイの論点は？

  A. couples with children talk about difficulty of raising them

Q3 エッセイの全体的な主張は？

  A. all mothers and fathers required to attend childcare courses = agree

本体1 賛成する理由1

Q4 最初の理由は？

  A. parents are not experts at raising children (esp. 1st child)

Q5 その具体例・詳細は？

  A. have limited knowledge regarding how babies/infants develop
    physically/mentally

Q6 ほかの例・詳細は？

  A. if take courses from qualified teachers, child-rearing will be easier &
    more enjoyable

本体2 賛成する理由2

Q7 2つ目の理由は？

  A. after having a child, parents ought to continue attending courses

Q8 その具体例・詳細は？

  A. will encourage them to reflect on raising 1st child & improve parenting
    skills further

Q9 ほかの例・詳細は？

    A. research into how children develop = processing → new data, parents

      access findings from teachers

本体3 賛成する理由3

Q10 3つ目の理由は？

    A. can receive advice/support from other parents

Q11 その具体例・詳細は？

    A. will talk about experiences, discuss worries, pass on knowledge

Q12 ほかの例・詳細は？

    A. will enable them to overcome parenting problems more easily

結論

Q13 主張はどのように言い換えられている？

    A. every mother and father should attend childcare courses

Q14 主張を裏づける総括的な理由は？

    A. will benefit parents & children → happier families

Task 2

2. タイプ別セルフスタディ1

225

若者の大半は、人生のどこかのタイミングで親になる。これに関連して、すでに子どもがいるカップルは、子育ての大変さをよく口にする。そこで、すべての母親と父親が育児を学ぶための講座を受講することが提案されていて、この考えに、私は完全に賛同する。

第1に、親は子育ての専門家ではなく、特に第1子の親はそうだ。赤ちゃんや幼児が心身ともにどのように成長するのか、親は限られた知識しかなく、そのため多くの困難に直面する。しかし、子どもの発達を理解する有資格者の指導を受ければ、子育てはもっと楽に、もっと楽しくなるはずだ。

子どもが生まれた後も、親は定期的に講座を受け続けるべきだ。そうすることで、第1子を育てた経験についてよく考えることを促し、育児能力をさらに伸ばすことにつながる。また、子どもの発達に関する研究は日進月歩で、新しいデータが定期的に出てくる。そのため、育児講座の講師から最新の知見に触れることができるのは、親にとって有益だ。

親が育児講座に参加することに賛成する最後の理由として、ほかの親から助言や支援を受けられる、ということがある。受講中に、親たちは自分の経験や考えを話したり、悩みを相談したり、第1子や第2子育児中に得た知識を伝えたりすることだってできる。そのようなコミュニケーションによって、親は自分たちだけで何とかしようとするよりも、子育ての問題を乗り越えやすくなる。

私の立場をまとめると、すべての母親と父親は育児講座受講を法律で義務づけられるべきだと強く思う。そうすることが、親や子どもたちのためになり、より家庭円満につながるだろう。

エクササイズ

エッセイ中の重要語句と表現をエクササイズで確認します。

語句に当てはまる訳の番号を選んでください。※訳は同じものが2つあります。

_____ In relation to this,　　　　_____ reflect on

_____ the difficulty of　　　　_____ the latest findings

_____ childcare　　　　_____ advice

_____ experts　　　　_____ support

_____ develop　　　　_____ subsequent

_____ qualified teachers　　　　_____ overcome

_____ child-rearing　　　　_____ by law

_____ periodically

1. 専門家	5. 成長する	9. 有資格者の教師	13. …についてよく考える
2. 支援	6. 子育て・育児	10. 子育て・育児	14. …の大変さ
3. 助言	7. 次の、続いて起こる	11. 乗り越える	15. 最新の知見・発見
4. 法律で	8. 定期的に	12. これに関連して	

エッセイから、家族を表す語句を探して入力してください。

• parents　＝　m_____, f_____

• children　＝　b_____　＝　i_____

カッコ内を正しい順序に並べ替えてください。

• As such, [suggested / has / it / been] that ...

• A [favour / in / final / of / reason] parents joining childcare courses is that ...

• To [strongly / I / position, / my / feel / summarise] that ...

正解 12, 14, 6 [10], 1, 5, 9, 10 [6], 8, 13, 15, 3, 2, 7, 11, 4／mothers, fathers, babies, infants／it has been suggested, final reason in favour of, summarise my position, I strongly feel　227

物事の両面と意見を述べる ①

タイプ別にモデルエッセイを分析・再構築することで、重要表現を身につけてライティング力を高めます。

Many people keep animals in their homes.
Discuss the pros and cons of owning a pet for the animals and for society.

モデルエッセイ ◀)35

Owning a pet is a common occurrence in most societies since people enjoy the company of animals and they both benefit in various ways. Yet this beneficial relationship is not always the case, as there are certain drawbacks, too.

In terms of benefits, treasured pets normally lead happy, safe and healthy lives. This is due to the fact that loving owners provide their animals with food, a comfortable home and medical treatment when they are injured or ill. As for society, children learn to value and look after living creatures. In addition, animals provide companionship, which is important for people who live alone, especially the elderly. Moreover, people who have lost the ability to see or hear can function better in daily life because of their guide dogs.

Unfortunately, though, some pets suffer because of their circumstances. For instance, without the freedom to go outdoors, they may feel great stress, which can lead to illness. Also, when the novelty of pet ownership wears off, owners sometimes abuse and even abandon their animals somewhere. In terms of society, one negative point is that powerful and aggressive pet dogs sometimes attack and bite strangers. In extreme cases, they can even kill people, particularly small children. Moreover, when other dangerous animals such as pet snakes escape from homes, it causes great public alarm.

Based on the above, pet ownership clearly has advantages and disadvantages for animals, owners and society. Yet, on the whole, I believe the merits outweigh the demerits because animals play valuable roles in our lives and bring us much joy and comfort. Therefore, before deciding to keep a pet, it is important for people to truly consider the responsibility and requirements of such a long-term commitment.

(285 words – 16 sentences)

Self-Study!

　モデルエッセイを分析していきます。エッセイの英文をもとに質問に**英語で**答えてください。回答がそのままエッセイを書く材料になります。

導入

Q1 エッセイのトピックは？

Q2 エッセイの一方の論点・主張は？

Q3 エッセイのもう一方の論点・主張は？

本体1 動物＆社会にとって良い点

Q4 ペットにとっての恩恵は？

Q5 その具体例は？

Q6 社会にとっての恩恵は？

Q7 2つ目の恩恵は？

Q8 3つ目の恩恵は？

本体2 動物＆社会にとって悪い点

Q9 ペットにとっての不利益は？

Q10 その具体例・詳細は？

Q11 2つ目の不利益は？

Q12 社会にとって好ましくない点は？

Q13 その具体例・詳細は？

Q14 もう1つの好ましくない点は？

結論

Q15 エッセイのトピック、論点、主張はどう要約されている？

Q16 筆者の個人的な意見は？

Q17 どのような注意・忠告を述べている？

以下の回答例や自分の分析した結果をもとにエッセイを書きましょう。

導入

Q1 エッセイのトピックは？

A. owning a pet = common occurrence in most societies

Q2 エッセイの一方の論点・主張は？

A. people enjoy company of animals ← → both benefit

Q3 エッセイのもう一方の論点・主張は？

A. both do not always benefit → certain drawbacks, too

本体1 動物＆社会にとって良い点

Q4 ペットにとっての恩恵は？

A. pets lead happy, safe and healthy lives

Q5 その具体例・詳細は？

A. owners provide food, comfortable home & medical treatment

Q6 社会にとっての恩恵は？

A. children learn to value & look after living creatures

Q7 2つ目の恩恵は？

A. animals provide companionship (people living alone, esp. elderly)

Q8 3つ目の恩恵は？

A. people who cannot see/hear function better in daily life ← guide dogs

本体2 動物＆社会にとって悪い点

Q9 ペットにとっての不利益は？

A. some pets suffer

Q10 その具体例・詳細は？

A. no freedom to go outdoors → stress → illness

[Q11] 2つ目の不利益は？

A. novelty of pet ownership wears off → owners abuse/abandon pets

[Q12] 社会にとって好ましくない点は？

A. powerful/aggressive dogs sometimes attack/bite strangers

[Q13] その具体例・詳細は？

A. extreme cases = kill people (small children)

[Q14] もう1つの好ましくない点は？

A. other dangerous animals (snakes) escape → causes public alarm

結論

[Q15] エッセイのトピック、論点、主張はどう要約されている？

A. pet ownership = advantages & disadvantages

for animals/owners/society

[Q16] 筆者の個人的な意見は？

A. merits outweigh demerits: animals play valuable roles, bring joy/comfort

[Q17] どのような注意・忠告を述べている？

A. before keeping pet, people should consider

responsibility/requirements of such commitment

Task 2

2. タイプ別セルフスタディ1

231

人は動物とのふれあいを楽しみ、双方が様々な意味で恩恵を受けることから、ペットを飼うことはほとんどの社会で一般的なことだ。しかし、この、互いに恩恵のある関係はいつもそうだというわけではなく、いくつかの欠点もある。

恩恵としては、大事にされているペットは通常、幸せで、安全で、健康的な生活を送ることになる。これは、愛情を持った飼い主が、飼っている動物に食事や快適な住まいを与え、けがや病気の時には医療手当を受けさせるからだ。社会的には、子どもたちが生き物を大切にし、世話をすることを学ぶことができる。また、動物は人に寄り添ってくれ、それは一人暮らしの人、特に高齢者にとって大事なことだ。さらには、目や耳が不自由になった人は、盲導犬、聴導犬のおかげで、より良い日常生活を過ごせるようになる。

しかし残念なことに、境遇によって苦しむペットもいる。例えば、外に出る自由がないと、大きなストレスを感じ、病気になってしまうことがある。また、ペットを飼うことの目新しさが失われると、時として飼い主が自分のペットを虐待したり、どこかに捨ててしまったりする場合がある。社会的には、1つの否定的な点として、力があって攻撃的な飼い犬が、見知らぬ人を襲ったりかみついたりすることがある。極端な例では、人、特に小さな子どもを殺してしまう場合もある。さらには、飼っているヘビなどの危険な動物が家から逃げ出すと、大きな社会不安を引き起こす。

以上のように、ペットを飼うことは、動物にとっても、飼い主にとっても、社会にとっても、利点と欠点があることは明らかだ。しかし全体として見れば、動物は私たちの生活の中で貴重な役割を果たし、多くの喜びと安らぎをもたらしてくれることから、メリットがデメリットを上回ると私は考えている。したがって、ペットを飼うと決める前に、それほど長期的な関わりを持つことに伴う、責任や必要条件について、真剣に考えることが大切になってくる。

エクササイズ

エッセイ中の重要語句と表現をエクササイズで確認します。

語句に当てはまる訳の番号を選んでください。

_____ a common occurrence	_____ freedom
_____ the company of	_____ wears off
_____ injured or ill	_____ abandon
_____ living creatures	_____ escape
_____ companionship	_____ public alarm
_____ the elderly	_____ responsibility
_____ guide dogs	_____ long-term commitment
_____ circumstances	

1. すり減る、消える	5. 境遇、状況	9. 捨てる	13. けがをした、
2. 社会的な不安	6. 日常的な出来事	10. 生き物	または病気で
3. 自由	7. …との交流	11. 高齢者	14. 責任
4. 盲導犬	8. 長期的な関わり・責務	12. 交わり、友好	15. 逃げる

次の文にコンマを3つ入れてください。

• For instance without the freedom to go outdoors they may feel great stress which can lead to illness.

カッコ内を正しい順序に並べ替えてください。

• Yet [the / always / is / case / beneficial / not / this / relationship], [as / are / drawbacks / there / certain], too.

• Based [the / above / on], pet ownership [and / clearly / for / disadvantages / has / advantages] animals, owners and society.

正解　6, 7, 13, 10, 12, 11, 4, 5, 3, 1, 9, 15, 2, 14, 8／For instance, ... go outdoors, ... great stress, ... ／ this beneficial relationship is not always the case, as there are certain drawbacks, on the above, clearly has advantages and disadvantages for

問題と解決策を提示する①

タイプ別にモデルエッセイを分析・再構築することで、重要表現を身につけてライティング力を高めます。

Overpopulation leads to various problems in society.
Describe a few of them and suggest at least one solution.

モデルエッセイ　　　　　　　　　　　　　　◀)36

It is common knowledge that the world's population is rapidly expanding year by year. As a result of this continuous growth, society suffers from numerous issues that must be dealt with in effective ways. This essay will highlight some of the issues and put forward potential solutions.

One problem often caused by overpopulation is a rise in crime. With a limited number of jobs, many people remain unemployed and do not have enough money to survive. As a result, some inevitably turn to crime in order to pay for food and other daily necessities. A further issue concerns welfare and medical services, since they become burdened with demands for food, accommodation, schooling and medical services. In most cases, to cover these costs requires governments to raise taxes, which becomes a financial burden on taxpayers.

To counter the problems stated above, governments need to implement appropriate measures. First and foremost, they must ensure that unemployed people are occupied. One way is to create opportunities for them to take advanced educational courses or vocational training while receiving basic living costs from state funds. However, this is not the only action governments should take. They ought to create more jobs in regions with high rates of unemployment by offering subsidies to companies that establish offices and factories there. In particular, they should try to attract construction companies in order to build more homes for the swelling population.

To conclude, when populations expand there is usually an increase in crime and a greater reliance on government support. However, the key to tackling these problems depends on providing education, training and employment opportunities. With lower crime rates and higher employment, the actual burden on taxpayers is mitigated.

(282 words – 17 sentences)

Self-Study!

　モデルエッセイを分析していきます。エッセイの英文をもとに質問に**英語で**答えてください。回答がそのままエッセイを書く材料になります。

導入

Q1 エッセイのトピックは？　　　Q3 エッセイの全体的な主張は？

Q2 エッセイの論点は？

本体1　人口過剰の問題点

Q4 1つの問題点は？

Q5 どのような例が挙げられている？

Q6 その結果は？

Q7 人口過剰が引き起こすもう1つの問題は？

Q8 その具体例・詳細は？

Q9 その結果は？

本体2　解決策

Q10 段落の導入文の内容は？

Q11 最初の解決策は？

Q12 その具体例・詳細は？

Q13 2つ目の解決策は？

Q14 その具体例・詳細は？

Q15 ほかの例・詳細は？

結論

Q16 2つの問題はどうまとめられている？

Q17 問題の解決策はどうまとめられている？

Q18 結果の概要は？

以下の回答例や自分の分析した結果をもとにエッセイを書きましょう。

導入

[Q1] エッセイのトピックは？

A. world's population is expanding

[Q2] エッセイの論点は？

A. society suffers from numerous issues

[Q3] エッセイの全体的な主張は？

A. essay will highlight some and put forward potential solutions

本体1 人口過剰の問題点

[Q4] 1つの問題点は？

A. rise in crime

[Q5] その具体例・詳細は？

A. limited jobs, many people = unemployed, not enough money to survive

[Q6] その結果は？

A. some people commit crimes to pay for food/daily necessities

[Q7] 人口過剰が引き起こすもう1つの問題は？

A. welfare & medical services become burdened

[Q8] その具体例・詳細は？

A. demands for food, accommodation, schooling, medical services

[Q9] その結果は？

A. governments raise taxes → burden on taxpayers

本体2 解決策

[Q10] 段落の導入文の内容は？

A. governments need to implement appropriate measures

Q11 最初の解決策は？

　A. ensure unemployed people are occupied

Q12 その具体例・詳細は？

　A. create opportunities: advanced educational courses or vocational

　　 training (while receiving basic living costs from state funds)

Q13 2つ目の解決策は？

　A. create jobs in regions with high unemployment

Q14 その具体例・詳細は？

　A. offer subsidies to companies that establish office/factories there

Q15 ほかの例・詳細は？

　A. in particular, try to attract construction companies to build homes

結論

Q16 2つの問題はどうまとめられている？

　A. populations expand = increase in crime & greater reliance on

　　 government support

Q17 問題の解決策はどうまとめられている？

　A. key = providing education, training, employment opportunities

Q18 結果の概要は？

　A. lower crime rates & higher employment: burden on taxpayers =

　　 mitigated

Task 2

2. タイプ別セルフスタディ 1

世界の人口が年々急速に増加していることは、周知の事実だ。この継続した増加の結果、社会は多くの問題に直面しており、効果的な対処が求められている。このエッセイでは、いくつかそのような問題を取り上げ、解決策の候補を提示する。

人口過剰がしばしばもたらす問題の1つに、犯罪の増加がある。職の数が限られているため、多くの人が失業したままであり、生きていくために十分なお金を持っていない。その結果、中には食べ物やその他の生活必需品を買うために、犯罪に手を染めざるを得なくなる人が出てくる。さらに、福祉や医療サービスに関する問題もあり、なぜなら食料、住居、学校教育、医療サービスなどの要求が、負担を与えるからだ。ほとんどの場合、こうした費用に対処するために、政府は増税を余儀なくされ、それは納税者の経済的負担となる。

上記のような問題に対処するには、政府は適切な対策を講じる必要がある。まず何よりも、政府は失業者が何かに従事できるようにしなければならない。基本的な生活費を国費でまかないながら、高度な教育課程や、職業訓練を受ける機会を設けるのも1つの方法だ。しかし、政府がとるべき行動はそれだけではない。失業率の高い地域に事業所や工場を設立する企業には補助金を出し、雇用を創出するべきだ。特に、建設会社を誘致して、増え続ける人口に対応するために住宅をもっと建設することが必要だ。

結論として、人口が増加すると、たいてい犯罪が増加し、政府の支援への依存が高くなる。しかし、これらの問題に対処する鍵は、教育、訓練、そして雇用の機会を提供することにある。犯罪率が下がり、雇用が増えれば、納税者の実際の負担は軽減される。

エクササイズ

エッセイ中の重要語句と表現をエクササイズで確認します。

語句に当てはまる訳の番号を選んでください。

_____ crime

_____ inevitably

_____ daily necessities

_____ welfare

_____ (be) burdened with

_____ financial burden

_____ taxpayers

_____ counter

_____ implement

_____ vocational training

_____ state funds

_____ subsidies

_____ establish

_____ reliance on

_____ mitigated

1. 生活必需品	4. 対処する	8. 納税者	12. 経済的負担
2. …という重荷を背負う	5. 必然的に	9. 職業訓練	13. 設立・設置する
	6. …への依存	10. 軽減される	14. 実行する
3. 福祉	7. 補助金	11. 国費	15. 犯罪

正しいつづりを選んでください。

• acommodation　/　accommodation　/　accomodation

• govermments　/　goverments　/　governments

• oppotunities　/　opportunities　/　oportunities

カッコ内を正しい順序に並べ替えてください。

• To [above / problems / stated / counter / the], governments need to …

• However, [the / not / is / this / action / only] governments should take.

• However, the [to / these / tackling / key / on / depends / problems] providing …

Task 2

2. タイプ別セルフスタディ1

議 論 を 評 価 す る ①

タイプ別にモデルエッセイを分析・再構築することで、重要
表現を身につけてライティング力を高めます。

Since most people have little connection with the daily news, it is a waste of time
for them to watch the news or read about it.
To what extent do you agree or disagree with this opinion?

モデルエッセイ ◀))37

The majority of the public receive the news through various kinds of media
including newspapers, radio, television and especially the internet. In relation to
this, it has been suggested that the news is irrelevant to most of us, which is a
viewpoint I only partly agree with.

On the one hand, to a certain extent it is true that watching news stories and
reading news articles is a waste of time. For instance, trivial stories about
celebrities have little to do with the lives of ordinary people. Moreover, the news
contains a great deal of financial information that is primarily of interest to
wealthy individuals who wish to invest money in stocks and shares.

Yet, for most people, the news is essential for everyday life. Firstly, it provides us
with daily and short-term forecasts about the weather. This helps us to choose
appropriate clothing and allows us to alter our plans depending on the reported
weather conditions. In addition, we learn about serious trends in health through
the news. For example, if a particular illness is becoming more prevalent or a
virus is rapidly spreading among the population, the media usually reports it,
and we can therefore take measures to protect ourselves. Thirdly, the public
receives vital information about politics and politicians. Since the party in power
has an important influence on our daily lives, it is important that we understand

current political situations and promises made by leaders.

In conclusion, while a small percentage of the news is unrelated to the lives of ordinary people, a large proportion directly affects our daily lives. Therefore, on the whole, it is not a waste of time to watch or read it.

(280 words – 14 sentences)

Self-Study!

　モデルエッセイを分析していきます。エッセイの英文をもとに質問に**英語で**答えてください。回答がそのままエッセイを書く材料になります。

導入

Q1 エッセイのトピックは？　　　　Q3 エッセイの全体的な主張は？

Q2 エッセイの論点は？

本体1　一部賛成

Q4 議論の弱い側（一部賛成）をどう紹介している？

Q5 最初の理由は？

Q6 2つ目の理由は？

本体2　主に反対

Q7 議論の強い側（主に反対）をどう　　Q10 2つ目の理由は？
　　紹介している？　　　　　　　　　Q11 その具体例・詳細は？

Q8 最初の理由は？　　　　　　　　　Q12 3つ目の理由は？

Q9 その具体例・詳細は？　　　　　　Q13 その具体例・詳細は？

結論

Q14 筆者の意見の配分は？

Q15 筆者の結論は？

以下の回答例や自分の分析した結果をもとにエッセイを書きましょう。

導入

Q1 エッセイのトピックは？

A. majority of public receive news through various kinds of media

Q2 エッセイの論点は？

A. suggested news is irrelevant to most people

Q3 エッセイの全体的な主張は？

A. partly agree (so mainly disagree)

本体1　一部賛成

Q4 議論の弱い側（一部賛成）をどう紹介している？

A. to a certain extent news is waste of time

Q5 最初の理由は？

A. trivial stories about celebrities have little to do with ordinary people

Q6 2つ目の理由は？

A. news contains financial information = of interest to wealthy people who invest in stocks/shares

本体2　主に反対

Q7 議論の強い側（主に反対）をどう紹介している？

A. for most people, news = essential for everyday life

Q8 最初の理由は？

A. provides daily & short-term forecasts about weather

Q9 その具体例・詳細は？

A. helps us choose appropriate clothing, can alter plans depending on weather

Q10 2つ目の理由は？

    A. we learn about serious trends in health

Q11 その具体例・詳細は？

    A. if illness/virus spreading → media reports it → we take measures to

    protect ourselves

Q12 3つ目の理由は？

    A. receive vital information about politics & politicians

Q13 その具体例・詳細は？

    A. party in power influences our lives → important we understand

    political situations and promises by leaders

結論

Q14 筆者の意見の配分は？

    A. while small percentage of news = unrelated to people, large proportion

    directly affects daily lives

Q15 筆者の結論は？

    A. therefore, not waste of time to watch/read it

市民の多くは、新聞、ラジオ、テレビ、そして特にインターネットなど、様々なメディアを通じてニュースを受け取っている。このことに関連して、ニュースはほとんどの人にとって無関係であると言われるが、私はこの見解には部分的にしか同意できない。

一方では、ニュースを見たり、記事を読んだりすることが時間の無駄であることも、ある程度は事実だ。例えば、有名人の取るに足らない話は、一般人の生活とはほとんど関係がない。また、ニュースには、主に株式などに投資したい裕福な人々が興味を持つような、金融情報が多く含まれている。

しかしほとんどの人にとって、ニュースは日常生活に欠かせないものである。まず、ニュースは毎日、短期の天気予報を提供してくれる。そのおかげで、私たちは伝えられる気象条件をもとに、適切な服装を選んだり、予定を変更したりすることができる。さらに、私たちはニュースを通じて、健康についての深刻な傾向を知ることができる。例えば、ある病気がはやっているだとか、あるウイルスが住民間で急速に広まっているというようなことがあれば、メディアがたいてい報道するので、私たちは自分の身を守るための対策をとることができる。第3に、国民は政治や政治家に関する重要な情報を受け取る。与党は私たちの生活に重要な影響を与えるため、現在の政治状況や、指導者たちの公約を理解することは重要だ。

結論として、ごく一部のニュースは一般人の生活と無関係だが、多くは、私たちの日常生活に直結するものだ。したがって、全体として見れば、ニュースを見たり読んだりすることは時間の無駄ではない。

エクササイズ

エッセイ中の重要語句と表現をエクササイズで確認します。

語句に当てはまる訳の番号を選んでください。

____ the public   ____ reported

____ irrelevant   ____ virus

____ partly agree   ____ politics and politicians

____ a waste of time   ____ the party in power

____ trivial   ____ influence

____ celebrities   ____ promises

____ stocks and shares   ____ leaders

____ short-term

1. 短期間の	5. 市民、一般大衆	9. 影響	13. 有名人
2. 約束	6. ウイルス	10. 取るに足らない	14. 時間の無駄
3. 部分的に同意する	7. 与党	11. 指導者	15. 報道される・
4. 無関係で	8. 政治と政治家	12. 株式	伝えられた

同じ意味になるよう、単語を答えてください。

- For instance,   =   For _____,
- Moreover,   =   In _____,

toまたはonを入れてください（2回ずつ使用）。

- ... the news is irrelevant (   ) most of us ...
- ... that is primarily of interest (   ) wealthy individuals ...
- ... depending (   ) the reported weather conditions.
- ... has an important influence (   ) our daily lives ...

Task 2

2. タイプ別セルフスタディ 1

原因とその影響を述べる①

タイプ別にモデルエッセイを分析・再構築することで、重要表現を身につけてライティング力を高めます。

More and more teenagers are going abroad to study at high school or university. Why do they choose to study overseas? What do they gain from such an experience?

モデルエッセイ　　　　　　　　　　　　　　　　　　◀)38

Leaving one's own country and studying abroad is becoming a popular choice for many young people these days. Naturally, there are various reasons for choosing this educational path, and the individuals concerned undoubtedly benefit in a variety of ways.

One reason teenagers study overseas is to improve their English skills. In many countries, children are taught English at primary and secondary school. However, this sometimes yields only slow and limited progress. Yet, by living and studying abroad, young people can quickly improve their foreign language ability and become fluent speakers in a short period of time. Moreover, by mixing with people of different nationalities, they become more globally-minded.

Another motivating factor is connected to independence. When teenagers live in their home country, many decisions are, of course, made by their parents. However, when they live and study at school abroad, teenage students cannot rely on their parents as much. Therefore, they have to consider various matters and make more decisions by themselves, and this responsibility teaches them to become more independent.

A third purpose is the desire to study a subject that is not offered at any university in one's home country, and possibly with course modules taught by famous professors or lecturers. By studying at a foreign university under such teachers, students can gain a deep insight into their particular area of academic interest.

To conclude, when teenagers decide to study overseas, they have various purposes in mind. Among them, this essay has highlighted three, which are possibly the main ones. If such young people can communicate well in English, be independent thinkers and satisfy their specific academic interests, it will help them to succeed in today's global world. *(280 words – 16 sentences)*

Self-Study!

　モデルエッセイを分析していきます。エッセイの英文をもとに質問に**英語で**答えてください。回答がそのままエッセイを書く材料になります。

導入

Q1 エッセイのトピックは？　　　Q3 エッセイの全体的な主張は？

Q2 エッセイの論点は？

本体1 理由と恩恵1

Q4 理由の1つは？　　　　　　Q6 その恩恵は？

Q5 それを裏づける詳細は？

本体2 理由と恩恵2

Q7 ほかの理由は？　　　　　　Q9 その恩恵は？

Q8 それを裏づける詳細は？

本体3 理由と恩恵3

Q10 さらなる理由は？　　　　　Q12 その恩恵は？

Q11 それを裏づける詳細は？

結論

Q13 エッセイの主張はどう言い換えられている？

Q14 主要なポイントはどうまとめられている？

Q15 どのような結果が述べられている？

以下の回答例や自分の分析した結果をもとにエッセイを書きましょう。

導入

Q1 エッセイのトピックは？

A. studying abroad = popular choice for many young people

Q2 エッセイの論点は？

A. various reasons for this educational path

Q3 エッセイの全体的な主張は？

A. individuals benefit in variety of ways

本体1 理由と恩恵1

Q4 理由の1つは？

A. to improve English skills

Q5 それを裏づける詳細は？

A. taught English at primary/secondary school = slow/limited progress

Q6 その恩恵は？

A. living/studying abroad = become fluent in short time, become more globally-minded

本体2 理由と恩恵2

Q7 ほかの理由は？

A. independence

Q8 それを裏づける詳細は？

A. when live with parents = decisions made by parents

when live abroad = cannot rely on parents as much

Q9 その恩恵は？

A. have to make decisions → responsibility → become more independent

本体3 理由と恩恵3

[Q10] さらなる理由は?

　A. to study subject not offered at university in home country

[Q11] それを裏づける詳細は?

　A. taught by famous professors/lecturers

[Q12] その恩恵は?

　A. studying at foreign university under such teachers = can gain deep
　　 insight into area of interest

結論

[Q13] エッセイの主張はどう言い換えられている?

　A. teenagers study overseas = various purposes, essay highlighted three

[Q14] 主要なポイントはどうまとめられている?

　A. can communicate in English, be independent thinkers, satisfy academic
　　 interests

[Q15] どのような結果が述べられている?

　A. will help them succeed in global world

自分の国を離れて海外で勉強することは、最近多くの若者にとって人気のある選択になっている。もちろん、この教育の道を選ぶ理由はいろいろあり、間違いなく、当事者たちは様々な恩恵を受ける。

10代の若者が留学する理由の1つに、英語力の向上がある。多くの国で、子どもたちは小学校や中学校で英語を教わる。しかし、これは時として、遅く、限定的な進歩しかもたらさない。しかし、海外で生活し、勉強することによって、若者は短期間で外国語能力を向上させ、流暢に話せるようになる。さらに、様々な国籍の人たちと交流することで、より世界思考になる。

もう1つの動機づけは、自立と関わる。10代の若者が母国で生活する場合、当然ながら、多くの決断は親が行う。しかし、海外で生活し、学校で学ぶとなると、10代の学生は、あまり親に頼ることができない。そのため、自分でいろいろなことを考え、決断しなければならないことが多くなり、その責任感から自立心を養うことができる。

第3の目的は、自国の大学では開講されていない科目を、場合によっては有名な教授や講師が教えるモジュール（授業の単位）で勉強したい、というものだ。海外の大学で、そうした先生のもとで学ぶことで、学生は自分の興味のある学問分野を深く知ることができる。

結論として、10代の若者が海外留学を決意する時、様々な目的を持っている。その中で、このエッセイでは、主要なものと思われる3つを取り上げた。そのような若者が英語でのコミュニケーションがとれて、自立した思考を持ち、自分の学問的興味を満たすことができれば、今日のグローバル社会で成功するのに役立つだろう。

エクササイズ

エッセイ中の重要語句と表現をエクササイズで確認します。

語句に当てはまる訳の番号を選んでください。

____ abroad		____ motivating factor	
____ educational path		____ independence	
____ undoubtedly		____ decisions	
____ primary school		____ rely on	
____ secondary school		____ insight	
____ progress		____ have ... in mind	
____ fluent		____ academic interests	
____ globally-minded			

1. 自立	的な視野を持つ	8. …に頼る	12. 教育・学問の道
2. 進歩	5. 学問的興味	9. 決断	13. …を考えている
3. 流暢な	6. 小学校	10. 海外で	14. 洞察・見識
4. 世界思考の、国際	7. 中学校	11. 動機となる要因	15. 間違いなく

正しいつづりを選んでください。

- particuler / paticular / particular
- professors / professers / proffesors
- lecturars / lecturers / lectuers
- indipendent / independant / independent

エッセイを参考に、下線の単語を言い換えてください。

- One reason teenagers study <u>abroad</u> is to improve their English <u>ability</u>.
- By studying at <u>an overseas</u> university under such teachers, students can ...

正解 10, 12, 15, 6, 7, 2, 3, 4, 11, 1, 9, 8, 14, 13, 5 / particular, professors, lecturers, independent / overseas, skills, a foreign

賛成・反対を述べる②

タイプ別にモデルエッセイを分析・再構築することで、重要表現を身につけてライティング力を高めます。

Some people argue that advertisements are not needed if products are good.
Do you agree or disagree with this opinion?

モデルエッセイ 🔊39

Companies today produce an abundance of high-quality goods that shoppers mostly learn about through advertising. Yet some individuals feel this method of marketing is unnecessary if the products are good. As for me, I tend to disagree with this opinion and believe advertisements are essential for consumers.

One reason is that word of mouth alone is not enough to spread information about good products. People may directly tell their family and friends about a wonderful item they have purchased, or they may do it by social media, especially nowadays. In either case, the number of people who receive the information is still limited. In contrast, commercial advertising reaches a far wider market that encompasses people of varying ages, genders and backgrounds, and often covers numerous countries.

Secondly, through advertising, shoppers can save time and money. Essentially, each advert is the summary of a product's main features, so different adverts for similar products enable us to compare them quickly and easily without wasting time searching for information. Furthermore, adverts inform us about new products, seasonal offers and special discounts, which all have obvious attractions for consumers.

A final point is that adverts often help the public to discover and buy products that benefit our lives. While watching television, for example, we might see a commercial for a home security system and purchase it. Without the advert, we may never have considered buying the system even though it would clearly protect and keep us safe in times of rising crime.

In conclusion, I strongly feel that advertisements for good products are vital since they inform many consumers about the products, save us time and money and can contribute to improving our quality of life. *(282 words – 15 sentences)*

Self-Study!

　モデルエッセイを分析していきます。エッセイの英文をもとに質問に**英語で**答えてください。回答がそのままエッセイを書く材料になります。

導入

Q1 エッセイのトピックは？　　Q3 エッセイの全体的な主張は？

Q2 エッセイの論点は？

本体1 反対の理由1

Q4 広告が必要な1つ目の理由は？　Q6 どんな対比が行われている？

Q5 それを裏づける詳細は？

本体2 反対の理由2

Q7 2つ目の理由は？　　　　Q9 ほかの例・詳細は？

Q8 それを裏づける詳細は？

本体3 反対の理由3

Q10 3つ目の理由は？　　　Q11 それを裏づける詳細は？

結論

Q12 主張はどう言い換えられている？

Q13 主な理由はどう要約されている？

以下の回答例や自分の分析した結果をもとにエッセイを書きましょう。

導入

Q1 エッセイのトピックは？

　　A. companies produce high-quality goods, shoppers learn about them through advertising

Q2 エッセイの論点は？

　　A. some individuals feel method is unnecessary if products are good

Q3 エッセイの全体的な主張は？

　　A. disagree – think advertisements are essential

本体1　反対の理由1

Q4 広告が必要な1つ目の理由は？

　　A. word of mouth is not enough to spread information

Q5 それを裏づける詳細は？

　　A. people tell family/friends, by social media (esp. nowadays) = number of people is limited

Q6 どんな対比が行われている？

　　A. commercial advertising reaches wider market, encompasses different people, often numerous countries

本体2　反対の理由2

Q7 2つ目の理由は？

　　A. shoppers can save time and money

Q8 それを裏づける詳細は？

　　A. advert = summary of product features → can compare products quickly & easily

Q9 ほかの例・詳細は？

A. adverts inform us about new products, seasonal offers, special discounts

本体3 反対の理由3

Q10 3つ目の理由は？

A. public discover products that benefit our lives

Q11 それを裏づける詳細は？

A. might see commercial on TV for home security system and purchase it, without advert, may never consider system but it protects & keeps us safe

結論

Q12 主張はどう言い換えられている？

A. advertisements for good products are vital

Q13 主な理由はどう要約されている？

A. inform many consumers about products, save us time & money, contribute to quality of life

今日の企業は高品質な商品を数多く生産しており、買い物客は主に広告を通じてその存在を知ることになる。しかし、中には商品が良ければ、このマーケティング手法は必要ない、と考える人もいる。私はこの意見に反対で、広告は消費者にとって必要不可欠なものだと考えている。

その理由の1つに、良い商品に関する情報を拡散するのに口コミは不十分だ、ということがある。自分が購入した素晴らしい商品のことを、家族や友人に直接伝えたり、とりわけ最近はソーシャルメディアを通じて発信したりするかもしれない。どちらの場合でも、情報を受け取る人の数はやはり限られる。それに対して、商業広告は様々な年齢、性別、そして背景を持つ人々を含む、はるかに広い市場に届き、数多くの国を対象としていることが多い。

第2に、広告を通じて、買い物客は時間とお金を節約することができる。基本的に、各広告は商品の主な特徴をまとめたものなので、似たような商品の異なる広告を見れば、情報収集で時間を無駄にすることなく、素早く簡単に商品を比較することができる。さらに、広告は新商品や季節ごとのセール、特別割引なども知らせてくれるので、これらはすべて消費者にとって明白な魅力だ。

最後の点として、広告は、人々が自分の生活に有益な商品を発見して購入するのに役立つことも多い。例えば、テレビで家庭用防犯システムのコマーシャルを見て、それを買う可能性もある。犯罪が増加する今の時代に、そうしたシステムが私たちを守り、安全を確保してくれることは確かであっても、広告がなければ購入を検討することもないかもしれない。

結論として、良い商品の広告はとても重要だと強く感じている。それは、広告がそうした商品のことを多くの消費者に知らせ、私たちの時間とお金を節約し、生活の質向上に貢献することができるからだ。

エクササイズ

エッセイ中の重要語句と表現をエクササイズで確認します。

語句に当てはまる訳の番号を選んでください。※訳は同じものが2つあります。

_____ an abundance of   _____ adverts/advertisements

_____ goods   _____ seasonal offers

_____ shoppers   _____ special discounts

_____ word of mouth   _____ obvious

_____ item   _____ a commercial

_____ social media   _____ protect

_____ commercial advertising   _____ contribute

_____ Essentially,

1. 買い物客	5. 口コミ	9. 商業広告	13. 守る
2. 明らかな	6. 広告	10. 特別割引	14. 製品、商品
3. 基本的に、本質的に	7. 貢献する	11. 季節のセール	15. ソーシャルメディア
4. 大量の…	8. コマーシャル、CM	12. 製品、商品	

同じ意味になるよう、単語を答えてください。

- goods = p_ _ _ _ _ _ _
- shoppers = c_ _ _ _ _ _ _ _
- essential = v_ _ _ _
- buy = p_ _ _ _ _ _ _

間違いを3箇所探してください。

- A final point is that advert often help the public to discover and buy product that benefit our live.

正解 4, 12[14], 1, 5, 14[12], 15, 9, 3, 6, 11, 10, 2, 8, 13, 7 / products, consumers, vital, purchase / adverts, products, lives

257

物事の両面と
意見を述べる ②

タイプ別にモデルエッセイを分析・再構築することで、重要表現を身につけてライティング力を高めます。

Some individuals feel that historic buildings ought to be preserved in their original forms. Others disagree and think this is unnecessary.
Discuss these two attitudes and indicate your opinion.

モデルエッセイ ◀)) 40

Buildings that were constructed long ago are often valued for their architectural and cultural significance. For this reason, it has been suggested that they ought to be kept and maintained in their original condition. However, some individuals disagree, citing reasons against preservation efforts.

On the one hand, preserving historic buildings is often considered important because architecture is educational. For example, historical structures such as museums, castles, palaces and government buildings convey a nation's history of power and conflict. Therefore, at such sites, visitors can not only learn historical facts but also absorb the atmosphere of the past. Moreover, old architecture brings economic benefits in that it attracts both domestic and overseas tourists to various locations. When visiting beautiful, unique, old buildings, visitors spend money on transportation, accommodation and in restaurants, thus benefitting local economies.

In contrast, some people argue that old buildings ought not to be preserved. They insist that the maintenance costs are higher than the income gained from tourism, so public taxes are often used for preservation purposes. These opponents feel that public money should instead be spent on essential projects for society, such as improving or constructing housing and health facilities. A second argument against the preservation of historic buildings concerns modernization. Making them usable and safe involves installing lights, heating and fire safety systems, etc., which alters the original essence of the buildings.

To conclude, there are reasonable arguments both for and against the preservation of historic buildings. Personally, I think they should be preserved, as they create employment. Furthermore, they represent important symbols in every country's historical diary, so they ought to be visited and experienced by present and future generations.　　　　　　　　　　　*(276 words – 16 sentences)*

Self-Study!

　モデルエッセイを分析していきます。エッセイの英文をもとに質問に**英語で**答えてください。回答がそのままエッセイを書く材料になります。

導入

Q1　エッセイのトピックは？

Q2　エッセイの一方の論点・主張は？

Q3　エッセイのもう一方の論点・主張は？

本体1　保存の賛成意見

Q4　古い建物の保存に賛成する第1の点は？

Q5　その具体例・詳細は？

Q6　どのような結果が述べられている？

Q7　賛成する第2の点は？

Q8　その具体例・詳細は？

本体2　保存の反対意見

Q9　古い建物の保存に反対する第1の点は？

Q10　その具体例・詳細は？

Q11　反対する第2の点は？

Q12　その具体例・詳細は？

結論

Q13　エッセイの論点と主張をどのように言い換えている？

Q14　筆者の意見は？

以下の回答例や自分の分析した結果をもとにエッセイを書きましょう。

導入

Q1 エッセイのトピックは？

　　A. buildings constructed long ago = valued for architectural & cultural significance

Q2 エッセイの一方の論点・主張は？

　　A. ought to be kept & maintained in original condition

Q3 エッセイのもう一方の論点・主張は？

　　A. some individuals disagree → against preservation

本体1 保存の賛成意見

Q4 古い建物の保存に賛成する第1の点は？

　　A. architecture is educational

Q5 その具体例・詳細は？

　　A. historical structures convey history of power & conflict

Q6 どのような結果が述べられている？

　　A. visitors can learn historical facts & absorb atmosphere of the past

Q7 賛成する第2の点は？

　　A. old architecture brings economic benefits: attracts tourists

Q8 その具体例・詳細は？

　　A. spend money on transportation, accommodation, in restaurants

本体2 保存の反対意見

Q9 古い建物の保存に反対する第1の点は？

　　A. maintenance costs are higher than income from tourism

[Q10] その具体例・詳細は？

    A. public tax often used for preservation, instead should be spent on projects for society

[Q11] 反対する第2の点は？

    A. modernization

[Q12] その具体例・詳細は？

    A. making old buildings usable & safe alters original essence of buildings

結論

[Q13] エッセイの論点と主張をどのように言い換えている？

    A. there are reasonable arguments for and against preservation

[Q14] 筆者の意見は？

    A. should be preserved: – create employment

                     – represent historical symbols for future generations to visit & experience

Task 2

3. タイプ別セルフスタディ2

遠い昔に建てられた建物は、その建築的、文化的意義が高く評価されることが多い。そのため、原型のままの状態で保存、維持することが望ましいとされている。しかし、中には保存活動への反対理由を挙げて、異議を唱える人もいる。

一方では、建築は教育に役立つため、歴史的建造物の保存は重要であると考えられることが多い。例えば、博物館、城、宮殿、庁舎などの歴史的建造物は、その国の権力や争いの歴史を伝えるものだ。そのため、こうした場所で、訪問者は歴史的事実を学べるだけでなく、過去の雰囲気を吸収することができる。さらに、古い建築物は、国内外からの観光客を各地に呼び込むという、経済効果をもたらす。美しく、個性的な古い建物を訪れると、観光客は交通や宿泊、飲食などにお金を使い、地域経済に恩恵をもたらす。

対照的に、古い建物は保存すべきではない、という意見もある。観光収入よりも維持費の方が高いので、公租が保存のために使われることが多い、というのだ。反対派は、住宅や医療施設の整備や建設など、社会にとって基幹的な事業に公的資金を使うべきだと感じている。歴史的建造物の保存に対する第2の反論は、近代化に関するものだ。それらを使用できる、安全な建物にするには、照明や暖房、防火設備などを設置する必要があり、それでは建物の本質が変わってしまうからだ。

結論として、歴史的建造物の保存の賛否に関しては、どちらも妥当な論拠がある。個人的には、雇用を生み出すという意味で、保存するべきだと考えている。さらに、歴史的建造物は、どの国の歴史日記においても重要な象徴になっているので、現在、そして未来の世代が訪れ、体験すべきものだ。

エクササイズ

エッセイ中の重要語句と表現をエクササイズで確認します。

語句に当てはまる訳の番号を選んでください。※訳は同じものが2つあります。

_____ architectural   _____ economic benefits

_____ condition   _____ income

_____ preservation efforts   _____ opponents

_____ historic buildings   _____ modernization

_____ historical structures   _____ original essence

_____ convey   _____ symbols

_____ power and conflict   _____ future generations

_____ absorb

1. 建築上の	5. 未来の世代	9. 吸収する	13. 歴史的建造物
2. 伝える	6. 状態	10. 保存活動	14. 歴史的建造物
3. 権力と争い	7. 元の本質	11. 象徴	15. 収入
4. 近代化	8. 反対者	12. 経済効果	

以下の複数の例を1語で表してください。

• museums, castles, palaces and government buildings = _____

• improving or constructing housing and health facilities = _____

エッセイを参考にして、空所に適切な1語を入れてください。

• However, some individuals disagree, citing reasons (　　　　) preservation efforts.

• To conclude, there are reasonable arguments both (　　　　) and (　　　　) the preservation of historic buildings.

問題と解決策を提示する②

タイプ別にモデルエッセイを分析・再構築することで、重要表現を身につけてライティング力を高めます。

Nowadays, more and more people move overseas to live there.
What problems do they experience in their new locations?
How can they deal with the problems?

モデルエッセイ ◀))41

In modern society, an increasing number of people choose to relocate abroad. Mostly, they enjoy life in their new location. However, they also face various challenges they need to overcome.

One issue many newcomers face is feeling homesick. Initially, they tend to miss their family, relatives and close friends, and can feel isolated and stressed out. Moreover, since they are strangers in their new location, often there are few people they can talk with in order to alleviate their negative feelings. A further difficulty residents encounter in unfamiliar places is a language barrier. If they do not speak and understand the local language, it can be difficult for them to communicate and interact with local people, which can make their sense of loneliness and stress seem even worse.

To overcome the aforementioned problems, new residents ought to employ two strategies. Firstly, they should regularly keep in touch with family members and friends back home. By using social media apps such as Instagram and Line, they can stay in contact easily by sending text messages and making video calls for face-to-face communication. Secondly, regarding the language barrier, it is a good idea to study the language of a country before moving there. People can do it by themselves, take lessons at a school, or use the internet to make friends from that country. Then they will not only develop basic conversational skills but also learn about the country's customs and culture.

In conclusion, homesickness and communication are obstacles that people experience when they move overseas. However, by studying the local language before they go and maintaining regular contact with family and friends after they arrive, it will help them settle into their new environment more smoothly.

(285 words – 15 sentences)

Self-Study!

　モデルエッセイを分析していきます。エッセイの英文をもとに質問に**英語で**答えてください。回答がそのままエッセイを書く材料になります。

導入

Q1 エッセイのトピックは？　　　Q3 エッセイの全体的な主張は？

Q2 エッセイの論点は？

本体1　海外で生活する問題点

Q4 1つ目の問題は？　　　　　　Q7 2つ目の問題は？

Q5 その具体例・詳細は？　　　　Q8 その具体例・詳細は？

Q6 ほかの例・詳細は？　　　　　Q9 ほかの例・詳細は？

本体2　解決策

Q10 1つ目の問題の解決策は？　　Q13 その具体例・詳細は？

Q11 その具体例・詳細は？　　　　Q14 ほかの例・詳細は？

Q12 2つ目の問題の解決策は？

結論

Q15 2つの問題はどうまとめられている？

Q16 2つの解決策はどうまとめられている？

Q17 解決策を実行するとどうなる？

Task 2

3. タイプ別セルフスタディ2

以下の回答例や自分の分析した結果をもとにエッセイを書きましょう。

導入

Q1 エッセイのトピックは？

A. increasing number of people relocate abroad

Q2 エッセイの論点は？

A. mostly enjoy life in new location

Q3 エッセイの全体的な主張は？

A. also face challenges they need to overcome

本体1 海外で生活する問題点

Q4 1つ目の問題は？

A. feeling homesick

Q5 その具体例・詳細は？

A. miss family, relatives, close friends

Q6 ほかの例・詳細は？

A. feel isolated & stressed out, stranger — few people can talk with

Q7 2つ目の問題は？

A. language barrier

Q8 その具体例・詳細は？

A. difficult to communicate & interact with local people

Q9 ほかの例・詳細は？

A. can make loneliness & stress seem worse

本体2 解決策

Q10 1つ目の問題の解決策は？

A. keep in touch with family & friends back home

[Q11] その具体例・詳細は？

　A. use social media apps (Instagram, Line) → text messages & video calls

[Q12] 2つ目の問題の解決策は？

　A. study language of country before moving

[Q13] その具体例・詳細は？

　A. study alone, lessons at a school, make friends from country on internet

[Q14] ほかの例・詳細は？

　A. develop basic conversational skills & learn about country's culture

結論

[Q15] 2つの問題はどうまとめられている？

　A. homesickness & communication = obstacles overseas

[Q16] 2つの解決策はどうまとめられている？

　A. – study the language before they go

　　　– maintain regular contact with family & friends after they arrive

[Q17] 解決策を実行するとどうなる？

　A. will help settle into new environment more smoothly

Task 2

3. タイプ別セルフスタディ2

267

現代社会では、海外移住を選択する人が増えている。新しい土地での生活を楽しむ人がほとんどだ。しかし、その一方で、乗り越えなければならない様々な課題にも直面する。

新参者の多くが直面する問題の1つがホームシックだ。まず、家族、親戚、親しい友人などが恋しくなり、孤独やストレスを感じる。また、新しい土地ではよそ者であるため、そのような悲観的な気持ちを和らげるために相談できる相手も少ない。さらに、慣れない土地で居住者がさらに出くわすのが、言葉の壁だ。現地の言葉を話したり、理解したりできなければ、地元の人とコミュニケーションをとったり交流したりすることが難しく、孤独感やストレスがより一層強くなりかねない。

このような問題を解決するために、新たな住民は2つの戦略をとるのがよい。第1に、母国の家族や友人と定期的に連絡をとるべきだ。InstagramやLINEなどのソーシャルメディアアプリを使い、テキストメッセージを送ったり、ビデオ通話で対面のコミュニケーションをとったりすることで、簡単に連絡を取り合うことができる。第2に、言葉の壁については、移住する前にその国の言葉を勉強しておくとよい。自分で勉強してもいいし、学校で教えてもらってもいいし、インターネットを使って、その国の友人を作るのもいい。そうすれば、基本的な会話能力が身につくだけでなく、その国の習慣や文化も学ぶことができる。

結論として、ホームシックとコミュニケーションは、海外移住の際に人々が経験する障害だ。しかし、渡航前に現地の言葉を勉強し、到着後も家族や友人と定期的に連絡を取ることで、よりスムーズに新しい環境になじむことができるだろう。

エクササイズ

エッセイ中の重要語句と表現をエクササイズで確認します。

語句に当てはまる訳の番号を選んでください。

_____ relocate		_____ language barrier	
_____ challenges		_____ loneliness	
_____ newcomers		_____ new residents	
_____ miss		_____ employ two strategies	
_____ isolated		_____ face-to-face communication	
_____ strangers		_____ obstacles	
_____ encounter		_____ settle into	
_____ unfamiliar places			

1. 新参者、新人	5. 課題、挑戦	9. 移住・移転する	13. 慣れない場所
2. 新たな住民	6. 孤独な	10. よそ者	14. 対面のやりとり
3. 孤独	7. 障害	11. 遭遇する	15. 言葉の壁
4. 恋しく思う	8. …になじむ	12. 2つの戦略をとる	

エッセイを参考に idea, overcome, good, should のいずれかを空所に入れてください。

- To (   ) the aforementioned problems, ...

- Firstly, they (   ) regularly keep in touch with ...

- Secondly, regarding the language barrier, it is a (   ) (   ) to study ...

エッセイを参考に正しいものを選んでください。

- [It / If / Which] they do not speak and understand the local language, [if / it / which] can be difficult for them to communicate and interact with local people, [which / it / if] can make their sense of loneliness and stress seem even worse.

議 論 を 評 価 す る ②

タイプ別にモデルエッセイを分析・再構築することで、重要
表現を身につけてライティング力を高めます。

Governments should provide free university education and require everyone to
graduate with a degree.
To what extent do you agree or disagree with this statement?

モデルエッセイ ◀))42

Education is important in any society. For that reason, it has been proposed that
all young people be required by law to continue studying until they complete a
university degree if it is funded by the state. In principle, I agree with such a
policy, but think it should not apply to everyone.

To begin with, even if degree courses are free, not all families can afford to pay
the extra costs (student accommodation, textbooks, etc.) involved in university
education. Moreover, young people from poorer homes may need to start
earning money for their family immediately after graduating from secondary
school. A further point is that not all students are interested in academic study,
as some wish to gain practical skills by working.

However, where possible, I believe it is better for young people to obtain a
university degree, since it benefits not only each person but also society in general.
Firstly, with a degree, young people will be able to find jobs with higher salaries
and thus enjoy higher standards of living. Furthermore, it is a generally accepted
fact that a better educated society is a more prosperous one. As such, governments
will receive more funds from taxes to spend on improving public services and
facilities. Moreover, having a higher percentage of educated people generally
results in lower rates of crime, and therefore a safer environment for all citizens.

To conclude, I would say it is unnecessary for governments to force all young people to remain in education until they graduate from university. However, while individual choice must be respected, I feel that all young people should be strongly encouraged to obtain a degree due to the benefits of having a highly educated population.

(285 words – 13 sentences)

Self-Study!

　モデルエッセイを分析していきます。エッセイの英文をもとに質問に**英語で**答えてください。回答がそのままエッセイを書く材料になります。

導入

Q1 エッセイのトピックは？　　　Q3 エッセイの全体的な主張は？

Q2 エッセイの論点は？

本体1 部分的に反対（＝全員が大学に行くべき、というわけでない）

Q4 筆者にとって反対する1つ目の理由は？

Q5 2つ目の理由は？

Q6 3つ目の理由は？

本体2 主に賛成（＝ほとんどの人が大学に行くべき）

Q7 筆者が主に賛成する全体的な理由は？

Q8 1つ目の具体的な理由は？

Q9 2つ目の理由は？

Q10 3つ目の理由は？

結論

Q11 エッセイの主張をどう言い換えている？

Q12 筆者の控えめな意見は？

Q13 筆者の主要な意見は？

以下の回答例や自分の分析した結果をもとにエッセイを書きましょう。

導入

Q1 エッセイのトピックは?

A. education = important in society

Q2 エッセイの論点は?

A. proposed that all young people be required by law to complete university degree if funded by state

Q3 エッセイの全体的な主張は?

A. in principle, agree with such policy, but should not apply to everyone

本体1 部分的に反対（＝全員が大学に行くべき、というわけでない）

Q4 筆者にとって反対する1つ目の理由は?

A. not all families can afford extra costs of university education

Q5 2つ目の理由は?

A. people from poorer homes may need to start earning money for family

Q6 3つ目の理由は?

A. not all students = interested in study, some wish to gain practical skills by working

本体2 主に賛成（＝ほとんどの人が大学に行くべき）

Q7 筆者が主に賛成する全体的な理由は?

A. university degree benefits each person & society in general

Q8 1つ目の具体的な理由は?

A. can find jobs with higher salaries → higher standards of living

Q9 2つ目の理由は?

A. better educated society = prosperous one: governments receive more taxes to improve public services & facilities

Q10 3つ目の理由は？

A. higher % of educated people = lower crime rates & safer environment for all citizens

結論

Q11 エッセイの主張をどう言い換えている？

A. unnecessary for all people to graduate from university

Q12 筆者の控えめな意見は？

A. individual choice → respected

Q13 筆者の主要な意見は？

A. all young people → encouraged to obtain degree due to benefits of highly educated population

教育はどんな社会でも重要だ。そのため、国が資金を提供する場合は、すべての若者が大学の学位を取得するまで勉強を続けることを法律で義務づけることが提案されている。私はこの方針に基本的には賛成だが、すべての人に適用すべきではないと考える。

そもそも、学位取得のための課程が無料であっても、すべての家庭が大学教育にかかる余分な費用（学生寮、教科書など）を払えるわけではない。さらに、貧しい家庭の若者は、中学校を卒業したらすぐに家族のためにお金を稼ぎ始めなければならないかもしれない。さらに、すべての学生が学問に興味があるわけではなく、中には働くことで実践的な技能を身につけたいと考える学生もいる。

しかし可能な場合は、若者たちが大学の学位を取得する方がいいと私は考えている。個人だけでなく、社会全体にとっても有益だからだ。まず、学位があれば、若者はより高い給料の仕事に就くことができ、より高い生活水準を享受することができる。さらに、教育水準の高い社会がより豊かであることは一般に認められている事実だ。そのため政府は、より多くの公共サービスや施設の改善に費やすための資金を税収から得ることができる。さらに、教育を受けた人の割合が高いほど、一般的に犯罪率が低くなり、すべての市民にとってより安全な環境となる。

結論として、政府がすべての若者に、大学を卒業するまで教育を受けることを強制する必要はないだろう。ただ、個人の選択は尊重されなければならないが、高度な教育を受けた人々がいることの利点から、すべての若者が学位を取得するよう強く奨励されるべきだと私は思う。

エクササイズ

エッセイ中の重要語句と表現をエクササイズで確認します。

語句に当てはまる訳の番号を選んでください。

____ university degree		____ higher standards of living	
____ the state		____ prosperous	
____ In principle,		____ funds	
____ policy		____ public services and facilities	
____ afford to		____ citizens	
____ earning money		____ individual choice	
____ graduating from		____ be respected	
____ practical skills			

1. 尊重される	5. 個人の選択	8. …を卒業して	12. 資金
2. 繁栄している	6. 公共サービスと	9. 市民、国民	13. 〜する余裕がある
3. より高い生活水準	公共施設	10. 大学の学位	14. 国
4. 実践的な技能	7. 方針	11. 基本的に、おおむね	15. 金を稼ぐ

正しいつづりを選んでください。

- text books / textbooks
- imediately / immediately
- benefits / beneffits
- Further more / Furthermore

下線部をほかの1語で言い換えてください。

- Moreover, having a higher percentage of educated people <u>normally/usually</u> results in lower rates of crime, and <u>so</u> a safer environment for all citizens.

Task 2

3. タイプ別セルフスタディ2

原因とその影響を述べる②

タイプ別にモデルエッセイを分析・再構築することで、重要表現を身につけてライティング力を高めます。

Some countries suffer from regular shortages of food.
What are some reasons for this occurrence?
How does it affect the countries concerned?

モデルエッセイ ◀)43

An important responsibility of any nation is to provide an adequate supply of food for its people. However, in certain cases, countries are not able to guarantee this, and without enough food, there are serious consequences.

One reason for insufficient food supply relates to geographical circumstances. For instance, small countries with rising populations have limited land space for growing crops and raising animals. Moreover, regardless of size, a nation's terrain and soil may be unsuitable for agricultural purposes. A further cause of food shortages is natural disasters. Some regions of the world are prone to droughts, floods and typhoons, which destroy crops and wipe out entire harvests. Moreover, scientists point out that the increasing frequency of such disasters is due to man-made global warming.

With a growing global population, the aforementioned issues have negative implications for some nations. Clearly, the most immediate problems concern health and hunger. Food shortages lead to rises in food prices, so people with lower incomes cut back on what they eat. In addition, those living in poverty may suffer from hunger, and in extreme cases, starvation. Combined, these two factors lead to an increase in individuals with health issues, especially children, and this can become a burden on health care systems. Furthermore, violence can erupt on the streets as people struggle to find food and fight or riot over scarce supplies.

To conclude, it is evident that various factors, both natural and man-made, hinder the ability of some nations to produce an adequate supply of food to feed their citizens. As such, when countries do face a food shortage crisis, I believe it is the moral duty of nations with ample supplies to help them.

(280 words – 16 sentences)

Self-Study!

モデルエッセイを分析していきます。エッセイの英文をもとに質問に**英語で**答えてください。回答がそのままエッセイを書く材料になります。

導入

Q1 エッセイのトピックは？　　Q3 エッセイの全体的な主張は？

Q2 エッセイの論点は？

本体1　不足の原因

Q4 食料不足の原因の1つは？　　Q7 2つ目の原因は？

Q5 その具体例・詳細は？　　　Q8 その具体例・詳細は？

Q6 ほかの例・詳細は？　　　　Q9 3つ目の原因は？

本体2　不足の影響

Q10 影響はどのように紹介されている？

Q11 2つの影響は？

Q12 1つ目の影響の具体例・詳細は？

Q13 2つ目の影響の具体例・詳細は？

Q14 2つの影響の結果は？

Q15 3つ目の影響は？

結論

Q16 原因はどうまとめられている？

Q17 影響に関する筆者の意見は？

Task 2

3．タイプ別セルフスタディ2

277

以下の回答例や自分の分析した結果をもとにエッセイを書きましょう。

導入

Q1　エッセイのトピックは？

　　A. important responsibility of any nation = provide food

Q2　エッセイの論点は？

　　A. certain cases, countries = not able to guarantee this

Q3　エッセイの全体的な主張は？

　　A. without enough food = serious consequences

本体1　不足の原因

Q4　食料不足の原因の1つは？

　　A. geographical circumstances

Q5　その具体例・詳細は？

　　A. small countries with rising populations = limited land space

Q6　ほかの例・詳細は？

　　A. terrain & soil may be unsuitable for agricultural purposes

Q7　2つ目の原因は？

　　A. natural disasters

Q8　その具体例・詳細は？

　　A. droughts, floods, typhoons destroy crops & wipe out harvests

Q9　3つ目の原因は？

　　A. increasing frequency ←→ man-made global warming

本体2　不足の影響

Q10　影響はどのように紹介されている？

　　A. growing global population, issues = negative implications for nations

[Q11] 2つの影響は？

A. health & hunger

[Q12] 1つ目の影響の具体例・詳細は？

A. food shortages = rises in food prices → people with lower incomes eat less

[Q13] 2つ目の影響の具体例・詳細は？

A. people living in poverty suffer from hunger (extreme cases, starvation)

[Q14] 2つの影響の結果は？

A. increase in individuals with health issues → burden on health care systems

[Q15] 3つ目の影響は？

A. violence on streets → people fight/riot over scarce supplies

結論

[Q16] 原因はどうまとめられている？

A. various factors (natural & man-made) hinder ability of some nations to produce adequate food

[Q17] 影響に関する筆者の意見は？

A. when countries face food crisis, nations with ample food should help

あらゆる国家の重要な責務に、国民に十分な食料を供給する、というものがある。しかし場合によっては国家がこれを保証できないことがあり、十分な食料がないと、深刻な結果をもたらすことになる。

食料不足の原因の1つは、地理的な事情に関わる。例えば、人口が増加している小国では、農作物や家畜を育てるための土地に限りがある。また、広さに関係なく、国土の地形や土壌が農業に適していない場合もある。食料不足のさらなる原因として、自然災害が挙げられる。世界には干ばつ、洪水、そして台風などが起きやすい地域があり、そうした災害は農作物を駄目にし、収穫を全滅させる。さらに、このような災害が頻発しているのは、人為的な地球温暖化のせいだと科学者は指摘している。

世界人口の増加に伴い、上記のような問題は複数の国にとってマイナスの影響を及ぼしている。明らかに、最も差し迫った問題としては、健康と飢餓の問題が挙げられる。食料不足は食料価格の上昇を招き、収入が少ない人々は食べるものを控える。さらに、貧困にあえぐ人々は空腹、極端な場合には飢餓に苦しむことになる。この2つの要因が重なると、健康問題を抱える人、特に子どもが増え、医療制度に負担をかけることになるかもしれない。さらに、人々が食べ物を探すのに苦労し、少ない物資をめぐって争いや暴動を起こすようになると、路上で暴力が勃発することもある。

結論として、自然および人為的な様々な要因が、一部の国が国民を養うために十分な量の食料を生産する能力を妨げることは明白だ。そのため、国が食料不足の危機に直面した時、十分な供給力を持つ国が彼らを助けることは、道徳的な義務だと私は考える。

エクササイズ

エッセイ中の重要語句と表現をエクササイズで確認します。

語句に当てはまる訳の番号を選んでください。

_____ guarantee	_____ entire harvests
_____ geographical	_____ man-made global warming
_____ terrain and soil	_____ hunger
_____ agricultural	_____ poverty
_____ natural disasters	_____ starvation
_____ droughts, floods and typhoons	_____ hinder
_____ destroy crops	_____ face a food shortage crisis
_____ wipe out	

1. 全滅・絶滅させる	5. 飢え	9. 地理的な	12. 自然災害
2. 貧困	6. 飢餓、餓死	10. 妨げる	13. 農作物に被害を与える
3. 農業の	7. 保証する	11. 食料不足の危機	14. 干ばつ、洪水、台風
4. 地形と土壌	8. 全収穫物	に直面する	15. 人為的な地球温暖化

同じ意味になるよう、単語を答えてください。

- serious consequences　　=　　n_____ i_____
- without enough food　　=　　f_____ s_____

下線部をほかの語句に言い換えてください。

- An important responsibility of any nation is to provide a sufficient supply of ...

- One reason for not enough food supply relates to ...

- ... as people struggle to find food and fight or riot over a lack of supplies.

- I believe it is the moral duty of nations with lots of supplies to help them.

正解　7, 9, 4, 3, 12, 14, 13, 1, 8, 15, 5, 2, 6, 10, 11 ／ negative implications, food shortages ／ an adequate, insufficient, scarce, ample

賛成・反対を述べる ③

タイプ別にモデルエッセイを分析・再構築することで、重要表現を身につけてライティング力を高めます。

Some individuals think the arts (painting, music, literature, dance, cinema, etc.) do not play very important roles in our lives today.
Do you agree or disagree with this point of view?

モデルエッセイ　◀)44

In spite of the fact that people are constantly surrounded by different forms of art in their daily lives, it has been suggested that the arts are relatively unimportant. From a personal perspective, I wholly disagree with this suggestion and feel they are an essential component of society.

First of all, the arts are extremely important in education, as literature is used to teach social concepts and initial language skills to small children. For instance, through picture books they learn about right and wrong behaviour and the importance of being kind to others. Moreover, they learn to read, and quickly expand their knowledge of vocabulary through storybooks.

Secondly, the various forms of art help children and teenagers to deal with feelings and emotions. For children, it is often difficult to express themselves in words. However, through drawing and painting pictures, they can communicate their thoughts and feelings in a simple way. Moreover, music and dance, which are especially popular among teenagers, help young people to release stress and cope with the daily pressure they encounter in school and at home.

Thirdly, the arts contribute to the well-being of people. For instance, individuals who suffer from mental or psychological problems are often advised by therapists to draw or paint pictures. Apparently, this approach is very effective in helping patients to recover. Moreover, many hobbies are based on the arts. So taking photographs or visiting art galleries and museums, for example, provides people with enjoyable leisure activities, even during retirement.

Overall, it is evident that the arts are crucial for living in today's world. In fact, it is hard to imagine our lives without the arts, since they benefit members of society in different ways.

(283 words – 16 sentences)

Self-Study!

　モデルエッセイを分析していきます。エッセイの英文をもとに質問に**英語で**答えてください。回答がそのままエッセイを書く材料になります。

導入

Q1 エッセイのトピックは？　　Q3 エッセイの全体的な主張は？

Q2 エッセイの論点は？

本体1 反対の理由1

Q4 芸術が重要な1つ目の理由は？　　Q6 ほかの例・詳細は？

Q5 その具体例・詳細は？

本体2 反対の理由2

Q7 2つ目の理由は？　　Q9 ほかの例・詳細は？

Q8 その具体例・詳細は？

本体3 反対の理由3

Q10 3つ目の理由は？　　Q12 ほかの例・詳細は？

Q11 その具体例・詳細は？

結論

Q13 主張はどう言い換えられている？

Q14 主張を裏づける総括的な理由は？

Task 2

4. タイプ別セルフスタディ3

以下の回答例や自分の分析した結果をもとにエッセイを書きましょう。

導入

Q1 エッセイのトピックは？

A. people are constantly surrounded by art

Q2 エッセイの論点は？

A. has been suggested that arts are unimportant

Q3 エッセイの全体的な主張は？

A. wholly disagree: arts = essential component of society

本体1 反対の理由1

Q4 芸術が重要な1つ目の理由は？

A. arts = important in education

Q5 その具体例・詳細は？

A. literature teaches social concepts & language skills to small children

Q6 ほかの例・詳細は？

A. picture books = learn right & wrong behaviour,
   learn to read & expand vocabulary through storybooks

本体2 反対の理由2

Q7 2つ目の理由は？

A. help children & teenagers deal with feelings/emotions

Q8 その具体例・詳細は？

A. children = difficult to express in words, however, through drawing &
   painting can communicate thoughts & feelings

Q9 ほかの例・詳細は？

A. music & dance, (esp. popular → teenagers), help young people cope
   with pressure at school/home

本体2　反対の理由3

Q10 3つ目の理由は？

A. arts contribute to well-being of people

Q11 その具体例・詳細は？

A. individuals with mental/psychological problems draw/paint =

effective in helping patients recover

Q12 ほかの例・詳細は？

A. many hobbies = based on arts & provide enjoyable leisure activities

結論

Q13 主張はどう言い換えられている？

A. arts are crucial

Q14 主張を裏づける総括的な理由は？

A. benefit members of society in different ways

日常生活において、人々は常に様々な形の芸術に囲まれているにもかかわらず、芸術は比較的重要でないと言われている。個人的な見解だが、この意見にはまったく反対で、芸術は社会にとって必要不可欠な構成要素だと考えている。

まず、幼い子どもたちに社会的概念や初期の言語能力を教えるために文学が使われるなど、教育において芸術は非常に重要だ。例えば、絵本を通して正しい行いや間違った行い、人に親切にすることの大切さを学ぶ。さらに、物語の本によって読むことを学び、語彙の知識を素早く増やしていく。

第2に、様々な芸術の形は子どもやティーンエージャーが気持ちや感情と向き合う手助けしてくれる。子どもたちにとって、言葉で自分を表現することは難しいことが多い。しかし、絵を描くことで、自分の考えや気持ちをわかりやすく伝えることができる。さらに、特にティーンエージャーに人気のある音楽やダンスは、若者が学校や家庭で遭遇する日々のプレッシャーに対処し、ストレスを発散するのに役立つ。

第3に、芸術は人々の幸福に貢献する。例えば、精神的、心理的な問題を抱えた人は、セラピストから絵を描くようすすめられることが多い。どうやらこの方法は、患者の回復に非常に効果的であるらしい。さらに、多くの趣味は、芸術に基づいている。だから、例えば写真を撮ったり、美術館や博物館を訪れたりすることは、退職後の生活にも楽しい余暇を提供することになる。

全体として、芸術は現代の世界を生きるために大変重要であることは明らかだ。実際、芸術は社会の人々にいろいろな方法で恩恵をもたらすことから、芸術のない生活は考えづらい。

エクササイズ

エッセイ中の重要語句と表現をエクササイズで確認します。

語句に当てはまる訳の番号を選んでください。

＿＿ literature	＿＿ psychological
＿＿ right and wrong behaviour	＿＿ therapists
＿＿ vocabulary	＿＿ Apparently,
＿＿ emotions	＿＿ approach
＿＿ express ... in words	＿＿ helping patients to recover
＿＿ release stress	＿＿ leisure activities
＿＿ daily pressure	＿＿ retirement
＿＿ well-being	

1. 語彙	5. どうやら	10. 余暇の活動	14. 感情
2. 患者が回復する	6. 方法	11. 退職	15. 文学
のに役立って	7. 日々のプレッシャー	12. 正しい行いと間	
3. 幸福	8. …を言葉で表現する	違った行い	
4. 心理的な	9. ストレスを解消する	13. セラピスト	

下線部をほかの1語で言い換えてください。

• From a personal <u>viewpoint</u>, I <u>completely</u> disagree with this suggestion and feel they are an essential <u>part</u> of society.

動詞に続く前置詞を答えてください。

• surrounded ＿＿＿＿＿

• deal ＿＿＿＿＿

• cope ＿＿＿＿＿

• contribute ＿＿＿＿＿

• suffer ＿＿＿＿＿

正解 15, 12, 1, 14, 8, 9, 7, 3, 4, 13, 5, 6, 2, 10, 11 ／ perspective, wholly, component ／ by, with, with, to, from

物事の両面と意見を述べる③

タイプ別にモデルエッセイを分析・再構築することで、重要表現を身につけてライティング力を高めます。

In most countries, governments rely too heavily on charities and voluntary organisations to provide assistance and funding for disabled people.
Discuss further ways that society and governments could help such people.

モデルエッセイ ◀)45

People with physical or mental disabilities require various kinds of support. Yet governments depend too much on non-profit organisations to provide it. Therefore, additional measures are necessary to assist the disabled and improve their quality of life, and there are various options available.

Firstly, the general public could help disabled individuals in small ways. For example, in local communities, people could give a little of their free time and take turns helping disabled neighbours with daily tasks, such as shopping for food. Also, they could take them to local events like festivals, since disabled people rarely attend or participate in them.

A second idea is that celebrities and other famous people volunteer to generate much-needed funds for the disabled. For instance, musicians could hold charity concerts and big, wealthy sports clubs could hold charity matches or competitions. Then the money raised from the sales of tickets and related goods could be used for the benefit of people with disabilities.

Lastly, governments could allocate a higher proportion of tax revenue in order to train and employ more care workers to assist the disabled. For this purpose, I feel that society would strongly support such a move even if it meant paying a new kind of tax. At the same time, governments should make it mandatory for companies to employ a larger percentage of staff who are disabled. Naturally, each person can be given appropriate work, depending on the severity of his or her disability.

In summary, charities and voluntary organisations play important roles in looking after the welfare and needs of disabled people. However, more action is necessary and, as outlined above, ordinary citizens, famous people and governments can contribute in this respect. *(280 words – 15 sentences)*

Self-Study!

　モデルエッセイを分析していきます。エッセイの英文をもとに質問に**英語で**答えてください。回答がそのままエッセイを書く材料になります。

導入

- Q1 エッセイのトピックは？
- Q2 エッセイの論点は？
- Q3 エッセイの全体的な主張は？

本体1　一般市民

- Q4 障害のある人を助ける1つ目の方法は？
- Q5 その具体例・詳細は？
- Q6 ほかの例・詳細は？

本体2　有名人・著名

- Q7 2つ目の方法は？
- Q8 その具体例・詳細は？
- Q9 ほかの例・詳細は？

本体3　政府・企業

- Q10 3つ目の方法は？
- Q11 その具体例・詳細は？
- Q12 ほかの方法は？
- Q13 ほかの例・詳細は？

結論

- Q14 トピックはどう言い換えられている？
- Q15 エッセイの主なアイデアはどう要約されている？

以下の回答例や自分の分析した結果をもとにエッセイを書きましょう。

導入

Q1 エッセイのトピックは？

A. people with mental/physical disabilities require support

Q2 エッセイの論点は？

A. governments depend too much on non-profit organisations

Q3 エッセイの全体的な主張は？

A. additional measures are necessary — various options available

本体1 一般市民

Q4 障害のある人を助ける1つ目の方法は？

A. general public could help in small ways

Q5 その具体例・詳細は？

A. helping disabled neighbours with daily tasks (shopping for food)

Q6 ほかの例・詳細は？

A. take them to local events (festivals), since disabled rarely

attend/participate

本体2 有名人・著名人

Q7 2つ目の方法は？

A. celebrities & famous people could volunteer to generate funds

Q8 その具体例・詳細は？

A. musicians hold concerts, sports clubs hold matches/competitions

Q9 ほかの例・詳細は？

A. money from sales of tickets & related goods → benefit people with

disabilities

本体3 **政府・企業**

Q10 3つ目の方法は？

A. governments could allocate more tax revenue to train & employ more care workers

Q11 その具体例・詳細は？

A. society would support this, even if meant new tax

Q12 ほかの方法は？

A. governments make companies employ larger percentage of disabled staff

Q13 ほかの例・詳細は？

A. each person given appropriate work, depending on disability

結論

Q14 トピックはどう言い換えられている？

A. charities & volunteer organisations = important roles in welfare & needs of disabled people

Q15 エッセイの主なアイデアはどう要約されている？

A. more action is necessary: citizens, famous people & governments can contribute

身体的、または精神的な障害のある人たちは、様々な支援を必要としている。しかし、政府はその提供について、非営利団体に頼りすぎている。したがって、障害のある人を支援し、彼らの生活の質を向上させるためには、さらなる対策が必要であり、様々な選択肢が存在する。

まず、一般市民が小さな方法で障害のある人を支援することができる。例えば、地域社会では、人々が自分の自由な時間を少し提供して、交代で食料の買い出しなど日常的な作業をすることで、近隣の障害のある人を手助けすることができる。また、障害のある人がめったに訪れたり参加したりしないお祭りなどの地域行事に連れていくこともできる。

2つ目のアイデアは、有名人や著名人に、障害のある人が本当に必要としている資金を捻出するための活動をボランティアでやってもらうことだ。例えば、ミュージシャンがチャリティーコンサートを開いたり、大規模で裕福なスポーツクラブがチャリティー試合や競技会を開いたりする。そうすれば、そのチケットや関連グッズの販売で得たお金を、障害のある人の利益のために使うことができる。

最後に、政府は障害のある人を支援する介護福祉士をより多く養成し、雇用するために、より高い割合の税収を配分することができる。そのためなら、たとえ新しい税金を払うことになっても、社会はそのような動きを強く支持するのではないかと思う。同時に、政府は企業に対して、障害者雇用率を高めることを義務づけるべきだ。当然ながら、1人ひとりが障害の程度に応じて、適切な仕事が提供されることになる。

要約すると、慈善団体やボランティア組織は、障害のある人の福祉やニーズを見守るうえで重要な役割を担っている。しかし、さらなる行動が必要であり、上記のように、一般市民、著名人、そして政府は、この点において貢献することができる。

エクササイズ

エッセイ中の重要語句と表現をエクササイズで確認します。

語句に当てはまる訳の番号を選んでください。

＿＿ disabilities	＿＿ revenue
＿＿ non-profit	＿＿ care workers
＿＿ neighbours	＿＿ mandatory
＿＿ daily tasks	＿＿ appropriate
＿＿ participate in	＿＿ severity
＿＿ much-needed	＿＿ needs
＿＿ charity	＿＿ in this respect
＿＿ allocate	

1. この点で	5. チャリティー、慈善	9. 適切な	14. 必要なもの
2. 非営利の	6. 義務の、強制的な	10. 厳しさ、深刻さ	15. 介護士
3. 割り当てる	7. 収入	11. …に参加する	
4. 待ち望んだ、本当に必要な	8. 日常的な作業・仕事	12. 障害 13. 隣人	

間違いを5箇所探してください。

- For instance, musician could hold charity concert and big, wealthy sports club could hold charity match or competition.

カッコ内を正しい順序に並べ替えてください。

- Therefore, [necessary / are / to / measures / additional] assist the disabled and improve their quality of life, and [options / are / various / there / available].

Task 2

4. タイプ別セルフスタディ 3

問題と解決策を
提示する③

タイプ別にモデルエッセイを分析・再構築することで、重要
表現を身につけてライティング力を高めます。

Most people know about the need to protect the Earth's environment, but in general, we take little action.
What are some causes of our environmental problems? What can we do to help solve them?

モデルエッセイ ◀))46

The general public are aware of the environmental issues facing our planet today. Even so, we fail to make real efforts to preserve it for ourselves and our children. However, as we cause the problems associated with the environment, we are responsible for resolving them.

One major reason for the negative impacts on our environment is overconsumption. In order to maintain economic growth, governments constantly encourage the consumption of more and more products. Consequently, many natural resources used to manufacture the products are being quickly depleted, and flora and fauna are disappearing. A further cause is the burning of fossil fuels. These include coal, oil and petrol, which are burned to produce energy for electricity and transportation. When they are burned, poisonous gases are released into the air, thus polluting it.

In order to tackle the aforementioned problems and protect the Earth, governments must alter their way of thinking and adhere more to the United Nations' Sustainable Development Goals (SDGs). Rather than pursue rapid economic growth, they ought to aim for slower, sustainable growth rates. For this to happen, people also need to consider the SDGs and change their everyday habits. First and foremost, we need to cut our unnecessary purchases of products and reduce, reuse and recycle more than we do at present. In addition, we must conserve the energy we use at home and in other buildings. Finally, we have to walk, cycle and use public transport whenever possible, so as to reduce pollution from private vehicles.

To conclude, overconsumption and the burning of fossil fuels are two causes of environmental destruction. However, if governments and the public follow the suggestions outlined above, we may be able to pass on a healthier planet to future generations.

(288 words – 17 sentences)

Self-Study!

モデルエッセイを分析していきます。エッセイの英文をもとに質問に**英語で**答えてください。回答がそのままエッセイを書く材料になります。

導入

Q1 エッセイのトピックは？　　Q3 エッセイの全体的な主張は？

Q2 エッセイの論点は？

本体1　環境問題の原因

Q4 原因の1つ目は？　　　　　Q7 ほかの原因は？

Q5 その具体例・詳細は？　　　Q8 その具体例・詳細は？

Q6 この原因の結果は？　　　　Q9 この原因の結果は？

本体2　解決策

Q10 解決策の1つ目は？　　　　Q12 2つ目の解決策は？

Q11 その具体例・詳細は？　　　Q13 その具体例・詳細は？

結論

Q14 再び述べられている2つの原因は？

Q15 それらはどのように解決できる？

Q16 どんな結果になる可能性がある？

以下の回答例や自分の分析した結果をもとにエッセイを書きましょう。

導入

Q1 エッセイのトピックは？

A. public are aware of environmental issues facing our planet

Q2 エッセイの論点は？

A. we fail to make efforts to preserve it

Q3 エッセイの全体的な主張は？

A. we cause the problems, so responsible for resolving them

本体1 環境問題の原因

Q4 原因の1つ目は？

A. overconsumption

Q5 その具体例・詳細は？

A. governments encourage consumption of more products

Q6 この原因の結果は？

A. natural resources = depleted, flora & fauna = disappearing

Q7 ほかの原因は？

A. burning of fossil fuels

Q8 その具体例・詳細は？

A. coal, oil, petrol burned for electricity & transportation

Q9 この原因の結果は？

A. when burned, poisonous gases released into air & polluting it

本体2 解決策

Q10 解決策の1つ目は？

A. governments must alter thinking, adhere more to the SDGs

Q11 その具体例・詳細は？

　　A. ought to aim for slower economic, sustainable growth

Q12 2つ目の解決策は？

　　A. people also need to consider SDGs & change habits

Q13 その具体例・詳細は？

　　A. - cut unnecessary purchases, reduce, reuse & recycle more

　　　　- conserve energy at home & other buildings

　　　　- walk, cycle, use public transport whenever possible

結論

Q14 再び述べられている2つの原因は？

　　A. overconsumption & burning fossil fuels

Q15 それらはどのように解決できる？

　　A. if governments and people follow the suggestions

Q16 どんな結果になる可能性がある？

　　A. may be able to pass on healthier planet to future generations

私たちの住む地球が今日直面している環境問題については、一般の人々も認識している。それにもかかわらず、自分たちや子どもたちのために地球を守る真の努力を、私たちはできていない。しかし、環境にまつわる問題を引き起こしているのは私たち自身である以上、それを解決するのも私たちの責任だ。

環境に悪影響を与えている大きな原因の1つは、過剰な消費だ。経済成長を維持するために、政府は常により多くの製品の消費を促している。その結果、製品の製造に使われる多くの天然資源が急速に枯渇し、動植物も消滅しつつある。さらなる原因に化石燃料の燃焼がある。これらには、石炭、石油、そしてガソリンが含まれ、これらを燃やして電気や輸送のためのエネルギーを生産している。これらが燃やされると有害なガスが大気中に放出され、大気汚染につながる。

これらの問題を解決し、地球を守るために、政府は考え方を変えて今よりも国連の持続可能な開発目標（SDGs）に沿って行動することが必要だ。急激な経済成長を目指すのではなく、ゆるやかで持続可能な成長率を目指すべきだ。そのためには、国民もSDGsを意識し、日々の生活習慣を変えていく必要がある。まず何よりも無駄な買い物を減らし、リデュース（減らす）、リユース（再利用）、リサイクルを、今以上に進めなくてはならない。加えて、家庭やその他の建物で使用するエネルギーを節約することも必要だ。最後に、可能な限り歩いたり、自転車に乗ったり、公共交通機関を利用して、自家用車による公害を減らさなければならない。

結論として、過剰消費と化石燃料の燃焼が環境破壊の2つの原因だ。しかし政府や一般市民が上記の提案を守れば、より健全な地球を未来の世代に引き継ぐことができるかもしれない。

エクササイズ

エッセイ中の重要語句と表現をエクササイズで確認します。

語句に当てはまる訳の番号を選んでください。

_____ fail to preserve

_____ associated with

_____ overconsumption

_____ depleted

_____ flora and fauna

_____ fossil fuels

_____ coal, oil and petrol

_____ poisonous gases

_____ tackle

_____ adhere to

_____ United Nations

_____ Sustainable Development Goals

_____ pursue rapid economic growth

_____ reduce, reuse and recycle

_____ vehicles

1. …に関連した
2. リデュース、リユース、リサイクル
3. 過剰な消費
4. 急激な経済成長
5. 激減した
6. 取り組む
7. 保存・保護できない
8. 国際連合
9. SDGs、持続可能な開発目標
10. 化石燃料
11. 動植物
12. …を厳守する
13. 有害なガス
14. 乗り物、車
15. 石炭、石油、ガソリン
   … を追求する

空所に共通する1語を入れてください。

- In _____ to maintain economic growth, ...

- In _____ to tackle the aforementioned problems ...

正しいつづりを選んでください。

- environmental / enviromental

- dissapearing / disappearing

- electrisity / electricity

- unecessary / unnecessary

- pollution / polution

正解 7, 1, 3, 5, 11, 10, 15, 13, 6, 12, 8, 9, 4, 2, 14／order／environmental, disappearing, electricity, unnecessary, pollution

299

Task 2

4. タイプ別セルフスタディ3

議論を評価する③

タイプ別にモデルエッセイを分析・再構築することで、重要表現を身につけてライティング力を高めます。

Museums are no longer necessary because we can get a lot of information about subjects such as art, history and science from the internet.
How far do you agree or disagree with this opinion?

モデルエッセイ ◀))47

Visiting museums is one way the public learn about art, history and science. However, it has been stated that the invention of the internet means it is no longer necessary to visit such places to gain knowledge about those fields. As for me, I primarily disagree with this point of view and believe that museums are essential.

In certain respects, it is true that the internet has benefits when gathering information. To begin with, it is much quicker to get data from a variety of online resources, including journals and studies carried out by researchers and scientists. Furthermore, unlike museums, people can access this information 24 hours a day. In addition, if you live in a very rural or remote location, it is inconvenient to visit museums since they are usually located in cities.

Despite the aforementioned merits of the internet, museums are necessary for several reasons. Firstly, it is more rewarding to see original works of art and ancient fossils with your own eyes. Only then can you truly appreciate their unique qualities. This is one reason why millions of people visit the Louvre Museum in Paris to see the Mona Lisa. Additionally, not all the information we find on the internet is reliable. However, museum exhibits are genuine and their descriptions are carefully researched and accurate. Finally, each museum, whether old or new, has a unique architectural structure and atmosphere. Accordingly, these qualities give visitors a special feeling and experience that cannot be gained from a computer screen.

In summary, for the reasons stated above, I think museums are vital and should be maintained regardless of how internet technology progresses.

(272 words – 16 sentences)

Self-Study!

モデルエッセイを分析していきます。エッセイの英文をもとに質問に**英語で**答えてください。回答がそのままエッセイを書く材料になります。

導入
- Q1 エッセイのトピックは？
- Q2 エッセイの論点は？
- Q3 エッセイの全体的な主張は？

本体1　一部賛成
- Q4 議論の弱い側（一部同意）をどう紹介している？
- Q5 1つ目の理由は？
- Q6 2つ目の理由は？
- Q7 3つ目の理由は？

本体2　主に反対
- Q8 議論の強い側（主に反対）をどう紹介している？
- Q9 1つ目の理由は？
- Q10 その具体例・詳細は？
- Q11 2つ目の理由は？
- Q12 その具体例・詳細は？
- Q13 3つ目の理由は？
- Q14 その具体例・詳細は？

結論
- Q15 主張はどう言い換えられている？
- Q16 どんな意見が加えられた？

以下の回答例や自分の分析した結果をもとにエッセイを書きましょう。

導入

Q1 エッセイのトピックは？

　A. museums = one way public learn about art, history, science

Q2 エッセイの論点は？

　A. invention of internet = no longer necessary to visit such places

Q3 エッセイの全体的な主張は？

　A. primarily disagree: museums = essential

本体1　一部賛成

Q4 議論の弱い側（一部同意）をどう紹介している？

　A. internet = benefits when gathering information

Q5 1つ目の理由は？

　A. quicker to get data from online resources (journals, studies)

Q6 2つ目の理由は？

　A. unlike museums, can access 24 hours/day

Q7 3つ目の理由は？

　A. if live in rural/remote location = inconvenient to visit museums

本体2　主に反対

Q8 議論の強い側（主に反対）をどう紹介している？

　A. museums are necessary for some reasons

Q9 1つ目の理由は？

　A. more rewarding to see original works & fossils with own eyes — can
　　　truly appreciate unique qualities

Q10 その具体例・詳細は？

　A. millions visit Louvre to see Mona Lisa

Q11 2つ目の理由は？

    A. not all information on internet = reliable

Q12 その具体例・詳細は？

    A. exhibits are genuine, descriptions = carefully researched & accurate

Q13 3つ目の理由は？

    A. each museum = unique architectural structure & atmosphere

Q14 その具体例・詳細は？

    A. qualities give visitors special feeling & experience

結論

Q15 主張はどう言い換えられている？

    A. museums are vital

Q16 どんな意見が加えられた？

    A. should be maintained regardless of how internet technology progresses

Task 2

4. タイプ別セルフスタディ3

303

美術館や博物館を訪れることは、一般の人々が芸術、歴史、そして科学について学ぶ方法の1つだ。しかしインターネットの発達により、それらの分野の知識を得るために、そういった場所を訪れる必要はなくなったとも言われている。私自身はこの意見には主に反対で、美術館、博物館は非常に重要なものだと考えている。

ある意味、インターネットは情報収集する際に利点があることは確かだ。まず、研究者や科学者による学術論文や研究成果を含め、様々なオンラインの資料からデータを入手する方が、格段に速い。また、美術館、博物館と違って、24時間いつでも情報にアクセスすることができる。さらに、美術館や博物館は都市部にあることが多いので、田舎や遠隔地に住んでいる場合、足を運ぶことが難しい。

上記のようなインターネットの利点がある一方で、美術館や博物館が必要な理由もいくつかある。まず、美術品や古代の化石などの現物を自分の目で見ることは、さらに価値があることだ。そうすることで初めてその固有な性質がわかる。例えば、何百万人もの人々がモナリザを見るためにパリのルーブル美術館を訪れるのは、このような理由からだ。加えて、インターネット上の情報がすべて信頼できるわけではない。一方、美術館の展示物は本物であり、その説明も入念に調査されていて、正確だ。最後に、古くても新しくても、それぞれの美術館・博物館には、独特の建築構造と雰囲気がある。その結果、こうした性質は、コンピューターの画面からは得られない特別な感覚と経験を訪問者に与える。

まとめると、以上のような理由から、インターネット技術がどのように進歩しようとも、美術館、博物館は必要不可欠であり、維持されるべきだと考えている。

エクササイズ

エッセイ中の重要語句と表現をエクササイズで確認します。

語句に当てはまる訳の番号を選んでください。

_____ fields   _____ unique qualities

_____ online resources   _____ reliable

_____ journals   _____ exhibits

_____ researchers   _____ genuine

_____ inconvenient   _____ descriptions

_____ rewarding   _____ accurate

_____ ancient fossils   _____ regardless of

_____ appreciate

1. 観賞する、正当に評価する
2. …にかかわらず
3. オンラインの資料
4. 価値がある
5. 分野
6. 説明
7. 研究者
8. 古代の化石
9. 不便な
10. 正確な
11. 本物の
12. 学術誌
13. 頼りになる、確かな
14. 固有の性質
15. 展示物

間違いをそれぞれ2箇所探してください。

• Further more, unlike museums, people can access this information 24 hour a day.

• This is one reason why millions of people visit the Louvre museum in Paris to see the Mona lisa.

カッコ内を正しい順序に並べ替えてください。

• As for me, I [with this / believe that / view and / primarily disagree / point of] museums are essential.

正解 5, 3, 12, 7, 9, 4, 8, 1, 14, 13, 15, 11, 6, 10, 2／Furthermore, hours, Museum, Lisa／primarily disagree with this point of view and believe that

原因とその影響を述べる③

タイプ別にモデルエッセイを分析・再構築することで、重要
表現を身につけてライティング力を高めます。

Foreign shows, dramas and films are regularly shown on television in many countries.

Why are they shown and what impacts do they have on audiences?

モデルエッセイ ◀)48

Television is arguably the most common form of entertainment in the world today. Yet among the programmes aired on TV, a growing proportion are imported from other countries, which raises the question of what influence they have on local audiences.

In spite of differences in language and culture, foreign shows, dramas and films are enjoying a boom in popularity. In showing them, television networks understand that audiences are genuinely interested in other cultures, and television can bring culture directly into their homes. A further reason for their popularity is due to a lack of funds. Wealthy nations can spend a lot of money on making expensive films with famous international stars. However, it is far less expensive for poorer countries to import such films and dub them or add subtitles in local languages rather than produce films themselves.

It could be argued that imported television influences audiences in two ways. On the negative side, some people criticise the content because they believe it is not appropriate in their culture. For example, it may show scenes of violence, or content that is against their religious beliefs. Yet, in the main, the reaction to imported productions is positive, hence their popularity. Audiences enjoy peering into the lifestyles of people in other countries even if the content is sometimes exaggerated. In addition, the programmes enable viewers to gain a better understanding of other cultures.

To summarise, foreign programmes are shown due to interest in other cultures and reasons related to cost. Furthermore, since it is human nature to be interested in others, it is no surprise that imported programmes are enjoying growing popularity around the globe. *(273 words – 15 sentences)*

Self-Study!

　モデルエッセイを分析していきます。エッセイの英文をもとに質問に**英語
で**答えてください。回答がそのままエッセイを書く材料になります。

導入

Q1 エッセイのトピックは？　　Q3 エッセイの全体的な主張は？

Q2 エッセイの論点は？

本体1 放映される理由

Q4 段落の導入文の内容は？　　Q7 2つ目の理由は？

Q5 1つ目の理由は？　　　　　Q8 その具体例・詳細は？

Q6 その具体例・詳細は？　　　Q9 ほかの例・詳細は？

本体2 視聴者への影響

Q10 段落の導入文の内容は？　　Q14 1つ目の肯定的な影響は？

Q11 1つ目の否定的な影響は？　 Q15 2つ目の肯定的な影響は？

Q12 その具体例・詳細は？

Q13 肯定的な影響はどう紹介されて
　　 いる？

結論

Q16 海外の番組が放映される理由はどうまとめられている？

Q17 筆者の結論は？

Task 2

4.タイプ別セルフスタディ3

以下の回答例や自分の分析した結果をもとにエッセイを書きましょう。

導入

Q1 エッセイのトピックは？

A. television = arguably most common entertainment in world

Q2 エッセイの論点は？

A. among programmes, growing proportion = imported

Q3 エッセイの全体的な主張は？

A. what influence on local audiences?

本体1 放映される理由

Q4 段落の導入文の内容は？

A. foreign shows etc. = enjoying boom in popularity

Q5 1つ目の理由は？

A. TV networks understand audiences are interested in other cultures

Q6 その具体例・詳細は？

A. TV brings culture directly into homes

Q7 2つ目の理由は？

A. lack of funds

Q8 その具体例・詳細は？

A. wealthy nations can make expensive films with famous international stars

Q9 ほかの例・詳細は？

A. less expensive for poorer countries to import films and dub or add subtitles

本体2　視聴者への影響

Q10 段落の導入文の内容は？

　　A. imported television influences audiences in two ways

Q11 1つ目の否定的な影響は？

　　A. people criticise content because not appropriate in their culture

Q12 その具体例・詳細は？

　　A. scenes of violence, or content that is against religious beliefs

Q13 肯定的な影響はどう紹介されている？

　　A. in the main, reaction to imported productions = positive

Q14 1つ目の肯定的な影響は？

　　A. audiences enjoy peering into lifestyles in other countries

Q15 2つ目の肯定的な影響は？

　　A. viewers gain better understanding of other cultures

結論

Q16 海外の番組が放映される理由はどうまとめられている？

　　A. shown due to interest in other cultures, cost

Q17 筆者の結論は？

　　A. human nature = interested in others → imported programmes

　　　= growing popularity

Task 2

4.
タイプ別セルフスタディ3

テレビは、今日、世界で最も一般的な娯楽の形だと言っても過言ではない。しかし、テレビで放送される番組の中で、外国から輸入される番組の割合が増えており、それらが地元の視聴者にどのような影響を与えるのかが問題になっている。

言葉や文化の違いにもかかわらず、海外の番組、ドラマ、映画は人気だ。それらを放映しているテレビ局は、視聴者が純粋に異文化に興味を持ち、テレビが文化を家庭に直接持ち込むことができることを理解している。人気のもう1つの理由は、予算の制約によるものだ。裕福な国は、国際的な有名スターを起用した豪華な映画を作るために、莫大な資金を使うことができる。したがって、貧しい国にとっては、自分たちで映画を制作するよりも、そうした映画を輸入して現地の言葉で吹き替えや字幕をつけた方が、はるかにコストがかからないのだ。

輸入されたテレビが視聴者に与える影響は2通りあると言える。否定的な面としては、その内容が自国の文化に適さない、と批判する人がいる。例えば、暴力シーンや宗教的信条に反する内容が含まれているかもしれない。しかし、輸入された作品に対する反応はおおむね肯定的であり、それゆえに人気がある。たとえ内容が誇張されている場合があったとしても、視聴者は他国の人々のライフスタイルをのぞき見ることを楽しんでいるのだ。また、そうした番組によって、視聴者は異文化をより理解することができる。

まとめると、海外の番組は異文化への興味とコストに関わる理由から放映されている。さらに、他者に関心を持つのは人間の本質であるため、輸入された番組が世界中でますます人気となっているのは、当然だ。

エクササイズ

エッセイ中の重要語句と表現をエクササイズで確認します。

語句に当てはまる訳の番号を選んでください。※訳は同じものが2つあります。

____ arguably	____ criticise
____ the most common form of	____ violence
____ imported	____ religious beliefs
____ audiences	____ peering into
____ a boom in popularity	____ exaggerated
____ televisions networks	____ viewers
____ dub	____ human nature
____ subtitles	

1. 視聴者
2. 宗教的信条
3. テレビ網
4. …の最も一般的な形
5. 吹き替えをつける
6. 暴力
7. 視聴者
8. …をのぞき見て
9. 誇張した
10. ほぼ間違いなく、議論の余地はあるが
11. 人気の高まり
12. 字幕
13. 人間の本質
14. 輸入される
15. 批判する

下線部をほかの1語で言い換えてください。

- ... raises the question of what <u>impact</u> they have on ...
- ... culture, <u>overseas</u> shows, dramas and films are enjoying ...
- <u>Rich</u> nations can spend ...

正しい1語を選んでください。

- In [type / order / spite / way] of differences in language and culture, ...
- A further reason for their popularity is [because / due / since / as] to a lack of funds.
- Yet, in the [most / past / minor / main], the reaction to imported productions is positive, ...

正解　10, 4, 14, 1[7], 11, 3, 5, 12, 15, 6, 2, 8, 9, 7[1], 13／influence, foreign, Wealthy／spite, due, main

賛成・反対を述べる④

タイプ別にモデルエッセイを分析・再構築することで、重要表現を身につけてライティング力を高めます。

It is said that many languages with few speakers will disappear over the next 100 years.
Do you agree or disagree that efforts should be made to save such languages?

モデルエッセイ 🔊49

Presently, there are around 7,000 languages on Earth. While dominant ones are expected to survive in the future, some people believe that minor ones will become extinct, which I think is a great loss. As such, it is my strong belief that we ought to preserve languages with few speakers.

First and foremost, human culture is rich because of its diversity, and a key aspect of that diversity is languages. Therefore, if we lose many languages spoken on Earth, humanity will become culturally poorer. Imagine travelling around the world a century from now and encountering the same language wherever you go. In this scenario, communication would be easier but your experiences would be far less enjoyable due to a lack of difference in language.

Secondly, when a language becomes extinct, we lose ways of thinking that define the culture of its speakers. For instance, in the Cherokee language, there is no word for 'goodbye'. Instead, these Native American Indians say 'I will see you again'. Moreover, since many minor languages are unrecorded and have dwindling numbers of speakers, such precious differences in human thought are permanently lost when a language dies.

A final point is that governments, organisations and ordinary members of the public put a great deal of time and energy into protecting endangered species of animals and plants from extinction. Therefore, it seems only natural that minor languages, which are an inherent part of humanity, should be protected, too.

To sum up my position, efforts should be made to stop minor languages from disappearing, since they enrich humanity in various ways. If they are not protected, important aspects of the world's cultural treasure will be eroded and possibly lost forever. *(282 words – 15 sentences)*

Self-Study!

　モデルエッセイを分析していきます。エッセイの英文をもとに質問に**英語で**答えてください。回答がそのままエッセイを書く材料になります。

導入

Q1 エッセイのトピックは?　　Q3 エッセイの全体的な主張は?

Q2 エッセイの論点は?

本体1 賛成の理由1

Q4 言語を保護する1つ目の理由は?　　Q6 ほかの例・詳細は?

Q5 その具体例・詳細は?

本体2 賛成の理由2

Q7 2つ目の理由は?　　Q9 ほかの例・詳細は?

Q8 その具体例・詳細は?

本体3 賛成の理由3

Q10 3つ目の理由は?　　Q11 その具体例・詳細は?

結論

Q12 主張はどう言い換えられている?

Q13 その理由は?

Q14 何もしなかった結果、どんなことが起こり得る?

Task 2

5. タイプ別セルフスタディ4

313

以下の回答例や自分の分析した結果をもとにエッセイを書きましょう。

導入

Q1 エッセイのトピックは？

A. 7,000 languages on Earth

Q2 エッセイの論点は？

A. some people believe: dominant ones = survive, minor ones = extinct

Q3 エッセイの全体的な主張は？

A. great loss, ought to preserve languages with few speakers

本体1　賛成の理由1

Q4 言語を保護する1つ目の理由は？

A. human culture = rich due to diversity ← → languages

Q5 その具体例・詳細は？

A. if lose many languages = culturally poorer

Q6 ほかの例・詳細は？

A. imagine same language everywhere a century from now

communication = easier but experiences less enjoyable

本体2　賛成の理由2

Q7 2つ目の理由は？

A. we lose ways of thinking that define culture of speakers

Q8 その具体例・詳細は？

A. Cherokee language: no 'Goodbye' → 'I will see you again'

Q9 ほかの例・詳細は？

A. minor languages = unrecorded & dwindling speakers, so precious

differences in human thought lost when language dies

本体3 賛成の理由3

Q10 3つ目の理由は？

A. governments (etc.) put time & energy into protecting endangered animals & plants from extinction

Q11 その具体例・詳細は？

A. minor languages (part of humanity) should be protected, too

結論

Q12 主張はどう言い換えられている？

A. efforts should stop minor languages from disappearing

Q13 その理由は？

A. they (lang.) enrich humanity in various ways

Q14 何もしなかった結果、どんなことが起こり得る？

A. if not protected, important aspects of cultural treasure eroded → possibly lost forever

現在、地球上には約7000の言語が存在する。優勢な言語は今後も生き残ると予想されるが、少数言語は絶滅するという説もあり、これは大きな損失だと思う。だから、話者の少ない言語は保護していくべきだというのが私の強い考えだ。

まず何よりも、人間の文化は多様だからこそ豊かなのであって、言語はその多様性の重要な側面だ。したがって、地球上で話されている言語の多くを失えば、人類は文化的に貧しくなる。今から100年後に世界中を旅して、どこへ行っても同じ言語に出合うことを想像してみてほしい。この筋書きでは、コミュニケーションは簡単になるが、言語の違いがないことで、はるかに楽しくない体験となるはずだ。

第2に、言語が消滅すると、その言語を話す人の文化を特徴づける思考方法が失われる。例えば、チェロキー語には「さようなら」という言葉がない。その代わり、このネイティブアメリカンのインディアンたちは「また会おう」と言う。さらに、少数言語の多くが記録されておらず、話者も減少しているので、言語が滅ぶと、人間の思考のこうした貴重な違いは永久に失われてしまうのだ。

最後の点として、政府や組織、一般の人々は、存続の危機にさらされた動物や植物を絶滅から守るために多大な時間とエネルギーを費やしている。したがって、人類の本質的な部分である少数言語も保護されるべきなのは当然に思える。

私の考えをまとめると、少数言語は様々な形で人類を豊かにしているので、消滅しないよう努力すべきだ。もし保護されなければ、世界の文化的財産の重要な側面が侵食され、永遠に失われることになるだろう。

エクササイズ

エッセイ中の重要語句と表現をエクササイズで確認します。

語句に当てはまる訳の番号を選んでください。

____ dominant		____ human thought	
____ survive		____ endangered species	
____ extinct		____ extinction	
____ diversity		____ an inherent part of	
____ humanity		____ enrich	
____ define		____ cultural treasure	
____ unrecorded		____ eroded	
____ dwindling numbers of			

1. 絶滅危機にある種	5. 優勢な	9. 豊かにする	14. 絶滅した
2. 損なわれた、むしばんだ	6. …に生まれつき備わっている部分	10. 人間の思考	15. 特徴づける、定義する
3. 文化的財産	7. 記録されていない	11. 多様 (性)	
4. …の (数の) 減少	8. 人類	12. 生き残る	
		13. 絶滅	

同じ意味になるよう、語句を答えてください。

- Today/Nowadays = _____

- one-hundred years later = _____

- for always = _____

エッセイと1文字目を参考に空所を完成させてください。

- As such, it is my strong b_ _ _ _ _ that ...

- ... and a key a_ _ _ _ _ of that ...

- Therefore, it seems only n_ _ _ _ _ _ that ...

正解 5, 12, 14, 11, 8, 15, 7, 4, 10, 1, 13, 6, 9, 3, 2／Presently, a century from now,
permanently/forever／belief, aspect, natural

物事の両面と
意見を述べる④

タイプ別にモデルエッセイを分析・再構築することで、重要表現を身につけてライティング力を高めます。

Some people believe that sending criminals to prison is not the best way to deal with them.
Discuss the merits and demerits of prison systems.

モデルエッセイ ◀))50

When a perpetrator is found guilty of committing a crime, one of the most common punishments he or she receives is a prison sentence. However, some members of society believe this is not the best way to deal with people who break the law. As such, this essay will consider imprisonment in terms of its advantages and disadvantages.

Regarding merits, prisons help many convicts to return to society as law-abiding citizens. Since they are deprived of a normal lifestyle and freedom, inmates miss the outside world, especially their family and friends. Moreover, imprisonment gives them time to reflect on their crimes and how they affected the victims. In addition, it is said that an educated society is a safer society. Accordingly, modern prisons are equipped with libraries and computers, thereby encouraging prisoners to study, raise their level of education and follow a different path in life after being released.

Yet every issue has two sides, so it can be argued that imprisonment has certain demerits. For instance, modern prisons are relatively comfortable, and unlike in the outside world, prisoners do not pay for food, rent, heating or medical costs. For this reason, after being released from prison, some people deliberately commit further offences in order to return there. A second drawback concerns the fact that offenders are surrounded by other convicts rather than ordinary citizens. In this situation, some become more aggressive and violent in order to protect themselves during their prison sentence.

To sum up, there are relevant arguments both for and against prison systems. Clearly, this is a difficult issue, but overall I believe prisons are necessary, especially to deal with people who commit serious crimes, and thus keep society safer. *(283 words – 15 sentences)*

Self-Study!

　モデルエッセイを分析していきます。エッセイの英文をもとに質問に**英語で**答えてください。回答がそのままエッセイを書く材料になります。

導入

Q1 エッセイのトピックは？　　　Q3 エッセイの全体的な主張は？

Q2 エッセイの論点は？

本体1 刑務所のメリット

Q4 刑務所のメリットは？　　　　Q7 2つ目のメリットは？

Q5 その具体例・詳細は？　　　　Q8 その具体例・詳細は？

Q6 ほかの例・詳細は？

本体2 刑務所のデメリット

Q9 段落の導入文の内容は？　　　Q12 2つ目のデメリットはどう紹介

Q10 1つ目のデメリットはどう紹介　　　 されている？

　　 されている？　　　　　　　 Q13 2つ目のデメリットは？

Q11 1つ目のデメリットは？

結論

Q14 エッセイの主張はどう言い換えられている？

Q15 筆者の意見は？

以下の回答例や自分の分析した結果をもとにエッセイを書きましょう。

導入

Q1 エッセイのトピックは？

A. perpetrator commits crime, common punishment = prison sentence

Q2 エッセイの論点は？

A. some believe: not best way to deal with people who break law

Q3 エッセイの全体的な主張は？

A. essay will consider imprisonment: advantages & disadvantages

本体1 刑務所のメリット

Q4 刑務所のメリットは？

A. convicts return to society as law-abiding citizens

Q5 その具体例・詳細は？

A. deprived of normal lifestyle and freedom, miss outside world, esp. family & friends

Q6 ほかの例・詳細は？

A. gives inmates time to reflect on crimes and how affected victims

Q7 2つ目のメリットは？

A. educated society = safer, so prisons = equipped with libraries & computers

Q8 その具体例・詳細は？

A. prisoners study, raise education level → follow different path in life after released

本体2 刑務所のデメリット

Q9 段落の導入文の内容は？

A. every issue = two sides: imprisonment has demerits

Q10 1つ目のデメリットはどう紹介されている？

A. modern prisons = comfortable, prisoners do not pay for food, etc.

Q11 1つ目のデメリットは？

A. after released, some commit further crimes to return

Q12 2つ目のデメリットはどう紹介されている？

A. offenders surrounded by other convicts

Q13 2つ目のデメリットは？

A. some become more aggressive and violent to protect themselves

結論

Q14 エッセイの主張はどう言い換えられている？

A. relevant arguments for/against prison systems

Q15 筆者の意見は？

A. prisons = necessary, esp. for people who commit serious crimes, & keep society safer

Task 2

5. タイプ別セルフスタディ4

加害者が罪を犯したことで有罪になった場合、人が受ける最も一般的な罰の1つが実刑判決だ。しかし社会の一部の人たちは、法律を破った人への対処法として、これが最善ではないと考えている。そこで、このエッセイでは懲役刑について、その利点と欠点という観点から考える。

メリットについては、刑務所は多くの受刑者が法を守る市民として社会に復帰するのを助ける。普通の生活や自由を奪われることから、受刑者は外の世界、特に家族や友人を恋しく思う。さらに、刑務所に入ることで、自分の犯罪や、それが被害者に与えた影響について考える時間が与えられる。さらに、教育された社会はより安全な社会だと言われる。そのため、現代の刑務所には図書館やコンピューターが設置されていて、それによって受刑者が勉強し、自分の教育水準を上げて、出所後に別の道を歩むことを促している。

しかしどんな問題にも2つの面があり、刑務所にはいくつかデメリットもある。例えば、現代の刑務所は比較的快適で、外の世界と違って囚人は食費、家賃、暖房費、医療費などを支払う必要がない。そのため、出所後、刑務所に戻るためにわざと罪を犯す人もいる。第2の欠点は、犯罪者が普通の市民ではなく、ほかの囚人に囲まれている、という事実に関わる。このような状況においては、服役中に自分の身を守るため、より攻撃的で暴力的になる者もいる。

要約すると、刑務所制度の賛否にはどちらも妥当な論拠がある。明らかにこれは難しい問題だが、全体として、私は刑務所が必要だと考えている。理由は、特に重大な罪を犯した人間に対処し、社会をより安全に保つためだ。

エクササイズ

エッセイ中の重要語句と表現をエクササイズで確認します。

語句に当てはまる訳の番号を選んでください。

_____ committing a crime   _____ (be) equipped with

_____ punishments   _____ thereby

_____ a prison sentence   _____ the outside world

_____ deal with   _____ deliberately

_____ break the law   _____ offences

_____ imprisonment   _____ aggressive

_____ law-abiding citizens   _____ relevant arguments

_____ victims

1. 犯罪	5. 被害者	9. 法を守る市民	13. 投獄、懲役刑
2. それによって	6. 罰	10. 外の世界	14. …に対処する
3. 妥当な根拠	7. 法を破る	11. 故意に	15. …が設置されている
4. 攻撃的	8. 罪を犯して	12. 実刑判決、実刑	

類似する意味になるよう、1文字目を参考に単語を答えてください。

• perpetrator = c_____ = i_____ = p_____ = o_____

エッセイを参考にして、動詞に続く前置詞を答えてください。

• guilty _____

• deprived _____

• reflect _____

• pay _____

正解　8, 6, 12, 14, 7, 13, 9, 5, 15, 2, 10, 11, 1, 4, 3 ／ convict, inmate, prisoner, offender ／ of, of, on, for

Self-Study!
問題と解決策を提示する④

タイプ別にモデルエッセイを分析・再構築することで、重要表現を身につけてライティング力を高めます。

Obesity is on the rise in various countries around the world.
What are some of the causes? How can society resolve this issue?

モデルエッセイ ◀)51

Changing lifestyles are dramatically affecting societies in many parts of the world, and one result is a sharp rise in the number of overweight people. This essay will explore some causes related to this negative phenomenon and offer potential solutions.

One obvious cause of obesity concerns unhealthy eating habits. People today tend to consume a lot of high-calorie food and drinks (sweets, fast food, fizzy drinks, etc.) containing large amounts of salt, fat and sugar. Moreover, the media constantly advertises such products, thus encouraging consumption among populations. Another reason is our sedentary lifestyles, as advances in technology mean that people spend much more time sitting than moving, especially in front of computers, smartphones and television screens.

To counter this unhealthy trend, I believe three approaches are necessary. First of all, governments must force food companies to reduce the amounts of additives and preservatives in their products and ban advertisements for junk food. Furthermore, frequent media campaigns ought to encourage parents to provide their children with balanced meals containing more fruit and vegetables. Finally, and perhaps most important of all, schools should place greater emphasis on teaching students about healthy eating habits. Then they might continue to eat nutritious food as they get older. If these three measures are taken, more people will avoid health issues, including heart attacks and cancer, later in life.

To conclude, in order to reduce obesity in society, governments, the media and parents ought to make efforts that encourage everyone in society, especially children, to eat healthier meals. By doing so, we should see tangible results in that people will be healthier and will live longer lives.

(271 words – 15 sentences)

Self-Study!

　モデルエッセイを分析していきます。エッセイの英文をもとに質問に**英語で**答えてください。回答がそのままエッセイを書く材料になります。

導入

Q1 エッセイのトピックは？　　　　Q3 エッセイの全体的な主張は？

Q2 エッセイの論点は？

本体1　肥満の原因

Q4 肥満の1つ目の原因は？　　　　Q7 その具体例・詳細は？

Q5 その具体例・詳細は？　　　　　Q8 3つ目の原因は？

Q6 1つ目と関連する2つ目の原因は？　Q9 その具体例・詳細は？

本体2　解決策

Q10 解決策はいくつ必要？　　　　　Q13 3つ目の解決策は？

Q11 肥満の増加に対する1つ目の　　Q14 具体的にはどんな結果が述べ
　　解決策は？　　　　　　　　　　　　られている？

Q12 2つ目の解決策とその結果は？

結論

Q15 解決策はどうまとめられてる？

Q16 全体的な結果はどう述べられている？

以下の回答例や自分の分析した結果をもとにエッセイを書きましょう。

導入

Q1 エッセイのトピックは？

A. changing life patterns = dramatically affecting societies in world

Q2 エッセイの論点は？

A. one result = sharp rise in number of overweight people

Q3 エッセイの全体的な主張は？

A. essay will explore causes and offer solutions

本体1 肥満の原因

Q4 肥満の1つ目の原因は？

A. unhealthy eating habits

Q5 その具体例・詳細は？

A. people consume a lot of high-calorie food & drinks (sweets, fast food, fizzy drinks)

Q6 1つ目と関連する2つ目の原因は？

A. media constantly advertises such products

Q7 その具体例・詳細は？

A. encourages consumption

Q8 3つ目の原因は？

A. sedentary lifestyles ← technology

Q9 その具体例・詳細は？

A. more time sitting than moving (computers, smartphones, television)

本体2 解決策

Q10 解決策はいくつ必要？

A. three approaches

Q11 肥満の増加に対する１つ目の解決策は？

A. governments force food companies to reduce additives & preservatives, ban junk food advertisements

Q12 ２つ目の解決策とその結果は？

A. media campaigns encourage parents to provide children with balanced meals (more fruits & vegetables)

Q13 ３つ目の解決策は？

A. schools → more emphasis on teaching healthy eating habits

Q14 具体的にはどんな結果が述べられている？

A. if measures taken, more people will avoid health issues later in life

結論

Q15 解決策はどうまとめられている？

A. governments, media, parents encourage everyone (esp. children) to eat healthier meals

Q16 全体的な結果はどう述べられている？

A. people will be healthier and live longer lives

生活様式の変化は、世界各地で社会に劇的な影響を及ぼしている。その結果の1つが、太り過ぎの人が急増していることだ。このエッセイでは、この負の現象に関連する原因をいくつか探り、可能性のある解決策を提案する。

肥満の明らかな原因の1つは、不健康な食習慣に関係する。現代人は塩分、脂肪分、そして糖分を多く含む、高カロリーな食べ物や飲み物（お菓子やファーストフード、炭酸飲料など）を多く摂取する傾向にある。さらに、メディアは常にそのような製品を宣伝し、人々の間で消費を促している。もう1つの理由として私たちの座りっぱなしの生活様式がある。テクノロジーの進歩によって、動く時間よりも、特にパソコンやスマートフォン、テレビ画面の前で座っている時間の方がはるかに長くなっているためだ。

この不健康な傾向に対抗するためには、3つの方法が必要だと考える。まず、政府は食品会社に商品の添加物や保存料の量を減らすよう求め、ジャンクフードの広告を禁止するべきだ。さらに、頻繁なメディア・キャンペーンを通じて、今よりもフルーツや野菜を含む、バランスの取れた食事を子どもに与えるよう、親に推奨する必要がある。最後に、おそらく最も重要なのは、学校が生徒に健康的な食習慣を教えることにもっと注力すべき、という点だ。そうすれば、大人になっても栄養価の高い食事を続けるかもしれない。この3つの対策が行われれば、より多くの人が、後年、心臓発作やがんなどの健康問題を避けることができる。

結論として、社会の肥満を解消するために政府、メディア、そして親は、社会の誰もが、特に子どもたちがより健康的な食事ができるように尽力するべきだ。そうすれば、人々はより健康になり、より長生きできるようになるという具体的な結果が得られるはずだ。

エクササイズ

エッセイ中の重要語句と表現をエクササイズで確認します。

語句に当てはまる訳の番号を選んでください。

____ overweight ____ place greater emphasis on

____ consume ____ healthy eating habits

____ sedentary lifestyles ____ nutritious food

____ advances in ____ avoid

____ force ____ heart attacks

____ additives and preservatives ____ cancer

____ media campaigns ____ tangible results

____ balanced meals

1. 健康的な食習慣	5. メディアを使った	9. 座りがちな生活様式	13. 心臓発作
2. 強いる	キャンペーン	10. がん	14. …にもっと注力
3. バランスの取れた	6. …の進歩	11. 肥満の	する、…をさら
食事	7. 添加物と保存料	12. 具体的な・目に	に重んじる
4. 栄養価の高い食事	8. 避ける	見える結果	15. 飲食する

カッコ内を正しい順序に並べ替えてください。

• This essay will explore some [this / phenomenon / to / causes / negative / related] and [solutions / offer / potential].

1文字目を参考に空所に適切な1語を入れてください。

• First of all, governments m_ _ _ force food companies to ...

• Furthermore, frequent media campaigns o_ _ _ _ to encourage parents to ...

• Finally, and perhaps most important of all, schools s_ _ _ _ _ place greater emphasis on ...

正解 11, 15, 9, 6, 2, 7, 5, 3, 14, 1, 4, 8, 13, 10, 12 ╱ causes related to this negative phenomenon, offer potential solutions ╱ must, ought, should

Task 2

5. タイプ別セルフスタディ4

329

Task
2

タイプ4

Self-Study!

議論を評価する ④

タイプ別にモデルエッセイを分析・再構築することで、重要
表現を身につけてライティング力を高めます。

Some people fear that as globalisation connects more and more nations, it will
lead to the total loss of cultural identity.
To what extent do you think this will actually happen?

モデルエッセイ　　　　　　　　　　　　　　　　　　　　　　**◀))52**

There is no doubt that globalisation is accelerating with each passing day. As a
result of this phenomenon, there is a concern that people will eventually lose all
sense of cultural identity. Although I do not believe it will happen to this degree,
I do think cultural diversity will decline to a great extent.

On the one hand, certain features of individual cultures will never totally vanish.
For instance, despite a continuing rise in the popularity of Western-style fast
food around the world, people will still prefer their local ethnic food over foreign
food. In addition, art that reflects particular cultures will never be completely
lost. This point is supported by the fact that many examples of ancient and
traditional art have survived for hundreds and even thousands of years until
today.

However, as globalisation progresses, it is undeniable that many aspects of
cultural identity will be lost. Take clothing, for instance. Instead of wearing
traditional garments, people in the majority of the world's countries now wear
Western clothes, such as jeans, T-shirts, baseball caps and suits. Furthermore,
national currencies, which show symbols of each country, might disappear if all
nations decide to use a single currency in years to come. Moreover, there is a
high possibility that this shared global currency will be in digital form. Finally,
languages will be affected, too. In fact, many have already become extinct or are

in danger of disappearing soon on account of the spread of major languages such as English.

To conclude, globalisation will eventually lead to an extensive loss of cultural identity. Therefore, since humanity is rich because of its cultural differences, everyone should protect their cultural identity to avoid ending up with only one culture on Earth.

(287 words – 16 sentences)

Self-Study!

　モデルエッセイを分析していきます。エッセイの英文をもとに質問に**英語で**答えてください。回答がそのままエッセイを書く材料になります。

導入

Q1 エッセイのトピックは？　　　Q3 エッセイの全体的な主張は？

Q2 エッセイの論点は？

本体1 文化的アイデンティティを失わない

Q4 議論の弱い側（一部同意）を　　Q5 1つ目の具体例・詳細は？
　　どう紹介している？　　　　　Q6 2つ目の具体例・詳細は？

本体2 文化的アイデンティティを失う

Q7 議論の強い側（主に反対）を　　Q10 2つ目の具体例は？
　　どう紹介している？　　　　　Q11 その詳細は？

Q8 1つ目の具体例は？　　　　　Q12 3つ目の具体例は？

Q9 その詳細は？　　　　　　　　Q13 その詳細は？

結論

Q14 筆者の主な意見は？

Q15 筆者はどうコメントしている？

Q16 筆者はどんな行動を推奨している？

以下の回答例や自分の分析した結果をもとにエッセイを書きましょう。

導入

Q1 エッセイのトピックは?

A. globalisation = accelerating each passing day

Q2 エッセイの論点は?

A. there is concern people will lose sense of cultural identity

Q3 エッセイの全体的な主張は?

A. although not happen to this degree, cultural diversity will decline to great extent

本体1 文化的アイデンティティを失わない

Q4 議論の弱い側(一部同意)をどう紹介している?

A. certain features = never totally vanish

Q5 1つ目の具体例・詳細は?

A. Western-style food: despite rise in popularity, people will still prefer local food

Q6 2つ目の具体例・詳細は?

A. art: ancient, traditional art survived hundreds/thousands of years

本体2 文化的アイデンティティを失う

Q7 議論の強い側(主に反対)をどう紹介している?

A. undeniable that many aspects of cultural identity = lost

Q8 1つ目の具体例は?

A. clothing (traditional garments)

Q9 その詳細は?

A. instead, people now wear Western clothes (jeans, T-shirts, etc.)

[Q10] 2つ目の具体例は？

A. national currencies (show symbols of country) → might disappear if all nations use single currency

[Q11] その詳細は？

A. high possibility that global currency = digital form

[Q12] 3つ目の具体例は？

A. languages

[Q13] その詳細は？

A. many already extinct/disappearing on account of spread of major languages (English)

結論

[Q14] 筆者の主な意見は？

A. globalisation → extensive loss of cultural identity

[Q15] 筆者はどうコメントしている？

A. humanity = rich because of cultural differences

[Q16] 筆者はどんな行動を推奨している？

A. should protect cultural identity to avoid only one culture on Earth

グローバル化が日を追うごとに加速していることは疑いようがない。この現象の結果、やがて文化的アイデンティティの感覚が完全に失われてしまうのではないかと懸念されている。私はそこまで至らないにしても、文化の多様性は大きく損なわれると考えている。

一方で、完全に消えることはない個々の文化の特徴もある。例えば、西洋風のファーストフードの人気が世界中で続いているが、人々はやはり外国の料理よりも地元の民族料理を好むだろう。加えて、特定の文化を反映した芸術が完全に失われることはない。このことは、今日に至るまで数百年、数千年もの時を経て、古代芸術や伝統芸術が伝承されているという、多くの事例に裏づけられている。

しかし、グローバル化が進めば、文化的なアイデンティティの多くの側面が失われることは否定できない。例えば衣服がある。世界の大半の国の人々は伝統的な衣服ではなく、ジーンズやTシャツ、野球帽、スーツといった西洋の衣服を身につけるようになった。さらに、各国の象徴が描かれた自国通貨も、この先すべての国が単一通貨を使うことになれば、消滅してしまうかもしれない。しかも、この世界共通通貨は、デジタル化される可能性が高い。最後に、言語も影響を受けるだろう。実際、英語などの主要言語の普及により、多くの言語がすでに消滅し、また近い将来消滅する危機にひんしている。

結論として、グローバル化によって、文化的アイデンティティが大きく失われることになる。したがって、人類は文化の違いゆえに豊かであることを考慮すると、地球上にたった1つの文化しか残されていない、という結果にならないように、誰もが自分の文化的アイデンティティを守るべきだ。

エクササイズ

エッセイ中の重要語句と表現をエクササイズで確認します。

語句に当てはまる訳の番号を選んでください。

____ phenomenon		____ in years to come	
____ to this degree		____ in digital form	
____ reflects		____ on account of	
____ undeniable		____ eventually	
____ clothing		____ an extensive loss of	
____ traditional garments		____ rich	
____ national currencies		____ ending up with	
____ single currency			

1. 国の通貨	6. 反映する	9. …のために	14. 否定できない
2. …の多大な損失	7. …で終わって、	10. 単一通貨	15. 豊かな
3. 結局は	結局…となって	11. 伝統的な衣服	
4. 今後	8. これほど、このぐ	12. 現象	
5. 衣類	らいまで	13. デジタルの形式で	

同じ意味になるよう、語句を答えてください。

- lose = v_____ = d_____ = become e_____

正しい方を選んでください。

- This point is [support / supported] by the [fact / facts] that many
  [example / examples] of ancient and traditional art have survived for
  [hundreds / hundred] and even [thousands / thousand] of years
  [until / by / since] today.

原因とその影響を述べる④

タイプ別にモデルエッセイを分析・再構築することで、重要表現を身につけてライティング力を高めます。

In the history of humans, there have been many wars.
Why do such conflicts occur? What impacts do they have?

モデルエッセイ ◀53

Unfortunately, the majority of countries experience armed conflict at some point in their history. In some cases, the wars are domestic while others take place across international borders. This essay will highlight reasons for such confrontations and how they affect the people and places concerned.

One cause of war is the desire for revenge. This may be sought for a previous defeat or to punish a nation or particular region. For example, Germany was punished for World War I, and this was a key factor for the country starting World War II. A further motive is economic gain. Throughout history, countries have fought over natural resources, including gold, oil and land. Moreover, scientists believe that as the global population rises, future conflicts will arise mainly due to a scarcity of basic resources, especially food and water.

Needless to say, many soldiers and civilians are seriously injured or killed in war. Those who do survive often suffer trauma and anxiety for many years, especially children. Wars also create many refugees who try to escape to other countries, which can cause a burden there. As a result of these factors, communities are destroyed and families are torn apart.

In addition, there is mass destruction of cities and infrastructure, which can have long-lasting effects on a nation's economy. To rebuild a country, though, not only takes time but also requires an enormous amount of money. However, with a devastated infrastructure, it is difficult to quickly return to normal life and restart the economy.

In conclusion, two reasons for military conflicts are the desire for revenge and economic gain. However, war only leads to great human loss and suffering, and negatively affects economies during and long after the conflicts have ended.

(286 words – 18 sentences)

Self-Study!

　モデルエッセイを分析していきます。エッセイの英文をもとに質問に**英語で**答えてください。回答がそのままエッセイを書く材料になります。

導入

Q1 エッセイのトピックは？　　Q3 エッセイの全体的な主張は？

Q2 エッセイの論点は？

本体1 原因——戦争

Q4 戦争の原因の1つは？　　　Q7 もう1つの原因は？

Q5 その詳細は？　　　　　　 Q8 その詳細は？

Q6 その具体例は？　　　　　 Q9 将来の可能性は？

本体2 結果——人

Q10 戦争が人に与える影響の1つは？ Q13 地域社会や人々にとってどんな

Q11 その詳細は？　　　　　　　　　 結果をもたらす？

Q12 第2の影響は？

本体3 結果——国

Q14 戦争が国に及ぼす影響の1つは？ Q16 ほかの具体例・詳細は？

Q15 その詳細は？

結論

Q17 戦争の理由はどうまとめられている？

Q18 影響はどうまとめられている？

以下の回答例や自分の分析した結果をもとにエッセイを書きましょう。

導入

Q1 エッセイのトピックは？

　A. majority of countries experience armed conflict

Q2 エッセイの論点は？

　A. some cases = domestic, others = international

Q3 エッセイの全体的な主張は？

　A. essay will highlight reasons for confrontations, how they affect

　　people & places

本体1　原因──戦争

Q4 戦争の原因の1つは？

　A. desire for revenge

Q5 その詳細は？

　A. may be for previous defeat or to punish

Q6 その具体例は？

　A. Germany: punished for WWI = key factor for starting WWII

Q7 もう1つの原因は？

　A. economic gain

Q8 その詳細は？

　A. countries have fought over natural resources (gold, oil, land)

Q9 将来の可能性は？

　A. scientists: future conflicts ← scarcity of food & water

本体2　結果──人

Q10 戦争が人に与える影響の1つは？

　A. soldiers & civilians injured or killed

Q11 その詳細は？

A. survivors suffer trauma & anxiety (esp. children)

Q12 第2の影響は？

A. creates refugees → burden on other countries

Q13 地域社会や人々にとってどんな結果をもたらす？

A. communities = destroyed, families = torn apart

本体3 結果——国

Q14 戦争が国に及ぼす影響の1つは？

A. mass destruction of cities & infrastructure = lasting effects on economy

Q15 その詳細は？

A. to rebuild takes time & money

Q16 ほかの具体例・詳細は？

A. devastated infrastructure = difficult to quickly return to normal life & restart economy

結論

Q17 戦争の理由はどうまとめられている？

A. desire for revenge & economic gain

Q18 影響はどうまとめられている？

A. war → human loss & suffering, negatively affects economies during & after conflicts ended

Task 2

5. タイプ別セルフスタディ4

残念ながら、大多数の国はその歴史のある時点で武力紛争を経験している。国内での戦争もあれば、国境を越えて行われる戦争もある。このエッセイでは、このような対立が起こる理由、そしてそれが関係する人々や場所にどのような影響を与えるのかに焦点を当てる。

戦争の原因の1つは復讐の欲求だ。これは以前の敗北に対するものであったり、国家や特定の地域を罰するためのものであったりする。例えば、ドイツは第一次世界大戦で処罰され、これが第二次世界大戦を始める大きな要因となった。もう1つの動機は経済的利益だ。歴史上、各国は金、石油、土地などの天然資源をめぐって争ってきた。さらに、科学者たちは世界人口の増加に伴い、将来的には主に食料と水といった基本的な資源の不足から紛争が起こると考えている。

言うまでもなく、戦争では多くの兵士や民間人が重傷を負ったり死亡したりする。生き残った人たちも、長年にわたってトラウマや不安にさいなまれることが多く、特に子どもたちがそうだ。また、戦争は他国に逃れようとする多くの難民を生み、その地にとって負担となることがある。これらの要素の結果として、地域社会が破壊され、家族が引き裂かれることになる。

さらに、都市やインフラの大規模な破壊が起こり、国の経済にも長期的な影響を及ぼしかねない。だが、国を再建するには、時間だけでなく、莫大な資金が必要となる。ところがインフラが破壊された状態では、すぐに通常の生活に戻り、経済を再開させることは困難だ。

結論として、軍事衝突の2つの理由は、復讐心と経済的利益だ。しかし戦争は大きな人的損失と苦痛をもたらすだけであり、紛争中も、紛争が終わった後にもずっと、経済に好ましくない影響を与えることになる。

エクササイズ

エッセイ中の重要語句と表現をエクササイズで確認します。

語句に当てはまる訳の番号を選んでください。 ※訳は同じものが2つあります。

＿＿ armed conflict	＿＿ civilians
＿＿ across international borders	＿＿ trauma and anxiety
＿＿ revenge	＿＿ refugees
＿＿ a previous defeat	＿＿ torn apart
＿＿ punish	＿＿ mass destruction
＿＿ economic gain	＿＿ devastated infrastructure
＿＿ a scarcity of	＿＿ military conflicts
＿＿ soldiers	

1. 以前の敗北	5. 経済的利益	9. 引き裂かれた	13. 難民
2. …の不足	6. 破壊されたインフラ	10. トラウマと不安	14. 国境を越えて
3. 民間人	7. 武力紛争、軍事紛争	11. 兵士	15. 武力紛争、軍事紛争
4. 大規模な破壊	8. 罰する	12. 復讐	

エッセイを参考にして、以下の表現を言い換えてください。

• During the whole of ＝ ＿＿＿＿＿＿＿

• Of course, ＝ ＿＿＿＿＿ ＿＿＿＿＿ ＿＿＿＿＿

• On account of ＝ ＿＿＿＿＿ ＿＿＿＿＿ ＿＿＿＿＿ ＿＿＿＿＿

but, not, also, only のいずれかを空所に入れてください。

• To rebuild a country, though, (　　　　) (　　　　) takes time

(　　　　) (　　　　) requires an enormous amount of money.

Task 2

5.
タ
イ
プ
別
セ
ル
フ
ス
タ
デ
ィ
4

正解 7[15], 14, 12, 1, 8, 5, 2, 11, 3, 10, 13, 9, 4, 6, 15[7]／Throughout, Needless to say, As a result of／not, only, but, also

問題例50

Task 2で出題が予想されるトピックについて、問題例を50用意しました。タイプ1〜5の順に並んだものが10セットあります。ご自身でエッセイを完成させて、ライティング力にさらに磨きをかけてください。

※問題のみです。モデルエッセイはありません。

1. FEWER WORKING DAYS　　Type 1

Some people have suggested that full-time work should be reduced from 5-6 days to 3-4 days per week.

Do you agree or disagree with this suggestion?

2. EDUCATION & GENDER　　Type 2

Some people feel that schools should be mixed with both girls and boys attending while others feel that genders ought to be separated.

Discuss both views and give your own opinion.

3. PEOPLE in HISTORY　　Type 3

Many young people today know more about international pop or film stars than about famous people in the history of their own country.

Why is this? What can be done to increase young people's interest in their country's famous people?

4. MOBILE PHONES　　Type 4

Many people think that mobile phones should be banned in public places such as libraries, shops and public transport.

How far do you agree or disagree with this way of thinking?

5. COOKING MEALS　　Type 5

Nowadays, fewer people are cooking food at home. Instead, they tend to eat out, buy ready-made meals from supermarkets and convenience stores or use food delivery services.

What are some causes of this tendency? What effects can it have?

6. PUBLIC CELEBRATIONS Type 1

Most countries have public celebrations (such as national holidays and festivals, etc.). However, some people believe they are expensive and unnecessary.

What is your opinion on this matter?

7. POPULARITY of SHOPPING Type 2

In many countries, shopping is now one of the most popular leisure activities among teenagers and young adults.

What are the positive and negative aspects of this trend?

8. SHORTAGE of FARMERS Type 3

Agriculture is very important, but in many countries there is a shortage of young people who want to become farmers.

What are some causes of this shortage? How can this issue be resolved?

9. TV vs LIVE ENTERTAINMENT Type 4

Watching a live performance such as a play, concert, or sporting event is more enjoyable than watching the same event on television.

To what extent do you agree or disagree?

10. AGEING POPULATION Type 5

Many countries are experiencing a steady rise in their ageing population. What are some causes of this phenomenon? How will it affect society in future years?

11. UNFAIR EARNINGS Type 1

Celebrities, famous entertainers and sports stars earn far too much money in comparison with ordinary people who do important jobs for the benefit of society.

Do you agree or disagree with this opinion?

■ 12. INTERNET for EDUCATION, BUSINESS ⟨ Type 2 ⟩

The number of people using the internet for educational and business purposes is rapidly increasing.

What are the merits and drawbacks of this trend?

■ 13. YOUNG PEOPLE & LEISURE ACTIVITIES ⟨ Type 3 ⟩

More and more young people stay indoors and use social media or play computer games for many hours per day.

What problems can this lead to? What can be done to solve this problem?

■ 14. SCHOOL SUBJECTS ⟨ Type 4 ⟩

Schools should primarily teach academic subjects so that students can pass exams, and practical skills such as cooking should not be taught.

How far do you agree or disagree?

■ 15. IMPORTED PRODUCTS ⟨ Type 5 ⟩

Nowadays, people like to buy a wide variety of products that are imported from other countries.

What are the reasons for this? Is this a positive or negative development?

■ 16. NATIONAL FOOD SUPPLY ⟨ Type 1 ⟩

Countries should produce most of the food that is eaten in their country and import as little as possible.

Do you agree or disagree?

■ 17. ANIMALS in CAPTIVITY ⟨ Type 2 ⟩

Many people think it is cruel to keep animals in places such as zoos, animal parks and aquariums just for public viewing. Others disagree and think such places are helpful in protecting animals.

Discuss both arguments and give your own opinion.

18. URBAN & RURAL TRANSPORT — Type 3

Many countries spend a lot of money on improving transport in urban areas while neglecting rural transport.

What are the problems associated with this? What are some possible solutions?

19. MASS MEDIA FOCUS — Type 4

The mass media tends to focus on problems rather than positive developments, and this is very harmful to society.

To what extent do you agree or disagree?

20. SINGLE-CHILD FAMILIES — Type 5

Recently, many married couples are deciding to have and raise only one child.

What are some causes for this decision? What are some effects?

21. CRIME & POLICE — Type 1

Many countries are struggling with increases in crime rates and some think that having more police on the streets is the best way to reduce these increasing levels of crime.

Do you agree or disagree?

22. TRAVEL during/after UNIVERSITY — Type 2

During their university studies or just after graduation, students in some societies are encouraged to travel for a year.

What are some merits of this? Are there any demerits?

23. VISITORS to MUSEUMS, ART GALLERIES — Type 3

In many countries, the number of visitors to different kinds of museums and art galleries has been steadily declining.

What are some reasons for this situation? What could be done to change it?

◼ 24. MALE vs FEMALE LEADERS 〔 Type 4 〕

Throughout history, male leaders have led populations into violence and conflict. Therefore, if there were more female leaders, the world would be more peaceful.

To what extent do you agree or disagree?

◼ 25. TYPES of POLLUTION 〔 Type 5 〕

Society suffers from various forms of pollution.

What are some different forms and their causes? What effects do they bring?

◼ 26. ANIMALS, PLANTS & EXTINCTION 〔 Type 1 〕

It is a natural process for some animals (e.g. dinosaurs) and plant species to become extinct. Therefore, it is not necessary to try and prevent this from happening.

Do you agree or disagree?

◼ 27. TECHNOLOGY and RICH & POOR 〔 Type 2 〕

Some people believe that advances in technology are widening the gap between the rich and poor while others think the opposite is happening. Discuss both sides and give your own opinion.

◼ 28. DIVORCE RATES 〔 Type 3 〕

In many societies, the percentage of married couples who divorce is continuing to rise.

What are some causes of this social trend? How can the percentage be reduced?

◼ 29. OTHER PLANETS 〔 Type 4 〕

In the future, it will become more difficult to live on Earth so more money should be spent researching how to live on other planets such as Mars.

To what extent do you agree or disagree?

■ 30. SPECIAL EVENTS   Type 5

Countries and cities often make great efforts to hold major international events such as the World Cup, the Olympic Games, and major festivals and carnivals, etc.

Why do they have this desire? What are the results of holding such major events for host countries and cities?

■ 31. FASHION & APPEARANCE   Type 1

Some people say that it is possible to tell a lot about a person's culture and character from their choice of clothes and other aspects of their appearance as well as the ways they talk.

Do you agree or disagree with this opinion?

■ 32. MUSIC in SOCIETY   Type 2

Many people believe that music is just a form of entertainment, whilst others believe that music has a much larger impact on society today since it has various roles.

Discuss both views and give your own opinion.

■ 33. ENVIRONMENT & ENERGY   Type 3

Scientists have been warning for many years about environmental protection and how important it is to limit our personal consumption of energy.

What are the causes of overconsumption of energy? How can people be encouraged to use less energy?

■ 34. INFORMATION TECHNOLOGY   Type 4

Information technology (e-mail, social media, apps) is changing many aspects of our lives and now dominates our home, work and leisure activities.

To what extent do the benefits of information technology outweigh the disadvantages?

◼ 35. RETIREMENT AGE Type 5

In some countries there are moves to raise the age of retirement while in other countries there are moves to lower it.

For what reasons do the countries want to make such changes? How would early or later retirement affect society?

◼ 36. SPORTS & MEDALS Type 1

Some countries invest great sums of money in building specialised sports and training facilities for top athletes to become world champions and win medals for their country.

Do you think it is necessary to spend such money or not?

◼ 37. UNIFORMS & SUITS Type 2

Many schools require students to wear uniforms and many companies require employees to wear uniforms or suits.

What are the positive and negative aspects of such requirements?

◼ 38. MENTAL, PHYSICAL ILLNESSES Type 3

The number of people suffering from physical or mental health problems is on the rise in many societies.

Why do you think it is increasing? How can this serious issue be addressed?

◼ 39. IMPACT of ADVERTISING Type 4

People are constantly surrounded by a large amount of advertising, and it has a mainly negative impact on our quality of life.

To what extent do you agree or disagree?

◼ 40. VIOLENCE, CRIME in ENTERTAINMENT Type 5

Violence and crime often appear in TV shows, films and video games, and these forms of entertainment are becoming more and more popular.

Why is this trend occurring? What effect is it having on society?

41. SALES METHODS — Type 1

The best way for businesses to attract customers and increase sales is through advertising on TV.

Do you agree or disagree?

42. CHILD CRIME & PUNISHMENT — Type 2

Some people believe that children who commit crimes should be punished. Others think their parents should be punished instead.

Discuss both views and give your own opinion.

43. WOMEN in the POLICE, MILITARY, etc. — Type 3

Compared to the number of men, there are far fewer women in the fire brigade, police force or military forces, such as the army or navy.

What are some reasons for this situation? What measures can be taken to change it?

44. EFFECTS of FAST FOOD — Type 4

Many claim that the fast-food industry had a negative effect on the environment, eating habits, and families.

To what extend do you agree or disagree?

45. FUTURE COMPUTERS & ROBOTS — Type 5

Scientists are trying to build computers and robots that will be more intelligent than human beings.

Why do they have such a goal? How will such technology positively and negatively impact our lives?

46. RAISING CHILDREN — Type 1

It is better for children if the whole family including grandparents, aunts, uncles and so on are involved in a child's upbringing, rather than just their parents.

Do you agree or disagree with this opinion?

■ 47. EXPERIMENTS, TESTING MEDICINES on ANIMALS `Type 2`

Some people think that using animals for conducting experiments and testing new medicines for humans is necessary while others disagree.

Discuss both views and give your own opinion.

■ 48. SCIENTIFIC RESEARCH `Type 3`

Scientific research and experiments take place in most countries of the world.

What problems can occur because of such work? How should those problems be resolved?

■ 49. CHILDREN'S DEVELOPMENT `Type 4`

Although families have an influence on children's development, nowadays factors outside the home have a bigger influence.

To what extent do you agree or disagree?

■ 50. COUNTRIES, PEOPLE & POVERTY `Type 5`

In many countries around the world, poverty is on the rise.

What are some reasons for this trend? What effects does it have on countries and their populations?

■ **参考：Task 1図表のデータ使用・参照リスト**

タスク別攻略	棒グラフ	Adapted source: www150.statcan.gc.ca
	折れ線グラフ	Adapted source: www.usa.gov/statistics
	表	Adapted source: www150.statcan.gc.ca
	円グラフ	Adapted unsource: www2.unwto.org
	異なるタイプの組み合わせ	Adapted source: www.ons.gov.uk
セルフスタディ①	棒グラフ	Adapted source: www.abs.gov.au
	折れ線グラフ	Adapted source: www.usa.gov/statistics
	円グラフ	Adapted source: www.abs.gov.au
セルフスタディ②	棒グラフ	Adapted source: www.stats.govt.nz
	折れ線グラフ	Adapted source: OECD
	表	Source: www.abs.gov.au
	円グラフ	Adapted source: www.ons.gov.uk
	異なるタイプの組み合わせ	Adapted source: www.ons.gov.uk
セルフスタディ③	棒グラフ	Adapted source: DfI Roads
	折れ線グラフ	Adapted source: OECD
	表	Adapted source: www.un.org
	円グラフ	Adapted source: www150.statcan.gc.ca

Anthony Allan（アンソニー・アラン）

イギリス・スコットランド生まれ、ロンドン育ち。英語教授法修士号（Master of Science in TESOL）取得。1992年より東京で、子どもから大人まで英語教育の普及に尽力。特にIELTSやTOEFL iBT対策について、日本人の弱点を考慮した効果的な教授法に定評がある。著書に『IELTS 32のドリル＋模試』『TOEFL iBT攻略！』（三修社）、『基礎英語3』（NHK出版）、『新セルフスタディ IELTS完全攻略［第2版］』（ジャパンタイムズ出版）など多数。文科省検定高校英語教科書『All Aboard! English Communication I, II, III』（東京書籍）の編集にも携わる。

ブックデザイン	山之口正和＋沢田幸平（OKIKATA）
DTP	株式会社創樹
英文校正	Owen Schaefer
翻訳	春日聡子
ナレーション	Guy Perryman, Rachel Smith
音声収録・編集	ELEC録音スタジオ

新セルフスタディ IELTSライティング完全攻略

2022年8月5日　初刷発行

著者	Anthony Allan
	© Anthony Allan, 2022
発行者	伊藤秀樹
発行所	株式会社ジャパンタイムズ出版
	〒102-0082 東京都千代田区一番町2-2
	一番町第二TGビル2F
	ウェブサイト　https://jtpublishing.co.jp/
印刷所	日経印刷株式会社

・本書の内容に関するお問い合わせは、上記ウェブサイトまたは郵便でお受けいたします。
・万一、乱丁落丁のある場合は、送料当社負担でお取りかえいたします。
　ジャパンタイムズ出版・出版営業部あてにお送りください。

定価はカバーに表示してあります。
Printed in Japan　ISBN978-4-7890-1819-7

本書のご感想をお寄せください。
https://jtpublishing.co.jp/contact/comment/

新セルフスタディ
IELTSライティング完全攻略

特別付録

【保存版】

IELTS
ミニ辞典

the japan times 出版

C o n t e n t s

Task 1のエッセイでは、多くの場合、過去のデータを説明する必要があります。動詞は過去形も合わせて覚えておきましょう。

■ 上昇

動詞		名詞	
increase - increased	増える	an increase	増加
go up - went up	上がる、伸びる	-	-
rise - rose	上がる	a rise	上昇
grow - grew	伸びる	growth	成長
climb - climbed	登る、上がる	a climb	上昇
edge upwards - edged upwards	少しずつ上昇する	-	-
shift upwards - shifted upwards	上昇する	an upward shift	上昇の動き
jump - jumped	急増・急騰する	a jump	急増、急騰
leap - leapt	急増・急騰する	a leap	急増、急騰
surge - surged	急増・急騰する	a surge	急増、急騰
shoot up - shot up	急上昇する	-	-
soar - soared	急増・急騰する	-	-
swell - swelled	増加・増大する	-	-
balloon - ballooned	急増・急騰する	-	-
double - doubled	2倍になる	-	-
triple - tripled	3倍になる	-	-
exceed - exceeded	越える、上回る	-	-
overtake - overtook	越える、上回る	-	-
surpass - surpassed	越える、上回る	-	-
peak at - peaked at	…で最高値に達する	(reach) a peak	最高値（に達する）

■ 下降

動詞		名詞	
decrease - decreased	減る	a decrease	減少
go down - went down	下降する	-	-
fall – fell	落ちる	a fall	下落
drop - dropped	下落する	a drop	下落
decline - declined	下がる	a decline	下降
dip - dipped	わずか［一時的］に減少する	a dip	沈下
edge downwards - edged downwards	少しずつ下降する	-	-
shift downwards - shifted downwards	下降する	a downward shift	下降の動き
contract - contracted	縮小する	a contraction	縮小、短縮
shrink - shrank	縮小・減少する	-	-
diminish - diminished	減少する	-	-
dwindle - dwindled	縮小・減少する	-	-
slump - slumped	急落・暴落する	a slump	急落、低迷
plunge - plunged	急落する	a plunge	急落
plummet - plummeted	急落する	a plummet	急落

■ その他

動詞		名詞	
start at/with - started at/with	…で始まる	-	-
finish at/with - finished at/with	…で終わる	-	-
show - showed	示す	-	-
stand at - stood at	数値が…である	-	-
represent - represented	示す、相当する	-	-
record - recorded	示す、表示する	-	-

動詞		名詞	
reflect - reflected	示す、反映する	-	-
constitute - constituted	構成する	-	-
register - registered	記録する、指し示す	-	-
account for - accounted for	…（割合など）を占める	-	-
mark - marked	示す	-	-
level off - levelled off	均一になる、横ばいである	-	-
plateau at - plateaued at	…で横ばいである	a plateau	横ばい、停滞
see a change - saw a change	変化がある	a change	変化
experience a change - experienced a change	変化がある	-	-
see/experience no change - saw/experienced no change	変化がない	no change	変化なし
stay/remain unchanged - stayed/remained unchanged	変化しないままである	-	-
stay/remain stable at - stayed/remained stable at	…で安定している	-	-
stay/remain steady at - stayed/remained steady at	…で安定している	-	-
stay/remain at - stayed/remained at	…の値を保つ	-	-
recover to - recovered to	…にもち直す	a recovery	回復
fluctuate - fluctuated	変動する	a fluctuation	変動
average - averaged	平均〜になる	an average	平均
range from ... to ~ - ranged from ... to ~	…から〜に及ぶ	a range of ... to ~	…から〜の範囲
equal - equalled	等しい、相当する	-	-
mirror - mirrored	反映する、重なる	-	-
parallel - paralleled	匹敵・一致する	a parallel	類似点
total - totalled	総計〜になる	a total	総計、総数

形容詞		副詞	
small	小さな	-	-
slight	わずかな	slightly	わずかに
minor	わずかな	-	-
minimal	最小限の	minimally	最小限に
marginal	わずかな	marginally	わずかに
modest	適度の、あまり大きく・多くない	modestly	適度に
moderate	ゆるやかな	moderately	ゆるやかに
noticeable	顕著な、著しい	noticeably	著しく
significant	かなりの、著しい	significantly	かなり
dramatic	劇的な	dramatically	劇的に
notable	顕著な	notably	顕著に
distinct	はっきりした	-	-
marked	著しい	markedly	著しく
major	大幅な	-	-
substantial	相当な	substantially	相当に
striking	著しい	strikingly	著しく
considerable	相当な	considerably	相当に
sharp	(変化が) 急激な、激しい	sharply	急激に
steep	急激な、大幅な	steeply	急激に
huge	大幅な	hugely	大幅に

Task 1　変化の速さを表す形容詞と副詞

形容詞		副詞	
slow	遅い	slowly	ゆっくりと
gradual	ゆるやかな	gradually	徐々に
steady	着実な	steadily	着実に
sudden	突然の	suddenly	突然に
rapid	急速な	rapidly	急速に
swift	素早い、即座の	swiftly	素早く、即座に

Task 1　未来について予測する表現

be + ...ed to		動詞 that + will	
be predicted to ...	…と予想されている	predict that ... will	…だろうと予想する
be expected to ...	…と期待されている	expect that ... will	…だろうと期待する
be likely to ...	…らしい	-	-
be forecast to ...	…と予想されている	forecast that ... will	…だろうと予想する
be projected to ...	…と予測されている	project that ... will	…だろうと予測する
be anticipated to ...	…と予想されている	anticipate that ... will	…だろうと予想する
be estimated to ...	…と推定されている	estimate that ... will	…だろうと推定する・見積もる

タスク説明文に1〜2つあるキーワードがわからないとエッセイを書き始めることができません。頻出キーワードを押さえておきましょう。

語句	訳
advantages, advantageous	優勢、利点；有利な
affect	影響を与える
argue	議論する
aspects	側面
attitudes	考え方
avoid	避ける
be addressed	取り組まれる
benefits, beneficial	恩恵、利点；有益な
challenges	課題
concerned	関係している、該当する
deal with	…に取り組む
disadvantages, disadvantageous	劣勢、欠点；不利な
drawbacks	欠点
effects	効果
impacts	影響、反響、効果
influence	影響を与える
issues	課題、問題
measures	方法、手段、方策

語句	訳
merits and demerits	長所と短所
methods	方式
negative developments	否定的な変化・発展
outweigh	〜より重要である、勝る
overcome	乗り越える
positive aspects	肯定的側面
prevent	防ぐ
pros and cons	賛否両論、長所と短所
reasons, causes, factors	理由、原因、要因
reduce	減らす
resolve	解決する
results	結果
solutions	解決法
strategies	戦略
suggest	提案する
tackle	取り組む

Task 2 で重要な形容詞

Task 2の様々なトピックで役立つ形容詞をまとめました。

形容詞	訳
accurate	正確な、的確な
attractive	魅力的な
available	利用できる、入手できる
beautiful	美しい
busy	忙しい、活気のある
beneficial	有益な
careful	注意深い
complex	複雑な
confident	自信に満ちた
considerable	（数量・大きさなどが）かなりの
difficult	難しい
efficient	効率的な
effective	効果的な
environmentally friendly	環境に優しい
excellent	極めて良い
expensive	値段が高い、費用のかかる
familiar	よく知っている
financial	財政の、金融の
frequent	頻繁な
full-time	常勤の、フルタイムの
generous	寛大な

形容詞	訳
global	世界的な、地球全体の
hard-working	勤勉な
illegal	不法の、違法の
important	重要な、大切な
interesting	面白い、興味を起こさせる
logical	論理的な、筋の通った
modern	現代の、近代の
motivated	動機づけられた、やる気のある
natural	自然の、天性の
negative	否定的な
nostalgic	郷愁の、懐かしい
numerous	多数の
nutritious	栄養のある
old-fashioned	古風な、旧式の
optimistic	楽観的な
part-time	非常勤の、パートタイムの
peaceful	平穏な、平和的な
pessimistic	悲観的な、厭世的な
positive	確かな、肯定的な、積極的な
previous	前の、以前の

形容詞	訳
reasonable	理性的な、妥当な
reliable	信頼できる、頼りになる
satisfied	満足した、納得した
selfish	利己的な
severe	深刻な、厳しい
shameful	恥ずべき
spacious	広々とした
skilful	熟練した
talented	才能のある
temporary	一時的な
traditional	伝統的な
trivial	ささいな、つまらない
trustworthy	信頼できる、当てになる
unfriendly	不親切な
unlikely	ありそうもない
unique	独特な、唯一の
unusual	普通でない、珍しい
urgent	緊急の
useful	役に立つ、有益な
valuable	高価な、貴重な
well-known/ famous	よく知られた／有名な

頻出トピック20個について、重要語句を名詞→動詞表現の順に掲載しています。チェックボックスも活用してください。

■ 1. People, Community & Culture

	語句	訳
☐	family and friends	家族と友人
☐	relatives	親戚、親族
☐	neighbours	近隣住民、隣近所
☐	neighbourhood	近所、近隣
☐	generation	一世代、同世代の人
☐	ancestors/descendants	先祖、祖先／子孫、末裔
☐	anniversary	記念日、〜周年
☐	resident	居住者、在住者
☐	accommodation	宿泊施設
☐	landlord/landlady	家主、地主／女家主、女地主
☐	tenant	借家人、借地人
☐	rent	家賃、賃借料
☐	customs	慣習、風習
☐	religion	宗教、信仰

	語句	訳
☐	mother tongue	母語
☐	beliefs	信仰、信念
☐	race	人種、民族
☐	ethic minority	少数民族
☐	discrimination	差別
☐	racism	人種差別（主義）
☐	equality	平等、対等
☐	(to) get along with	…と仲良くやっていく
☐	(to) communicate with	…（人）と連絡を取る
☐	(to) marry	結婚する
☐	(to) divorce	離婚する
☐	(to) die, (to) pass away	死ぬ、亡くなる
☐	(to) inherit	（財産を）相続する

■ 2. Consumer Trends

語句	訳
customers	顧客、取引先
consumers	消費者
department store	百貨店、デパート
shopping mall	ショッピングモール
retail stores	小売店
products/goods/items	製品、商品／品物／商品
fake goods	偽造品、模倣品
genuine products	純正品、真正商品
famous brands	有名ブランド
a large discount	大幅な値引き
bargain prices	特価、割引価格
reasonable prices	適正価格、妥当な値段
consumption tax	消費税
sales clerk/sales assistant	販売員／店員
(to) be on sale	売りに出されて、特価で
(can) afford to	～する金銭的余裕がある
(to) buy, (to) purchase	購入する
(to) shop online	オンラインで買う
(to) order	注文する
(to) pay in cash	現金で支払う
(to) pay by credit card	クレジットカードで支払う

■ 3. Tourism & Travel

語句	訳
the travel industry	旅行業界
tourists/travellers	観光客／旅行者
travel agency	旅行代理店
package tour	パック旅行
air tickets	航空券
flights	航空便
holiday destination	休暇の目的地
tourist resorts	観光地
exotic location	エキゾチックな場所
honeymoon	新婚旅行、ハネムーン
luggage, suitcases	手荷物、スーツケース
passport	パスポート
visa	査証、ビザ
journey	旅行
voyage	航海、船旅
economy class	エコノミークラス
business class	ビジネスクラス
passport control	出入国審査
customs and immigration	税関、出入国管理・審査
foreign currency	外貨
(to) pack your luggage	手荷物をまとめる
(to) go on holiday	旅行する、休暇で出かける
(to) travel by car/train/airplane	車／電車／飛行機で移動する
(to) take/go on a world cruise	世界一周の船旅をする

■ 4. Population Movement/Change

語句	訳
immigration	移住、移民
emigration	（自国から他国への）移住、移民
migrants	移住者、（季節）労働者
refugees	（国外への）避難者、難民
illegal aliens	不法滞在者、不法入国者
poverty	貧困
hardship	困難、困窮
financial support	経済的支援
social welfare/the welfare system	社会福祉／福祉制度
housing shortages	住宅不足
taxpayers	納税者
citizens	国民、市民
subsidies	（国家の）助成金、補助金
(to) escape from	…から脱する・逃れる
(to) arrive in	…に到着する
(to) claim benefits	給付金・手当を請求する
(to) provide housing	住居を提供する
(to) provide employment/work/jobs	雇用／仕事／職を提供する
(to) provide education	教育を提供する
(to) provide medical care	医療を提供する

■ 5. Internet & Social Media

語句	訳
☐ smartphones	スマートフォン
☐ computers	コンピューター
☐ mobile devices	モバイル機器、携帯機器
☐ internet access	インターネット接続
☐ network	ネットワーク、人脈
☐ Wi-Fi connection	Wi-Fi接続
☐ website	ウェブサイト
☐ app	アプリ
☐ online shopping	ネット通販
☐ e-mail	Eメール
☐ text messages	(携帯電話間の) テキストメッセージ、ショートメッセージ
☐ online harassment	ネット上の嫌がらせ行為
☐ an anonymous person	匿名の人
☐ a hacker	ハッカー
☐ (to) send text messages	テキストメッセージを送る
☐ (to) post stories on the internet	インターネットに話を投稿する
☐ (to) upload images	画像をアップロードする
☐ (to) download files	ファイルをダウンロードする
☐ (to) go viral	バズる、急速に拡散する
☐ (to) censor content	コンテンツを検閲する
☐ (to) block content	コンテンツをブロックする
☐ (to) hack into a computer	コンピューターに侵入する

■ 6. Mass Media & Advertising

語句	訳
TV commercials	テレビCM
adverts/advertisements	広告／広告、宣伝
advertising boards	広告板
advertising companies	広告会社
publishers	出版社
publications	出版物
daily (regional/national) newspapers	日刊（地方／全国）紙
the press	マスコミ、記者団
magazines	雑誌
reporters	記者
news articles/stories	ニュース記事
fake news	偽のニュース、フェイクニュース
readership	読者数、読者層
circulation	発行部数
press freedom	報道の自由
censorship	検閲
(to) attract customers	顧客を引きつける
(to) persuade consumers	消費者を勧誘する
(to) increase sales	売上を伸ばす
(to) be biased	偏見・偏りのある
(to) ban/prohibit	〜を禁止する
(to) censor articles	記事を検閲する

■ 7. Education & Learning

語句	訳
☐ curriculum	履修課程、カリキュラム
☐ nursery school	保育園
☐ kindergarten school	幼稚園
☐ primary school	小学校
☐ secondary school	中学校
☐ university, college	総合大学、単科大学
☐ technical/vocational school	専門／職業訓練学校
☐ teachers, professors	先生、教授
☐ students/pupils	学生／生徒
☐ classrooms	教室
☐ remote learning	遠隔学習
☐ academic subjects	(実技ではない) 学科の科目
☐ knowledge and skills	知識と技能
☐ homework assignments	宿題
☐ grades and results	成績の評点と成績
☐ extra-curricular activities	課外活動、部活
☐ university degree	大学の学位
☐ undergraduate student	大学の学部生
☐ postgraduate student	大学院生
☐ (to) take exams	試験を受ける、受験する
☐ (to) pass exams	試験に合格する
☐ (to) fail exams	試験に失敗する・落ちる
☐ (to) graduate	卒業する

■ 8. Nature & the Environment

語句	訳
greenery	緑樹、草木
forests	森林
rivers, seas, oceans	川、海、海洋
animal and plant life	動植物
living creatures	生き物
marine animals	海生動物
insects	昆虫
wildlife protection	野外生物保護
survival	生存
extinction	絶滅
natural habitat	自然生息地
ecosystem	生態系、エコシステム
natural resources	天然資源
depletion	（資源などの）枯渇、激減
pollution	汚染
rubbish and waste	ゴミと廃棄物
plastic packaging	プラスチック包装

語句	訳
a sustainable society	持続可能な社会
wind and solar power	風力・太陽光発電
fossil fuels	化石燃料
weather patterns	天候パターン
climate change	気候変動
natural disasters	自然災害、天才
fossil fuel emissions	化石燃料排出物
the ozone layer	オゾン層
toxic chemicals	有毒化学物質
soil/water contamination	土壌／水質汚染
(to) recycle	〜をリサイクルする・再生利用する
(to) protect	〜を保護する
(to) conserve water	節水する
(to) save energy	エネルギーを節約する
(to) contaminate	〜を汚染する

18

■ 9. Animal Welfare

語句	訳
pet owner	ペットの飼い主
pet shop	ペットショップ
cage	おり、鳥かご
laboratory experiments	研究室での実験
wild animal	野生動物
domesticated animal	家畜
guide dogs	盲導犬
rescue dogs	保護犬、救助犬
food and shelter	食べ物と住まい（保護施設）
endangered species	絶滅危惧種
animal rights	動物の権利
(to) keep/own a pet	ペットを飼う／所有する
(to) feed	～に食物を与える
(to) abuse	～を虐待する
(to) treat an animal badly	動物にひどい仕打ちをする
(to) abandon	～を遺棄する・捨てる

語句	訳
doctors, nurses, patients	医師、看護師、患者
a health/ medical check-up	健康診断
healthcare and health services	医療と公共医療サービス
medical equipment and supplies	医療機器と物資
illness/ sickness	病気
injury, infection	けが、感染
ambulance	救急車
treatment	治療、手当
medicine	薬、医薬品
virus	ウイルス
vaccine, vaccination	ワクチン、予防接種
disabled people/ the disabled	障害のある人
mental/ physical problem	精神的／身体的機能障害
stress	ストレス、緊張

語句	訳
depression	意気消沈、うつ病
nutrition	栄養（物）
longevity	長生き、長寿
a balanced diet	バランスの取れた食事
eating habits	食習慣、食生活
the food industry	食品産業
take-away food	持ち帰り用の料理
processed food	加工食品
a vegetarian	菜食主義者、ベジタリアン
a vegan	ヴィーガン、完全菜食主義者
(to) eat healthy food	健康的な食事をする
(to) exercise regularly	定期的に運動する
(to) have an allergy to	…にアレルギーがある
(to) get/have a vaccination	予防接種を受ける
(to) have surgery/ an operation	手術を受ける

■ 11. Sport, Leisure & Entertainment

語句	訳
stadium	競技場、スタジアム
venue	会場、開催地
spectators	観客
audiences	観衆
viewers	視聴者
competitions	試合、競争相手
sponsors	広告主、スポンサー
athletes and coaches	運動選手と指導者
banned substances	禁止薬物
leisure activities, hobbies	レジャー活動、趣味
taking walks/going for walks	散歩すること
going to live concerts	ライブのコンサートに行くこと
going to sports events	スポーツイベントに行くこと
going to the cinema	映画を観に行くこと
watching (animated) films	(アニメ) 映画を観ること
a box office hit	興行成績の良い作品
subtitles	字幕
main characters	主役、主人公
actors, actresses	俳優、女優
celebrities and stars	有名人とスター
(to) have a hobby	趣味がある
(to) go to the theatre	劇場に行く
(to) see/watch a play	芝居を観る

■ 12. The Arts

語句	訳
painting	絵画
sculpture	彫刻
literature	文学
architecture	建築
cinema	映画
music	音楽
theatre	演劇
drawings, sketches	描画、スケッチ
photographs	写真
sculptures	彫刻（作品）、彫像
fiction/ non-fiction novels	フィクション／ノンフィクション小説
drama	演劇、ドラマ
poetry	詩
interior design	インテリアデザイン
music and dance	音楽とダンス

語句	訳
theatre performances	舞台パフォーマンス
music concerts	音楽のコンサート
popular music	ポピュラー音楽、ポップ音楽
film-making	映画制作
museums	美術館、博物館
art galleries	画廊、アートギャラリー
concert halls	コンサートホール
funding	資金調達、財政的支援
(to) perform a play	芝居を上演する
(to) show a film/movie	映画を上映する
(to) hold a concert	コンサートを開催する
(to) hold an exhibition	展覧会を行う
(to) display/ show exhibits	展示品を陳列する

22

■ 13. Science & Technology

語句	訳
☐ scientists	科学者
☐ researchers	研究者
☐ theory	理論、学説
☐ experiments	実験
☐ laboratory	実験室、研究所
☐ research project	研究プロジェクト
☐ an innovative idea	革新的なアイデア
☐ a new invention	新発見、新発明
☐ artificial intelligence (AI)	人工知能
☐ humanoid robots	人型ロボット
☐ the atmosphere	（地球の）大気、大気圏
☐ planets	惑星
☐ space travel	宇宙旅行
☐ spaceship	宇宙船
☐ astronaut	宇宙飛行士
☐ (to) explore	〜を探索・探検する
☐ (to) do research on	…の研究を行う
☐ (to) design	〜を設計する
☐ (to) solve a problem	問題を解決する
☐ (to) invent	〜を発明・考案する
☐ (to) discover	〜を発見する
☐ (to) succeed	成功する
☐ (to) fail	失敗する

■ 14. Employment & Retirement

語句	訳
employer	雇用主
employee	従業員
employment rate	就業率
unemployment rate	失業率
career	職歴、専門的職業
job, occupation	仕事、職業
working hours	労働時間
workplace	職場
office equipment	オフィス設備
manager	経営者、部長
staff, co-workers/ colleagues	社員、同僚／同僚
teamwork	チームワーク
promotion	昇進、昇格
salary, income	給料、所得

語句	訳
fringe benefits	福利厚生、付加給付
breadwinner	（家庭の）稼ぎ手
networking	人脈作り
work-life balance	ワークライフ・バランス、仕事と生活の調和
pension	年金
(to) do an internship	実務研修をする
(to) attend an interview	面接を受ける
(to) be employed	雇われる
(to) do overtime	時間外勤務をする
(to) quit a job	仕事を辞める
(to) be fired from a job	解雇される
(to) retire	退職する、引退する

■ 15. Companies & Business

語句	訳
corporation	法人
parent company	親会社
subsidiary	子会社
businesspeople	実業家
management	経営、経営陣
recruitment	（仕事の）求人、（組織の）補充
manufacturing	製造（業）
marketing	マーケティング
brands	ブランド、銘柄
services	サービス、職務
supply and demand	需要と供給（英語とは順番が逆）
buyers and sellers	買い手と売り手
materials	原料、材料
suppliers	供給者、サプライヤー
competitors	競合相手
a branch shop/office	支店／支社
the car industry	自動車産業

語句	訳
the clothing industry	衣料産業
domestic/ international markets	国内／国際市場
the financial sector	金融部門
the stock market	株式市場
stocks and shares	株式
(to) trade	商売をする
(to) invest in	…に投資する
(to) make a profit	利益を得る
(to) make a loss	損をする
(to) have debts	負債がある
(to) go bankrupt	倒産する、破産する

■ 16. Construction & Urban Planning

語句	訳
infrastructure	社会基盤、インフラ
city planning	都市計画
inner cities	都心部、インナーシティー
urban areas	都市圏、市街地
suburbs/suburban areas	郊外／都市周辺地域
public facilities	公共施設
public housing	公営住宅
homes	家、住居
apartment buildings	アパート、共同住宅
office buildings	オフィスビル、事務所用ビル
factories	工場
concrete buildings	コンクリートのビル
skyscrapers	超高層ビル、摩天楼
roads and motorways	道路と高速道路
bridges	橋
public transport	公共交通機関
bus and rail networks	バス鉄道網
high-speed trains	高速鉄道
ports and harbours	港湾
roadworks	道路工事
sewage system	下水設備
power supplies	電力供給
(to) construct	～を建設・建造する
(to) demolish	～を破壊・解体する

■ 17. Politics & Government

語句	訳
politicians	政治家
leaders	指導者
the prime minister	首相
the president	大統領、国家主席
the state	国、国家
democracy	民主主義
elections	選挙
candidates	(立) 候補者
voters	有権者、選挙人
a political party	政党
a scandal	不祥事、スキャンダル
the ministry of finance/ education etc.	財務省／文部科学省等
a minister	大臣
a diplomat	外交官
association	協会、組合
organisation	組織、機構
(to) vote	投票する
(to) win/lose an election	選挙に勝つ／負ける
(to) run/govern a country	国を運営する／治める

■ 18. Crime & Law

語句	訳
☐ the police	警察
☐ police officers	警察官
☐ a crime, offence, illegal act	犯罪、違反、不法行為
☐ CCTV/surveillance cameras	監視カメラ
☐ perpetrators	犯人、加害者
☐ criminals	犯罪者
☐ victims	被害者
☐ court	裁判所
☐ judge and jury	裁判官と陪審員団
☐ punishment	処罰、刑罰
☐ a fine	罰金
☐ a prison sentence	実刑判決
☐ justice	正義、司法
☐ (to) commit a crime	罪を犯す
☐ (to) break the law	法律に違反する
☐ (to) investigate a crime	犯罪を捜査する
☐ (to) arrest a suspect	容疑者を逮捕する
☐ (to) go to court	裁判を起こす、提訴する
☐ (to) be fined	罰金を科せられる
☐ (to) receive a prison sentence	実刑判決を受ける
☐ (to) go to prison	投獄される
☐ (to) be released from prison	刑務所から釈放される、出所する

■ 19. War & Peace

語句	訳
international crisis	国際的危機
national security	国家安全保障
armed conflict	武力紛争
invasion	侵略、侵入
military action	軍事行動
armed forces (army, navy, air force)	国軍（陸軍、海軍、空軍）
soldiers	兵士、軍人
civilians	一般市民、民間人
prisoners	囚人、捕虜
survivors	生存者
tanks	戦車
warships	軍艦
submarines	潜水艦
peace treaty/agreement	平和条約／講和条約
nuclear bombs	核爆弾

語句	訳
chemical weapons	化学兵器
explosions	爆発
destruction	破壊
a defeat, a victory	敗北、勝利
(to) attack	〜を攻撃する・襲う
(to) capture	〜を占領する・捕らえる
(to) fight	〜と戦う
(to) kill	〜を殺す
(to) defend	〜を守る・防御する
(to) destroy	〜を破壊する・荒廃させる
(to) defeat	〜を負かす・倒す
(to) negotiate a peace treaty/agreement	平和条約締結／和平合意の交渉を行う

■ 20. Occupations

	語句	訳
☐	app developer	アプリ開発者
☐	archaeologist	考古学者
☐	architect	建築家、建築士
☐	author/writer	著者、執筆者／作家、筆者
☐	construction worker	建設労働者
☐	dentist	歯科医
☐	doctor, nurse	医師、看護師
☐	electrician	電気技師
☐	engineer	技術者、エンジニア
☐	entertainer	芸人、エンターテイナー
☐	estate agent	不動産仲介業者
☐	farmer	農場経営者、農夫
☐	fashion designer	ファッションデザイナー
☐	firefighter	消防士
☐	graphic designer	グラフィックデザイナー

	語句	訳
☐	journalist	ジャーナリスト、新聞雑誌記者
☐	lawyer	弁護士、法律家
☐	musician	音楽家
☐	plumber	配管工、水道業者
☐	politician	政治家
☐	presenter	（テレビなどの）司会者
☐	secretary	秘書、書記、事務官
☐	shopkeeper/shop owner	店主、商店経営者
☐	software developer	ソフトウェア開発者
☐	sports coach	スポーツ指導者
☐	systems engineer	システムエンジニア
☐	vet, animal doctor	獣医
☐	website designer/developer	ウェブサイト設計者／開発者

断定を避ける表現

　アカデミックな英語では、can、may、shouldといった、可能性や必要性、要求の度合いを表現する助動詞が使われます。また、世間によく知られている事実や定義に言及する場合を除き、断定を避ける表現が好まれます。

極端な表現	断定を避ける表現
Trains are always late.	Trains are often late.
Prices never decrease.	Prices rarely decrease.
People do not like animals.	A small percentage of people do not like animals.
All teenagers ...	Most/The majority of teenagers ...
There are no problems relating to health.	There are very few problems relating to health.
No one trusts the government.	Some people do not trust the government.
Everyone dreams of becoming famous.	Many people dream of becoming famous.

断定的な表現	婉曲的な表現
It is a bad system.	It may be a bad system.
There is a better solution.	There might be a better solution.
It is necessary for them to ...	It may be necessary to ...
The new measures will not be popular.	The new measures may not be popular.
It will cause ...	It could cause ...
This will become ...	This may become ...
Such steps will not result in ...	Such steps will probably not result in ...
These actions will lead to ...	These actions might lead to ...

　エッセイでは、論点を整理し、発展させて自分の見解を述べる必要があります。明快で筋の通った記述にするために役立つ表現をまとめました。

■ エッセイ導入部分

- In recent years there have been many changes/developments in ...

（近年、…で多くの変化・発展が見られる）

- ... has developed rapidly over the last few decades.

（…は、ここ20〜30年で急速に発展している）

- Over the last few decades, many people have ...

（ここ20〜30年で、多くの人々が…）

- One of the most important problems in our society today is ...

（今日の社会で、最も重大な問題の1つは…）

■ メインの論点をつなぐ

- Firstly, it is important to consider the issue of ...

（まず…という課題を検討することが重要だ）

- Another aspect to remember is ...　（覚えておくべきもう1つの側面は…）

- The final point to take into account is ...　（考慮すべき最後の点は…）

■ 例を挙げる

- One example is ...　（1つの例として）

- Another/A further example is ...　（もう1つの／さらなる例として…）

- Take X(s) as an example. It/They ...

（Xを例として挙げると、それ／それらは…）

■ 論点を明快にする

- It/This is not only ... but also ~ （それ／これは…だけでなく～も）

- There is no doubt in my mind that ... （…は間違いない）

■ 同意する／異議を唱える

- I would accept the view that ... （…という意見はもっともだと思う）

- I agree with the point of view that ... （…という意見に賛成だ）

- It is certainly true to say that ... （…と言うのも当然だ）

- I am not convinced that ... （…とは確信できない、…とは思えない）

- I cannot accept the view that ... （…という見解は受け入れられない）

- There is little evidence to suggest that ... （…と言うには根拠が足りない）

■ 結果の予測

- This might cause ... （これが原因で…になるかもしれない）

- This could lead to ... （これが…を導くかもしれない）

- It can result in ... （それが…という結果を生むかもしれない）

- This would have a positive/negative effect on ...

  （これが…に良い／悪い影響を及ぼすかもしれない）

■ エッセイ結論部分

- Considering all the points above it is clear that ...

  （上記のすべてを考慮すると、…ははっきりしている）

- Overall, it is evident that ... （全体的に見て…は明白である）

- Looking at all the arguments it is obvious that ...

  （議論を尽くした結果…は明らかだ）

- Overall, we can see that ... （全体として…ということがわかる）

　これらの表現は、ライティングはもちろん、スピーキングなどにも役に立ちます。文頭で使うことが多いものは大文字にしています。

Addition （付加・追加・拡張）	
and	そして
also	また
too	…も
… as well as ~	~同様…も
In addition,	加えて
likewise	同様に
not only … but ~	…だけでなく~も
similarly	同じく

Reason （理由）	
because/as/since	…なので
due to	…のため
owing to	…のため
because of	…のため
the reason why	なぜかというと
leads to	…につながる
cause	~の原因となる

Sequence （つなぎ・連続・連結）	
First/Firstly,	まず、第1に
Second/Secondly,	次に、第2に
To begin with,	始めに
Initially,	最初は、冒頭に
Then,	それから
Next,	次に
After this/that,	この／その後
Following this/that,	これ／それに続き
Lastly/Finally,	最後に／最終的に

Example （例・たとえ）	
for example	例として
for instance	例えば
such as	…のような
in particular	特に

Contrast（対比）	
but	しかし
However,	とはいえ
On the other hand,	一方で
On the contrary,	逆に
In/By contrast,	比べると
Although	…ではあるが
Even though	たとえ…でも
While	一方
Compared with	…と比較すると
Whereas	…であるのに、ところが…
Despite	…であるのに
In spite of	…にもかかわらず
Instead of	…の代わりに、…しないで
Alternatively,	代わりに

Result（結果）	
As a result,	結果として
So,	それで
Therefore,	したがって
consequently	結果的に
Thus,	したがって
Hence,	したがって
Accordingly,	したがって、その結果

Summary（要約）	
In summary,	要約すると
In conclusion,	結論は
To sum up,	要約すると

Condition（条件）	
If	もし…なら
Unless	もし…でなければ
Provided that	もし…とすれば
Whether	…であろうとなかろうと
So that	…するように
in order to	〜するために

ゆっくり矢印の方に引くとこの冊子を取り外すことができます。